ADAM SMITH

LECTURES

ON

JUSTICE, POLICE, REVENUE AND ARMS

Elibron Classics
www.elibron.com

Elibron Classics series.

ISBN 0-543-94074-8 (paperback)
ISBN 0-543-94073-X (hardcover)

This Elibron Classics Replica Edition is an unabridged facsimile of the edition published in 1896 by the Clarendon Press, Oxford.

LECTURES

OF

ADAM SMITH

London

HENRY FROWDE

Oxford University Press Warehouse
Amen Corner, E.C.

New York
THE MACMILLAN CO., 66 FIFTH AVENUE

LECTURES

ON

JUSTICE, POLICE, REVENUE AND ARMS

DELIVERED IN THE UNIVERSITY OF GLASGOW

BY

ADAM SMITH

REPORTED BY A STUDENT IN 1763

AND

EDITED WITH AN INTRODUCTION AND NOTES

BY

EDWIN CANNAN

Oxford

AT THE CLARENDON PRESS

1896

Oxford
PRINTED AT THE CLARENDON PRESS
BY HORACE HART
PRINTER TO THE UNIVERSITY

PREFACE

THE history of the manuscript now made public and the principles which I have followed in editing it are fully dealt with in the Introduction.

I have here only to express my gratitude to Mr. Thomas Raleigh, who, when I first took the work in hand, was Reader in English Law at Oxford and a Delegate of the University Press, and is now Registrar to the Judicial Committee of the Privy Council. Besides reading through the text, and making observations on passages which he thought corrupt or in need of explanation, he has since answered from time to time, with unwearied patience, the inquiries I have addressed to him on legal points, many of which must have appeared trivial to any one except an editor desirous of believing himself to be conscientious. It must be understood, however, that, as he has had no opportunity of seeing what use I have made of the information derived from him, he is no more responsible for anything which actually occurs in the notes than Mr. Serjeant Hawkins or any other legal authority whom I have consulted.

EDWIN CANNAN.

OXFORD,
August 1896.

CONTENTS

EDITOR'S INTRODUCTION.

INTRODUCTION.

PART I: OF JUSTICE.

PART III: OF REVENUE.

PART II: OF POLICE

(*Resumed*).

PART IV: OF ARMS.

PART V: OF THE LAWS OF NATIONS.

EDITOR'S INTRODUCTION

CHAPTER I. HISTORY OF THE REPORT.

'OF Mr. Smith's lectures while a professor at Glasgow, no part has been preserved, excepting what he himself published in the *Theory of Moral Sentiments* and in the *Wealth of Nations*.' This statement was made by Dugald Stewart in the 'Account of the Life and Writings of Adam Smith,' which he read before the Royal Society of Edinburgh early in 1793. He allowed it to be printed in the *Transactions* of the society in 1794 [1], and to be reprinted both in 1795 [2] and in 1811 [3] without alteration. For a little more than a century it has remained unquestioned, and, so far as Adam Smith's own lecture-notes are concerned, it is doubtless correct.

When setting out for London in April, 1773, Adam Smith wrote a letter to Hume, whom he had made his literary executor, giving instructions as to the disposal of his papers in case of his death. Except those which he carried along with him, that is to say, the manuscript of the *Wealth of Nations*, there were none, he said, worth publication, unless perhaps the fragment on the history of astronomical systems, to be found in a certain desk, might be printed as a portion 'of an intended juvenile work.' 'All the other loose papers which you will find in that desk,' the letter continues, 'or within the glass folding doors of a bureau which stands in my bedroom, together with

[1] Vol. iii. pt. i. p. 61.

[2] *Essays on Philosophical Subjects by the late Adam Smith, LL.D., to which is prefixed an Account of the Life and Writings of the Author by Dugald Stewart, F.R.S.E.* p. xv.

[3] *Biographical Memoirs of Adam Smith, LL D., of William Robertson, D.D., and of Thomas Reid, D.D., read before the Royal Society of Edinburgh. Now collected into One Volume, with some Additional Notes*, p. 12.

about eighteen thin folio paper books which you will likewise find within the same glass folding doors, I desire may be destroyed without any examination.' Fourteen years later, when again contemplating a visit to London, Adam Smith 'enjoined his friends to whom he had entrusted the disposal of his manuscripts, that in the event of his death, they should destroy all the volumes of his lectures, doing with the rest of his manuscripts what they pleased.' In July, 1790, ten days or a fortnight before he died, 'he spoke to his friends again upon the same subject. They entreated him to make his mind easy, as he might depend upon their fulfilling his desire. He was then satisfied. But some days afterwards, finding his anxiety not entirely removed, he begged one of them to destroy the volumes immediately. This accordingly was done, and his mind was so much relieved that he was able to receive his friends in the evening with his usual complacency.' He was unable, however, to sit up with them as usual, and retired to bed before supper, taking leave with the words, 'I believe we must adjourn this meeting to some other place'[1].

Dr. James Hutton, the narrator of this story, was one of the two friends to whom Adam Smith had entrusted the disposal of his manuscripts, Dr. Joseph Black being the other[2]. From his cautious use of the phrase 'one of them,' and the impersonal 'this was done,' most readers would infer that Hutton himself was the destroyer of the manuscripts, but Mackenzie, who was present at the supper, is reported to have told Samuel Rogers that Black did the deed[3]. No one who has tried to burn some hundreds of leaves of folio manuscript will feel any surprise that Adam Smith, in his feeble state, should have shrunk from attempting the task with his own hands, even if he was sitting up and had a fire on that July morning. What is suggested, however, by the wording of the narrative, taken in conjunction with the letter to Hume already quoted, is that Smith was in bed in the morning when his friend called on him, and that the 'thin folio paper books' were still, as they had been seventeen years before at Kirkcaldy, 'within the glass

[1] Dugald Stewart, in *Transactions of the Royal Society of Edinburgh*, vol. iii. pt. i. p. 131; in Adam Smith's *Essays*, p. lxxxviii; in *Biographical Memoirs*, p. 109, note.

[2] See *Essays*, pp. iii. iv., and Adam Smith's will in Bonar, *Catalogue of Adam Smith's Library*, pp. xvi, xvii.

[3] P. W. Clayden, *Early Life of Samuel Rogers*, p. 167.

folding doors of a bureau' in his bedroom, and thus in his sight, but, while he was so ill, before his revival in the evening, altogether out of his reach. Nothing could be more natural in these circumstances than that he should ask his visitor to take the manuscripts out of the bureau and destroy them at once, whether before his eyes in the bedroom or elsewhere.

The manuscripts having thus perished, three generations have been obliged to content themselves with the account of the lectures which Dugald Stewart obtained from John Millar, who seems to have heard all or most of the lectures himself[1]:—

'In the professorship of Logic, to which Mr. Smith was appointed on his first introduction into this University, he soon saw the necessity of departing widely from the plan that had been followed by his predecessors, and of directing the attention of his pupils to studies of a more interesting and useful nature than the logic and metaphysics of the schools. Accordingly, after exhibiting a general view of the powers of the mind, and explaining so much of the ancient logic as was requisite to gratify curiosity with respect to an artificial method of reasoning which had once occupied the universal attention of the learned, he dedicated all the rest of his time to the delivery of a system of rhetoric and *belles lettres*. . . .

'About a year after his appointment to the professorship of Logic, Mr. Smith was elected to the chair of Moral Philosophy. His course of lectures on this subject was divided into four parts. The first contained Natural Theology, in which he considered the proofs of the being and the attributes of God, and those principles of the human mind upon which religion is founded. The second comprehended Ethics strictly so called, and consisted chiefly of the doctrines which he afterwards published in his "Theory of Moral Sentiments." In the third part he treated at more length of that branch of morality which relates to *justice*, and which, being susceptible of precise and accurate rules, is for that reason capable of a full and particular explanation.

'Upon this subject he followed the plan that seems to be suggested by Montesquieu; endeavouring to trace the gradual progress of jurisprudence, both public and private, from the rudest to the most refined ages, and to point out the effects of those arts which contribute to subsistence and to the accumulation of property, in producing corresponding improvements or alterations in law and government. This important branch of his labours he also intended to give to the public; but this intention, which is mentioned in the conclusion of the "Theory of Moral Sentiments" he did not live to fulfil.

[1] See his *Historical View of the English Government*, p. 528, and Rae, *Life of Adam Smith*, pp. 43, 53.

'In the last part of his lectures, he examined those political regulations which are founded not upon the principle of *justice*, but that of *expediency*, and which are calculated to increase the riches, the power and the prosperity of a state. Under this view, he considered the political institutions relating to commerce, to finances, to ecclesiastical and military establishments. What he delivered on these subjects contained the substance of the work he afterwards published under the title of "An Inquiry into the Nature and Causes of the Wealth of Nations"'[1].

From a purely biographical point of view it would doubtless be extremely interesting to have before us the text or a full report of Adam Smith's lectures on rhetoric, belles lettres and natural theology. But these are not of historical importance. However excellent any of them may have been, they had not the opportunity of exercising a very wide influence in their own time, and it is of course idle to expect that anything first printed a century and a half after it was written will ever have much influence on human thought or action. Each generation requires to be addressed from a particular standpoint, and arguments which would have been convincing in 1763 will fall perfectly flat in 1896. There are indeed some classics which have been lost or have suffered total eclipse for a time and yet seem to have exercised an influence after their reappearance, but it will always be found on examination that the influence is really that of their commentators and critics, or even in some cases of their translators.

To the second part of Adam Smith's Moral Philosophy course, his lectures on 'Ethics strictly so called,' very little interest attaches, either for the historian or the biographer. There is no reason to doubt Millar's statement that it consisted chiefly of the doctrines contained in the *Theory of Moral Sentiments*, and as that work was published in 1759, while Smith still occupied the professorial chair, and only seven years after his appointment, it is scarcely possible that the publication of the lectures could add anything of much value to the history either of the lecturer or of his subject.

But the third and fourth parts of the Moral Philosophy course occupy an entirely different position. The influence of the

[1] *Transactions of the Royal Society of Edinburgh*, vol. ii pt. i. pp. 61-63; *Essays*, pp. xvi-xviii; *Biographical Memoirs*, pp. 12-15.

Wealth of Nations in politics has been so great that every inquirer into the history of political science must have regretted that he had no access to the third part, in which Adam Smith 'endeavoured to trace the gradual progress of jurisprudence, both public and private, from the rudest to the most refined ages, and to point out the effects of those arts which contribute to subsistence and to the accumulation of property, in producing corresponding improvements or alterations in law and government.' The fourth part of the course resembles the second in being said to have served as the foundation for a published book. But that book—the *Wealth of Nations*—was of incomparably greater importance than the *Moral Sentiments*, and it was not published till more than twelve years after Smith had ceased lecturing. Of this period a portion is known to have been spent in communion with the French *Économistes*, and nearly all the rest in research. There has consequently been good reason to believe that the lectures, if they could be obtained, would show exactly how certain economic ideas which were eventually received into public favour, grew up in the mind of the man who did most to commend them to the world.

No one could have been more sensible of the historical value of the last two parts of the lectures than I, but I can not claim any credit for having discovered the manuscript which is now published. On April 21, 1895, Mr. Charles C. Maconochie, Advocate, whom I then met for the first time, happened to be present when, in course of conversation with the literary editor of the *Oxford Magazine*, I had occasion to make some remark about Adam Smith. Mr. Maconochie thereupon immediately said that he possessed a manuscript report of Adam Smith's lectures on jurisprudence, which he regarded as of considerable interest.

This manuscript, which is copied in the present volume, forms an octavo book 9 in. high, $7\frac{1}{2}$ in. broad and $1\frac{1}{8}$ in. thick. It has a substantial calf binding, the sides of which, however, have completely parted company with the back, apparently, as often happens in the case of calf-bound books a century old, from age rather than from use. On the back there is some gilt-cross-hatching and the word JURIS PRUDENCE (thus divided between two lines) in gilt letters on a red label. There are in all 192 leaves. Two of these are fly-leaves of dissimilar paper and have their fellows pasted on the insides of the cover, front and back. The rest all consist of paper of homogeneous character, water-marked 'L. V. Gerrevink.'

The manuscript is written on both sides of the paper in a rectangular space formed by four red ink lines previously ruled, which leave a margin of about three-quarters of an inch. Besides the fly-leaves there are three blank leaves at the end and two at the beginning.

There is nothing to show conclusively whether the writing was first executed on separate sheets subsequently bound up, or in a blank note-book afterwards rebound, or in the book as it appears at present.

No characteristic of the orthography, handwriting or paper affords any reason for suspecting that the manuscript is of a later date than that which it bears on its title-page, namely, 1766. Mr. Falconer Madan of the Bodleian Library, before seeing that date, conjectured the handwriting to be as early as the second quarter of the eighteenth century. Paper water-marked 'L. V. Gerrevink' was in use fifteen years before, as is shown by the fact that there is in the Glasgow University Library a letter from Dr. Pearce, Bishop of Bangor, to Professor Rosse, written on such paper under the date June 20, 1751.

Inside the front cover, written large with a very thick pen, is the inscription 'J. A. Maconochie 1811,' near the top, and in the middle the same signature, without the date, is written small with a very fine pen over the remains of a book plate which has been unfortunately so ruthlessly cut away with a knife that nothing except the discovery of another copy would make identification possible. There is also Mr. C. C. Maconochie's signature with the date 1876. On the inside of the first blank-leaf '1/2' is marked in the top left-hand corner in ink as faded as that of the manuscript.

Mr. Maconochie gives the following account of the way in which the manuscript came into his possession:—

65 NORTHUMBERLAND STREET,
EDINBURGH,
June 12, 1896.

MY DEAR CANNAN,

I am sorry to say that I have entirely failed to trace the source from which the MS. of Adam Smith's lectures passed into the hands of my grand-uncle, James Allan Maconochie. It is not possible, looking to dates and other facts, that either he, his father, the first

Lord Meadowbank[1], or his brother, the second judge of that name[2], took the notes which were subsequently copied out, and I am inclined to think that the book must have been bought at a sale or elsewhere, as I cannot find at Meadowbank House any copy of a bookplate the scroll work of which at all resembles that of the obliterated plate on the cover of the MS.

James Allan Maconochie, who was an advocate and Sheriff of Orkney, died in 1845 unmarried. Many of his books are still at Meadowbank, where law books naturally accumulated in large numbers, as two judges and a Professor in the Faculty of Law in Glasgow University[3] have been among the proprietors of the estate during the last hundred and thirty years, and several other members of the family, as well as J. A. Maconochie, have been in the legal profession. A large number of these books, some of which were very bulky, had from time to time been stacked in heaps on the floor of a garret room, and in 1876, immediately before I was called to the Bar, I was given permission to take away such of them as I thought would be useful to me. Amongst others I took the MS. in question, and it has been in my possession since that date.

Believe me,

Yours very truly,

CHARLES C. MACONOCHIE.

That the manuscript is a fair copy and not the original notes taken at the lectures is shown, first, by the fact that the date on the title-page is 'MDCCLXVI,' whereas Adam Smith relinquished his professorial chair in January, 1764; secondly, by its clean and well-written character and the almost entire absence of abbreviations, coupled with the fact that the report is often obviously verbatim, and, thirdly, by the circumstance that some of the mistakes are evidently caused by misreading and not by mishearing.

That the fair copy was not made by the person who took the original notes is shown by the fact that though the original note-taker must have been able and intelligent, the transcrip-

[1] Allan Maconochie, born 1748, called to the bar 1770, Professor of Public Law in the University of Edinburgh 1779, appointed to the bench with the title of Lord Meadowbank 1796, died 1816.

[2] Alexander Maconochie, eldest son of the above, born 1777, called to the bar 1799, Solicitor-General 1813, Lord Advocate 1816, appointed to the bench with the title of Lord Meadowbank 1819, assumed the additional surname of Welwood 1854, died 1861.

[3] Allan Alexander Maconochie-Welwood, eldest son of the above, born 1806, called to the bar 1829, Professor of Civil Law in the University of Glasgow 1842, died 1885.

tion is evidently the work of a person who often did not understand what he was writing. For example, at a place where the context obviously requires 'one' he writes 'me,'[1] simply because the initial letter of 'one,' written narrow or blind, resembles the first part of the initial letter of 'me,' carelessly written with a loop. In other places he substitutes 'shop' for 'ship'[2] and 'corn' for 'coin,'[3] regardless of the sense. He habitually makes nonsense of the argument by dividing sentences and paragraphs at the wrong place. Moreover, his somewhat elaborate and characterless handwriting suggests the professional copyist of mature years rather than the young man who has just completed his academical course.

It does not seem possible to give a decided answer to the question whether the copyist copied directly from the original notes or from a fair copy made by the original note-taker. It is evident throughout the manuscript that he takes pains to make his pages correspond with the pages from which he was copying. He constantly spreads out or compresses his handwriting as he approaches the end of a page, and when unsuccessful in filling the page exactly, he does not scruple to leave the last line partially blank. For example, the last two lines on p. 134 and the first on p. 135 of the manuscript are written thus:

> 'a better chance for its being abolished, Because
> One Single Person is Lawgiver
> And the Law will not extend to him nor diminish—— '

and the last two lines on p. 223 and the first on p. 224 appear as follows:

> 'progress of Opulence both in Ancient and
> Modern Times,
> Which Causes shall be shown either to Affect—— '

The amounts contained in a page are very unequal. Page 104, for instance, contains twenty-six lines of manuscript which occupy twenty-five of print[4], while page 106 contains only twenty lines of manuscript, equal to nineteen lines of print[5], two of which, owing to the chances of paragraphing, are more

[1] Below, p. 181, note 4.
[2] P. 12, note 1.
[3] P. 200.
[4] P. 75, lines 8 to 32.
[5] P. 76, line 19, 'The reason,' to p. 77, line 5, 'her husband.'

nearly empty than any in the manuscript. Such great inequality makes it appear probable that the pagination of the original notes is followed, and this would scarcely have been the case unless an index existed to the original notes. Now it seems improbable that a student who was likely to make a fair copy of his notes would have made the index before instead of after making the fair copy, so that we might infer that the copyist copied directly from the original notes. But, on the other hand, it seems improbable that any rough notes, almost necessarily full of abbreviations, could have been clear enough for a not very intelligent copyist to reproduce without many more obvious blunders than are to be found in the manuscript.

The original notes were probably destroyed after the fair copy was made, and if the manuscript was copied from them direct, it may have been always unique, but in any case it is quite possible, and even probable, that there were at one time several copies in existence. 'In those days manuscript copies of a popular professor's lectures, transcribed from his students' note-books, were often kept for sale in the booksellers' shops. Blair's lectures on rhetoric, for example, were for years in general circulation in this intermediate state'[1]. There can, however, scarcely have been many copies, or Adam Smith himself and his literary executors would have become aware of the fact. The description of the burning of the manuscripts before Adam Smith's death makes it certain that none of the three parties concerned suspected such a thing.

Adam Smith lectured at Glasgow as Professor of Moral Philosophy from 1752 to the end of December, 1763, and perhaps for a few days at the beginning of January, 1764[2]. Internal evidence enables us to attribute the report of the lectures to the end of this period. Frequent references to the Seven Years' War as 'the late' or 'the last' war[3] indicate a date certainly not earlier than the beginning of the academical session of 1762–3, when negotiations were proceeding, and almost certainly not earlier than the signature of the treaty of Fontainebleau on November 3, 1762. If this indication of date be rejected on the ground that it would be natural after the

[1] Rae, *Life of Adam Smith*, p. 64. See Blair's preface to *Lectures on Rhetoric and Belles Lettres*, 1783.

[2] Rae, *Life of Adam Smith*, pp. 46, 169.

[3] Pp. 27, 32, 268, cf. p. 271.

conclusion of peace for the reporter or the transcriber to alter 'the war' or 'the present war' into 'the late war,' and if the correspondence of the price of wheat, mentioned on p. 182, with the price quoted in the newspapers for February, 1763 [1], be rejected for the very good reason that it is too slender a foundation on which to build, we are driven back upon the reference to 1760 or 1761 contained in the statement that 'a late minister of state raised twenty-three millions in one year,' [2] and upon the account of the ransom of the Litchfield prisoners, which was not settled till April, 1760 [3]. It is accordingly probable that the actual lectures from which the notes were taken were delivered either in the portion of the academical session of 1763-4 which preceded Adam Smith's departure, or in the session of 1762-3, almost certain that they were not delivered before 1761-2, and absolutely certain that they were not delivered before 1760-1.

In the present edition the punctuation of the manuscript has been entirely disregarded, the spelling has been modernized and sectional headings have been added. To have followed the punctuation of the manuscript would have been simply ridiculous, and would have made the work almost unreadable. If the spelling had been merely archaic, it would of course have been right to retain it, but in fact it is not so much archaic as outrageously erratic and inconsistent, even when judged by the easy standard prevailing in the middle of the eighteenth century [4]; to spell as Adam Smith himself would have spelled in 1763 was a counsel of perfection which soon in practice proved impossible to carry out with sufficient success to make the laborious task worth attempting. Without the addition of new headings and divisions, the work would have been in tediously long blocks, and the reader would have found it difficult to find his way, owing to the abrupt changes of subject not indicated by any outward marks. So far as possible, the new headings have been adapted from

[1] P. 182, note 1.

[2] P. 207.

[3] Pp. 63-4.

[4] The MS. usually spells 'naturally,' 'generally,' and similar words, with only one l, but occasionally they appear with two. 'Woemen,' 'cannon law,' 'seperate,' 'arsine' (arson) all occur. In a very few cases the incorrect or archaic spelling of the manuscript has been retained for special reasons. To alter 'Puffendorf' or 'Wittenagemot,' for example, seemed obviously undesirable. The Index too has been left unaltered except for the necessary adaptation of the numbers of the pages.

words used in the text and modelled on the headings in the *Moral Sentiments* and the *Wealth of Nations*. The added headings are distinguished from those which occur in the manuscript by being enclosed in square brackets.

No attempt has been made to amend the report itself, much less the lectures, but mere clerical errors of the copyist have been amended wherever there appeared to be no reasonable doubt as to the correct reading. In every such case, however trivial, the reading of the manuscript is placed on record, words left out or altered being printed in the notes, and words added being enclosed in square brackets[1].

The notes are purely explanatory and historical. They are intended to help the reader to understand the text, to judge of the accuracy of the report, and to compare it with the authorities open to Adam Smith and with the subsequent development of his thought in the *Wealth of Nations*. The most conscientious effort has been made to resist the temptation to which commentators on the *Wealth of Nations* have generally succumbed, of using the text as a mere clothes-line on which to hang editorial opinions on economic theory.

To estimate in every case the degree of the probability that Adam Smith used a particular work would have occupied too much space. Consequently, as a rule, the passages in earlier authors which he may possibly have used, and those which he almost certainly did use, are alike simply quoted or referred to without comment.

Except in a few cases where practical difficulties stood in the way, the references to earlier authors have been made to that edition of each work which Adam Smith is most likely to have used in 1763. The volume and page references to the *Wealth of Nations* (abbreviated to '*W. of N.*') are to Thorold Rogers' edition published by the Oxford University Press (2nd ed. 1880).

Chapter II. Value of the Report.

Doubts may well be felt as to whether it is right to publish a report of lectures which has been made by a University student. A lecturer generally finds that his apparently most

[1] The manuscript of course has no head-lines at the top of the pages. It is always legible, except that 'those' is usually indistinguishable from 'these.'

incorruptible ideas have considerably deteriorated when they have passed through the minds and note-books of his pupils. But, after all, the doctrines of more than one of the greatest teachers of antiquity have come down to us in no other way than by means of the records left by disciples who had listened to their oral instruction. If we were to reject all that has been transmitted to us in this way, we should be left with some very considerable gaps both in philosophy and religion. In the present case we know that the disciple was both faithful and intelligent. We have most unusual means for judging of the accuracy of his work, and we find that it stands the severest tests in a manner which might be envied by a modern reporter with the advantage of shorthand. It is unnecessary to give examples here. A reader who will take the trouble to look out a few of the hundred references to the *Wealth of Nations*, and of the four hundred other references given in the notes, may easily satisfy himself on the point.

Granting that the report is satisfactory in itself, the further objection to its publication may be made that it is an act of impiety towards Adam Smith's memory. It is an evasion of his last wishes, and if Black and Hutton had not honestly complied with those wishes, we should be inclined to condemn their action, even if we could not profess to regret it. Adam Smith himself, however, would not have judged harshly of disregard of wishes more than a century old. He did not trust even his good friends Black and Hutton to fulfil their solemn promise to destroy his manuscripts immediately after his death, and thirty years before he had taught the Glasgow students that 'piety to the dead can only take place when their memory is fresh in the minds of men: a power to dispose of estates for ever is manifestly absurd.'[1]

Moreover it is probable that if he had been acquainted with the criticisms which were to be passed upon his work, he would have withdrawn all objection to the publication of his lectures.

Du Pont de Nemours said, in his haste, of the *Wealth of Nations*, 'everything that is true in this respectable but tedious work in two fat quarto volumes is to be found in Turgot's *Reflexions on the Formation and Distribution of Riches*; everything added by Adam Smith is inaccurate, not

[1] Below, p. 124.

to say incorrect.'[1] At a later period he repented of this outbreak, and confessed to a certain want of knowledge of the English tongue which had prevented him from appreciating Smith's work as he ought to have done. But down to quite recent times, if not to the present day, writers of authority have often expressed belief that the *Wealth of Nations* owes much to Turgot's *Réflexions*. Du Pont's learned and able biographer, as lately as 1888, permitted himself to speak of 'the care with which' Adam Smith 'omits to quote' the principal works of the physiocrats and 'especially that of Turgot.'[2]

For the particular accusation, indeed, that Adam Smith does not acknowledge his obligations to Turgot, there never was much foundation. He certainly does not acknowledge obligations; but had he any to acknowledge? Turgot's book, though written in 1766, was only published six years before the *Wealth of Nations*, and then only in the periodical *Éphémérides du Citoyen*[3]. As this was not in the Advocates' Library at Edinburgh in 1776[4], and is not among the collections of Adam Smith's books which Dr. James Bonar has catalogued[5], we are not justified in assuming that Adam Smith had so much as seen the work. The internal evidence is of the weakest possible character. To rely on general similarities of doctrine in such a case is childish. Such similarities are constantly found in the writings of contemporary authors who cannot possibly have been acquainted with each other's works. The coincidence is to be explained simply by the fact that in literature, as in everything else, the same effects produce the same causes. There is surely nothing surprising in the fact that two men who have read the same books and observed the same events, should occasionally use the same arguments and arrive at the same conclusions. Something much more definite is needed, and

[1] 'Tout ce qu'il y a de vrai dans ce livre estimable, mais pénible à lire, en deux gros volumes in-4°, se trouve dans les *Réflexions* de Turgot sur la formation et la distribution des richesses; tout ce qu'Adam Smith y a ajouté manque d'exactitude et même de fondement.' Quoted in Schelle, *Du Pont de Nemours et l'École physiocratique*, 1888, p. 159.

[2] *Ibid.*, loc. cit.

[3] Schelle, *Pourquoi les 'Réflexions' de Turgot ne sont-elles pas exactement connues?* in the *Journal des Économistes* for July, 1888, pp. 3-5.

[4] *Catalogue of the Library of the Faculty of Advocates, Edinburgh*, pt. ii. 1776.

[5] *Catalogue of Adam Smith's Library*, 1894.

no serious attempt has ever been made to supply it by pointing out particular passages in the *Wealth of Nations* which appear to owe anything to the *Réflexions*[1].

Myths of this kind, however, die hard, and if the lectures had remained unknown, the statement that Adam Smith made much use of the *Réflexions* would probably have been repeated from text-book to text-book for at least another half-century. But as it now appears that the resemblance between the *Réflexions* and the lectures is just as close as that between the *Réflexions* and the *Wealth of Nations*, and as the *Réflexions* were not even written till after Adam Smith had ceased lecturing and had seen and conversed with Turgot, it may be supposed that the enthusiasts of plagiarism will now seek to show that instead of Smith stealing from Turgot, the truth was that Turgot stole from Smith.

But the report of the lectures does much more in regard to the *Wealth of Nations* than merely dispose finally of the Turgot myth. It enables us to follow the gradual construction of the work almost from its very foundation, and to distinguish positively between what the original genius of its author created out of British materials on the one hand and French materials on the other.

In the work of professors, as in many other things, a kind of atavism is often observable. A professor has rarely been a student under his immediate predecessor in the chair. While he has been obtaining experience in a less dignified post, or has been absent acquiring the honour which it is proverbially difficult for a prophet to obtain in his own country, his master has died or retired and been succeeded by a man of an intermediate generation, and probably of intermediate views, whom he very likely regards with that slight dash of contempt which men are apt to feel for those who are older than themselves, but yet not old enough to

[1] Professor Thorold Rogers, indeed, after stating in the preface to his edition of the *Wealth of Nations*, that 'in the First Book, particularly, passages will be found which are almost transcripts from Turgot's divisions and arguments' (p. xxiii), quotes Turgot seven times in the notes to Book I. In one case (p. 14) the text bears a remote resemblance to the passage quoted from Turgot, but an infinitely closer resemblance to passages in earlier English writers quoted below, p. 162, note 1. In the other six cases there is not the smallest resemblance between the text and the passage quoted.

obtain from them the respect universally and fortunately accorded to the surviving lights of a past age and an 'old school,' whose virtues have become uncommon, and whose weaknesses and eccentricities, instead of annoying or disgusting, afford kindly amusement. We should do well therefore to look in Adam Smith's work for important traces of the influence of Francis Hutcheson, who was Professor of Moral Philosophy at Glasgow from 1729 to 1746, even if Hutcheson had been but an undistinguished member of the series of professors, instead of a teacher of unusual ability and originality, to whom Adam Smith acknowledged obligations, and of whom he used warm words of praise [1].

In 1745 Hutcheson published in Latin a little volume entitled *Philosophiae moralis institutio compendiaria libris III. ethices et iurisprudentiae naturalis elementa continens.* Of this he authorised a translation, published in 1747 as *A Short Introduction to Moral Philosophy in three books, containing the Elements of Ethicks and the Law of Nature.* From it we may gather with sufficient accuracy what Smith was taught as a boy in the class-room at Glasgow before he left, at the age of barely seventeen, for his long stay at Oxford.

The address 'to the students in Universities,' which forms the preface to the work, opens thus:—

> 'The celebrated division of philosophy among the ancients was into the *rational* or *logical*, the *natural*, and the *moral*. Their moral philosophy contained these parts, *ethicks* taken more strictly, teaching the nature of virtue and regulating the internal dispositions; and the knowledge of the *law of nature*. This latter contained, 1. the doctrine of *private rights*, or the laws obtaining in natural liberty. 2. *Oeconomicks*, or the laws and rights of the several members of a family; and 3. *Politicks*, shewing the various plans of civil government, and the rights of states with respect to each other.'

The three Books are accordingly headed: 'The Elements of Ethicks,' 'Elements of the Law of Nature' (in the Latin '*Iurisprudentia privata*') and the 'Principles of Oeconomicks and Politicks.' The part of Smith's course which eventually grew into the *Theory of Moral Sentiments* obviously corresponds with Book I; 'Private Law,' the third division of his 'Justice,' corresponds with Book II; while 'Domestic Law' and 'Public

[1] Rae, *Life of Adam Smith*, pp. 13, 14, 411.

Jurisprudence,' the first two divisions of his 'Justice,' correspond with Book III. The mode of treatment is very different, as Adam Smith goes into legal particularities in a way quite foreign to Hutcheson, but the main subjects treated are, roughly speaking, the same. The Law of Nations is divided in Hutcheson between chapter xv of Book II, 'Rights arising from Damage done and the Laws of War,' and the last two chapters of Book III, on the 'Laws of War' and 'Of Treaties, and Ambassadors, and the entire dissolution of States.' Neither Smith's 'Revenue' nor his 'Arms' correspond to anything in Hutcheson, and nearly as much may be said of his 'Police.' Hutcheson has, however, a short chapter in Book II (ch. xii), 'Concerning the Values or Prices of Goods,' in which the causes of high and low price and the characteristics of good money are discussed.

Probably it is in this chapter that the germ of the *Wealth of Nations* is to be found. In writing the chapter Hutcheson simply followed Pufendorf, and he does not make its connexion with the adjoining chapters, 'Of Oaths and Vows,' and 'Of the Several Sorts of Contracts,' very distinct and obvious, so that Adam Smith may well have thought, when he began his lectures, that it would be an improvement in logical arrangement to transfer the whole to a new heading, 'Police,' since the regulation of prices and the creation of money by the state both came under the head of 'Police,' as the word was understood in his time. As he lectured year by year, however, he would be led from this by two ways towards the consideration of the question what constitutes opulence or wealth. He would perceive both that regulations which interfere with natural prices diminish plenty or opulence, and that mere additions to a nation's stock of money do not increase its opulence, as some at least of the more extreme mercantilists really believed, and as all of them to some extent tacitly or explicitly assumed. Observing the overwhelming importance of this question, he was not the man to be deterred by considerations as to the symmetry of his general scheme of arrangement from putting it in the principal place and allowing it to introduce various subjects which cannot possibly be regarded as part of police.

In some such way as this the second and only considerable portion of 'Police' assumed its present form, in which it consists of, first, a discussion of the material wants of mankind and of the great cause, division of labour, which enables them to be better satisfied in a civilized than in an uncivilized nation (§§ 1–6); next, the traditional inquiry as to prices and money (§§ 7, 8) with a large appendix explaining various evil consequences of the notion that money alone constitutes opulence (§§ 9–13) and corollaries as to interest (§ 14) and exchange (§ 15); thirdly, a dissertation on the causes why opulence does not increase as fast as might be expected (§ 16); and, lastly, a description of the influence of commerce (which, in consequence of the effects of the division of labour, is the great cause of opulence) on manners (§ 17). Even the Third Part of the whole scheme, 'Of Revenue,' is brought in as one of the causes of the slow progress of opulence. The portion of 'Jurisprudence' dealing with 'Police' thus became, with the exception of a scrap about security and a bare mention of sanitation, an 'Inquiry into the Nature and Causes of the Wealth of Nations.'

If the Contents of the *Wealth of Nations* and those of the lectures on 'Police,' 'Revenue,' and 'Arms' be compared, a close correspondence between them is observable. The first three chapters of the first book of the *Wealth of Nations*, on the division of labour, correspond with §§ 3–6 of 'Cheapness or Plenty' in the lectures; chapter iv, on money, corresponds with § 8, and chapters v, vi and vii, on prices, correspond with § 7; Book II, chapter iv, on stock lent at interest, corresponds with § 14; Book III, on the different progress of opulence in different nations, has practically the same subject as § 16; the first eight chapters of Book IV, on the mercantile system, treat of the same matter as §§ 9–12; Book V, on revenue, corresponds with Part III of the lectures, and also absorbs much of Part IV, 'Of Arms.'

Looking at the question first from the side of the lectures, we see that this leaves §§ 1, 2, 13, 15 and 17 of 'Cheapness or Plenty' unaccounted for. It is not easy to explain why the first two sections were omitted from the *Wealth of Nations*, and the fact will be regretted by those who ask for a theory of consumption as a preliminary to the other parts of political economy. The explanation of the omission of § 13 is given by Adam Smith himself. It was simply that the Mississippi scheme had been 'explained so fully, so clearly, and with so much order and distinctness by Mr. Du Verney' that it was unnecessary to give any account of it[1]. A mere summary of Duverney's description, however well suited for an academical lecture, could not properly appear in a great book. Exchange (§ 15) was doubtless omitted as too elementary, and § 17, on the influence of commerce on manners, finds no special place, because most of it was absorbed in Book V, chapter i. article ii. 'Of the Expense of the Institutions for the Education of Youth.'

Turning now to the consideration of the question from the side of the *Wealth of Nations*, we are at once struck by the fact that not only chapter ix of Book IV, on the system of the *Économistes* or physiocrats, but also chapter viii of Book I, on wages, chapter ix, on profits, chapter x, on differences of wages and profits, and chapter xi, on rent, are as yet unaccounted for. Further examination shows that the main ideas and many of the illustrations of chapter viii, of chapter ix, and still more of chapter x, are contained in the section of the lectures which deal with prices, but that there is no trace whatever in the lectures of the scheme of distribution which the *Wealth of Nations* sets forth. The main body of Book II, 'Of the Nature, Accumulation and Employment of Stock,' is also entirely unaccounted for. There is nothing at all about capital in the lectures, and stock is not given an important place, while there is no mention whatever of that distinction between productive and unproductive labour which is fundamental in the *Wealth of Nations*, and to which a large portion of Book II is devoted.

When Adam Smith went to France he found 'a few men of great learning and ingenuity' whose leader had constructed an elaborate table containing an arithmetical example of 'three sorts of expenses, their source, their advances, their distribution, their effects, their reproduction, their relation to each other, to population, to agriculture, to manufactures, to commerce, and to the general riches of a nation.' This table was regarded by the sect with extraordinary veneration, and doubtless every possible effort was made to explain it to Adam Smith. Its three sorts of expenses are productive expenses, expenses of revenue and sterile expenses, but of these three the middle one, expenses of revenue, is almost immediately divided between the other two. Productive expenses are annual advances in

[1] *W. of N.* bk. ii. ch. ii. vol. i. p. 318.

agriculture, and sterile expenses are annual advances in other industries. The *Reproduit totale*, estimated at the bottom of the table, is altogether the result of the productive expenses and operations, and not at all of the sterile. It is distributed between three classes, the productive class, the sterile class and the proprietors of land.

To us at the present day the table, with its tangle of zigzag lines, appears an almost childish toy, and its recent republication by the British Economic Association[1] excited very little interest. Nevertheless, in the fact that it attempts to give a comprehensive view of the total results of the industry of a year, it marks an enormous advance in economic theory, and we can easily imagine that an acute mind like Adam Smith's would immediately grasp its importance. To accept it as it stood he was not prepared, but he adopted the point of view of its author, and accordingly we find in the *Wealth of Nations* something which is absent from the lectures, namely, a definite conception of labour set in motion by a particular kind of expenditure and producing an aggregate annual produce which is 'distributed' into several large categories. The particular kind of expenditure which sets productive labour in motion is identified with the laying out of capital stock. It is assumed that all labour set in motion by this laying out of capital produces vendible objects, and argued that all such labour, and no other, is properly called productive. This new doctrine forms the main body of Book II, 'Of the Nature, Accumulation, and Employment of Stock' in the *Wealth of Nations*.

If the theory were thoroughly believed in, it would appear that Book II ought logically to have been placed first. According to the Introduction and Plan, the average produce per head of population 'must in every nation be regulated by two different circumstances; first, by the skill, dexterity, and judgement with which its labour is generally applied; and, secondly, by the proportion between the number of those who are employed in useful labour and that of those who are not so employed.' These two circumstances are evidently in the wrong order. We ought to consider what proportion of the population is employed in useful labour before we consider how skilfully and dexterously they work.

[1] *Tableau Oeconomique*, by François Quesnay, 1894.

'The number of useful and productive labourers,' we are assured, 'is everywhere in proportion to the quantity of capital stock which is employed in setting them to work, and to the particular way in which it is so employed,' and if this be so, an economic treatise ought surely to begin with a dissertation on capital. But Adam Smith had already, in his lectures, begun his treatment of the subject with his dissertation on the productive powers of labour, and had incidentally treated of stock in store not as something indispensable before labour can be set in motion, but merely as something required 'after the ages of hunting and fishing,' or 'when manufactures were introduced' and 'a great deal of time' required[1]. It would have been astonishing if he had been willing to relegate his own excellent disquisition on the division of labour to the second place, and consequently no surprise need be felt that capital is treated only in the second Book, in spite of the adoption of the view of the *Tableau* as to its function in governing the amount of productive labour[2].

It has always been obvious that in spite of the mention of the problem of distribution in the title of Book I of the *Wealth of Nations*[3], 'Adam Smith's theory of distribution, instead of being made one of the main subjects of the Book, is inserted in the middle of the chapter on prices as a mere appendage or corollary of his doctrine of prices'[4]. By way of explaining the discrepancy, it was possible to conjecture that 'in all probability the Book existed in a fairly complete form before Adam Smith became acquainted with the physiocratic doctrine,' and that when that event took place 'he may very well have thought that his theory of prices and his observations on wages, profit and rent made a very good theory of what the physiocrats called "distribution," and thus have been led to affix the present title of the Book and to interpolate the passage about the whole produce being parcelled out and distributed as wages, profit and rent'[5]. This conjecture

[1] Below, p. 181.

[2] In the Introduction to Book II, an attempt to combine the old and the new view is observable.

[3] 'Of the Causes of Improvement in the productive Powers of Labour, and of the Order according to which its Produce is naturally distributed among the different Ranks of the People.'

[4] Cannan, *History of the Theories of Production and Distribution in English Political Economy from* 1776 *to* 1848, 1893, p. 186.

[5] *Ibid.* p. 188.

is now shown to be substantially correct. The dissertations on the division of labour, money, prices, and the causes of the differences of wages in different employments, evidently existed very nearly in their present form before Adam Smith went to France, and the scheme of distribution, on the other hand, was wholly absent. It is plain that Smith acquired the idea of the necessity of a scheme of distribution from the physiocrats, and that he tacked his own scheme (very different from theirs) on to his already existing theory of prices[1].

Besides thus elucidating the composition of the *Wealth of Nations*, the lectures serve to settle the doubtless far less important but still interesting question of the nature of Adam Smith's proposed work on Justice, or that portion of jurisprudence not dealt with in the *Wealth of Nations.*

Millar, in the account of the Glasgow lectures quoted above, says that Smith intended to give to the public the substance of the third part of his course, the lectures on Justice, and that he mentioned this intention in the conclusion of the *Theory of Moral Sentiments.* Turning to the passage referred to, which is the same in the sixth as in the first edition, we find Adam Smith first condemning casuistry, and then declaring that the two useful parts of moral philosophy are ethics and jurisprudence. 'Every system of positive law,' he says, 'may be regarded as a more or less imperfect attempt towards a system of natural jurisprudence, or towards an enumeration of the particular rules of justice.' But, owing to various difficulties which he enumerates, the attempt is never perfectly successful. 'The reasonings of lawyers upon the different imperfections and improvements of the laws of different countries' might have been expected to 'have led them to aim at establishing a system of what might properly be called natural jurisprudence, or a theory of the general principles which ought to run through and be the foundation of the laws of all nations.' However, 'it was very late in the world before any such general system was thought of, or before the philosophy of law was treated by itself and

[1] Appended to this Introduction (pp. xxxv–xxxix) is a table of parallel passages in the lectures and the *Wealth of Nations.* The total number of pages occupied in Rogers' edition by each chapter are given in order to facilitate reference to other editions.

without regard to the particular institutions of any one nation.'

'Grotius,' Adam Smith concludes, 'seems to have been the first who attempted to give the world anything like a system of those principles which ought to run through and be the foundation of the laws of all nations; and his treatise of the laws of war and peace, with all its imperfections, is perhaps at this day the most complete work that has yet been given upon this subject. I shall in another discourse endeavour to give an account of the general principles of law and government and of the different revolutions they have undergone in the different ages and periods of society, not only in what concerns justice, but in what concerns police, revenue and arms, and whatever else is the object of law. I shall not, therefore, at present enter into any further detail concerning the history of jurisprudence.'

In the Preface to the sixth edition of the *Moral Sentiments*, published in 1790, after quoting from this passage the promise of 'another discourse,' Adam Smith says—

'In the *Enquiry concerning the Nature and Causes of the Wealth of Nations*, I have partly executed this promise; at least so far as concerns police, revenue and arms. What remains, the theory of jurisprudence, which I have long projected, I have hitherto been hindered from executing by the same occupations which had till now prevented me from revising the present work.'

It has always appeared somewhat strange that the publication of the *Wealth of Nations* should have been regarded by Adam Smith as a partial fulfilment of a promise to give an account of the general principles of law and government and of the different revolutions they have undergone in the different ages and periods of society in what concerns police, revenue and arms, even when we remember the wide sense then borne by the word 'police.' Nor has it been altogether clear how the *Wealth of Nations* fitted into the 'history of jurisprudence.'

The report clears up every difficulty. The lectures included in it are obviously the third and fourth part of the moral philosophy course described by Millar, and they are also the draft of the 'account of the general principles of law and government' or 'history of jurisprudence' contemplated as a future work by Adam Smith when he wrote the last page of the *Moral Sentiments* in 1759. Part I, 'Of Justice,' with perhaps the fifth part, entitled 'Of the Laws of Nations,' is the third part in Millar's description of the whole course, and is also the 'account of the general principles of law and government in what concerns justice' mentioned in 1759 'and the theory of jurisprudence' mentioned in 1790. Parts II, III and IV 'Of Police, Revenue and Arms,' are the fourth part in Millar's description of the course; serving as the first draft of the *Wealth of Nations*, they induced Adam Smith to say that he had fulfilled his promise as regards police, revenue and arms, though no one unacquainted with the lectures would have described the *Wealth of Nations* as a treatise on those three subjects in that order.

It does not seem probable that Adam Smith ever made much progress with the projected work on Justice. Mackenzie, if Rogers reports him correctly, seems to have believed that the manuscripts which were burnt by Black and Hutton consisted of this book in a nearly completed condition. Before he came that evening, he says, Adam Smith, with the assistance of Dr. Black, 'had burnt sixteen volumes in manuscript on Jurisprudence—the sum of one course of his lectures at Glasgow, as was the *Wealth of Nations* of another; but these had not received his last corrections, and from what he had seen he had formed a mean opinion of posthumous publications in general.' Little importance, however, need be attached to this, since, according to Rogers, Mackenzie also described Adam Smith, an only child, as 'an affectionate brother,' and stated that he died 'a few hours after' the supper, though he lived as a matter of fact for six days[1]. After the publication of the *Wealth of Nations* he must have had far greater distractions than before, and his official duties at the Board of Customs[2] must have occupied a portion of his time. In November, 1785, after mentioning a new edition of the *Moral Sentiments*, he wrote: 'I have likewise two other great works upon the anvil; the one is a sort of Philosophical History of all the different branches of Literature, of Philosophy, Poetry and Eloquence; the other is a sort of theory and History of Law and Government.' He had, it thus appears, failed to concentrate his energies on one work, and he could only say of the two that 'the materials of both are in a great measure collected, and

[1] P. W. Clayden, *Early Life of Samuel Rogers*, p. 167.

[2] He describes himself in 1787 as a regular attendant. Rae, *Life of Adam Smith*, p. 411.

some part of both is put into tolerable good order.' That he did indeed 'struggle violently' against 'the indolence of old age,' which he felt 'coming fast upon' him[1], we can well believe, but the failure of his health which took place soon afterwards forbids the supposition that he could have done much more before his death in 1790. It is therefore unlikely that the unfinished work ever consisted of very much more than those parts of the lectures on Justice which were not incorporated in the *Wealth of Nations*. What these parts were the reader has now the opportunity of judging for himself.

[1] Letter to the Duke de la Rochefoucauld, first published in the *Athenaeum*, December 28, 1895, and reprinted in the *Economic Journal*, March, 1896, pp. 165, 166.

TABLE OF PARALLEL PASSAGES

IN THE

WEALTH OF NATIONS.

INTRODUCTION (vol. i. pp. 1–4).

BOOK I.

CHAP. I (vol. i. pp. 5–14).

CHAP. II (vol. i. pp. 14–18).

CHAP. III (vol. i. pp. 18–23).

Chap. II (vol. i. pp. 283–331).

Chap. III (vol. i. pp. 332–53).

Chap. IV (vol. i. pp. 353–62).

BOOK III.

Chap. II (vol. i. pp. 386–98).

Chap. III (vol. i. pp. 398–409).

Chap. IV (vol. i. pp. 410–23).

BOOK IV.

CHAP. I (vol. ii. pp. 1–24).

CHAP. II (vol. ii. pp. 25–46).

CHAP. III (Digression, vol. ii. pp. 53-62; pt. ii. pp. 62–73).

CHAP. V (vol. ii. pp. 79–122).

CHAP. VI (vol. ii. pp. 122–34).

CHAP. VII (pt. i. vol. ii. pp. 134–44; pt. ii. pp. 144–70).

CHAP. VIII (vol. ii. pp. 226–46).

CHAP. IX (vol. ii. pp. 246–73).

BOOK V.

Chap. I (pt. i. vol. ii. pp. 274–92; pt. ii. pp. 292–305; pt. iii. art. 2, pp. 344–72).

Chap. II (pt. i. vol. ii. pp. 404–13; pt. ii. art. 1, pp. 413–40; art. 2, pp. 440–53; art. 4, pp. 463–506).

Chap. III (vol. ii. pp. 506–50).

NOTE

The title page opposite reproduces that of the manuscript as exactly as is possible in type and allowing for the fact that the manuscript is an inch wider.

JURIS PRUDENCE

or

Notes from the Lectures

on *Justice*, *Police*, *Revenue*, and *Arms*

delivered in the University of *Glasgow*

by

Adam Smith *Professor of Moral Philosophy.*

MDCCLXVI.

JURISPRUDENCE

INTRODUCTION

[§ 1. *Of Works on Natural Jurisprudence.*]

JURISPRUDENCE is that science which inquires into the general principles which ought to be the foundation of the laws of all nations. Grotius seems to have been the first who attempted to give the world anything like a regular system of natural jurisprudence, and his treatise On the Laws of War and Peace, with all its imperfections, is perhaps at this day the most complete work on this subject[1]. It is a sort of casuistical book for sovereigns and states, determining in what cases war may justly be made and how far it may be carried on. As states have no common sovereign and are with respect to one another in a state of nature, war is their only method of redressing injuries. He determines war to be lawful in every case where the state receives an injury which would be redressed by an equitable civil magistrate[2]. This naturally led him to inquire into the constitution of states and the principles of civil laws; into the rights of sovereigns and subjects; into the nature of crimes, contracts, property, and whatever else was the object of law, so that the two first books of

[1] *Moral Sentiments*, ad fin.   [2] Lib. ii. cap. i. § 2.

his treatise, which are upon this subject, are a complete system of jurisprudence.

The next writer of note after Grotius was Mr. Hobbes. He had conceived an utter abhorrence of the ecclesiastics, and the bigotry of his times gave him occasion to think that the subjection of the consciences of men to ecclesiastic authority was the cause of the dissensions and civil wars that happened in England during the times of Charles I and of Cromwell. In opposition to them he endeavoured to establish a system of morals by which the consciences of men might be subjected to the civil power, and which represented the will of the magistrate as the only proper rule of conduct. Before the establishment of civil society, mankind, according to him, were in a state of war; and in order to avoid the ills of a natural state, men entered into contract to obey one common sovereign who should determine all disputes. Obedience to his will, according to him, constituted civil government, without which there could be no virtue, and consequently it too was the foundation and essence of virtue.

The divines thought themselves obliged to oppose this pernicious doctrine concerning virtue, and attacked it by endeavouring to show that a state of nature was not a state of war, but that society might subsist, though not in so harmonious a manner, without civil institutions. They endeavoured to show that man in this state has certain rights belonging to him, such as a right to his body, to the fruits of his labour, and the fulfilling of contracts. With this design Puffendorf wrote his large treatise. The sole intention of the first part of it is to confute Hobbes, though it in reality serves no purpose to treat of the laws which would take place in a state of nature, or by what means succession to property was carried on, as there is no such state existing.

The next who wrote on this subject was the Baron de Cocceii, a Prussian. There are five volumes in folio of his works published, many of which are very ingenious and distinct, especially those which treat of laws. In the last volume he gives an account of some German systems[1].

Besides these there are no systems of note upon this subject.

[§ 2. *Of the Division of the Subject.*]

Jurisprudence is the theory of the general principles of law and government.

The four great objects of law are justice, police, revenue, and arms.

The object of justice is the security from injury, and it is the foundation of civil government.

The objects of police are the cheapness of commodities, public security and cleanliness, if the two last were not too minute for a lecture of this kind. Under this head we will consider the opulence of a state.

It is likewise necessary that the magistrate who bestows his time and labour in the business of the state should be compensated for it. For this purpose, and for defraying the expenses of government, some fund must be raised. Hence the origin of revenue. The subject of consideration under this head will be the proper means of levying revenue,

[1] Neither the works of Heinrich, Freiherr von Cocceii, nor those of his son Samuel are wholly comprised in five folio volumes. The volumes referred to are probably *Henrici de Cocceii sacrae regiae maiestati borussicae quondam a consiliis secretioribus Grotius illustratus*, Wratislaviae, 1744, 1746, 1747 and 1752, 4 vols. folio, published with observations by Samuel Freiherr von Cocceii long after his father's death, and *Samuelis L. B. de Cocceii summi regni borussici cancellarii ministri status intimi . . . Introductio ad Henrici L. B. de Cocceii Grotium illustratum*, Halae, 1748, 1 vol. folio. These and no other folio works of either author appear in the 1776 catalogue of the Edinburgh Advocates' Library, and all except vol. iv of *Grotius illustratus* are in Bonar, *Catalogue of Adam Smith's Library*. Dissertations X and XI in the *Introductio* deal with 'some German systems,' and the very lengthy Dissertation XII 'treats of laws.'

which must come from the people by taxes, duties, &c. In general, whatever revenue can be raised most insensibly from the people ought to be preferred; and in the sequel it is proposed to be shown, how far the laws of Britain and of other European nations are calculated for this purpose.

As the best police cannot give security unless the government can defend themselves from foreign injuries and attacks, the fourth thing appointed by law is for this purpose; and under this head will be shown the different species of arms with their advantages and disadvantages, the constitution of standing armies, militias, &c.

After these will be considered the laws of nations, under which are comprehended the demands which one independent society may have upon another, the privileges of aliens, and proper grounds for making war.

PART I: OF JUSTICE

[INTRODUCTION]

THE end of justice is to secure from injury. A man may be injured in several respects:

First, as a man.

Secondly, as a member of a family.

Thirdly, as a member of a state.

As a man he may be injured in his body, reputation, or estate.

As a member of a family he may be injured as a father, as a son, as a husband or wife, as a master or servant, as a guardian or pupil. For the two last are to be considered in a family relation, till such time as the pupil can take care of himself.

As a member of a state, a magistrate may be injured by disobedience, or a subject by oppression, &c.

A man may be injured:

First, in his body by wounding, maiming, murdering, or by infringing his liberty.

Secondly, in his reputation, either by falsely representing him as a proper object of resentment or punishment, as by calling him a thief or robber, or by depreciating his real worth, and endeavouring to degrade him below the level of his profession. A physician's character is injured when we endeavour to persuade the world he kills his patients instead of curing them, for by such a report he loses his business. We do not however injure a man when we do not give him all the praise that is due to his merit. We do not injure Sir Isaac Newton or Mr. Pope when we say that Sir Isaac was no better philosopher than Descartes, or that Mr. Pope was no better poet than the ordinary ones of his own time. By these expressions we do not bestow on them all the praise that they deserve, yet we do them no injury, for we do not throw them below the ordinary rank of men in their own professions. These rights which a man has to the preservation of his body and reputation from injury are called natural, or as the civilians express them *iura hominum naturalia*.

Thirdly, a man may be injured in his estate. His rights to his estate are called acquired or *iura adventitia*, and are of two kinds, real and personal.

A real right is that whose object is a real thing and which can be claimed *a quocumque possessore*. Such are all possessions, houses, furniture.

Personal rights are such as can be claimed by a law-suit from a particular person, but not *a quocumque possessore*. Such are all debts and contracts, the payment or performance of which can be demanded only from one person. If I buy a horse and have him delivered to me, though the former owner sell him to another, I can claim him *a quocumque possessore*; but if he was not delivered to me I can only pursue the seller.

Real rights are of four kinds, property, servitudes, pledges, and exclusive privileges.

Property is our possessions of every kind, which if any way lost, or taken from us by stealth or violence, may be redemanded *a quocumque possessore*.

Servitudes are burdens upon the property of another. Thus I may have a liberty of passing through a field belonging to another which lies between me and the highway, or if my neighbour have plenty of water in his fields and I have none in mine for my cattle, I may have a right to drive them to his. Such burdens on the property of another are called servitudes. These rights were originally personal, but the trouble and expense of numerous lawsuits in order to get possession of them, when the adjacent property which was burdened with them passed through a number of hands, induced legislators to make them real and claimable *a quocumque possessore*. Afterwards the property was transferred with these servitudes upon it.

Pledges, which include all pawns and mortgages, are securities for something else to which we have a right. The laws of most civilized nations have considered them as real rights, and give a liberty to claim them as such.

Exclusive privileges are such as that of a bookseller to vend a book for a certain number of years, and to hinder any other person from doing it during that period. These rights are for the most part creatures of the civil law, though some few of them are natural, as in a state of hunters even before the origin of civil government, if a man has started a hare and pursued her for some time, he has an exclusive privilege to hunt her, by which he can hinder any other to come in upon her with a fresh pack of hounds.

An heir has also an exclusive privilege of hindering any person to take possession of the inheritance left him while he is deliberating whether or not it will be for his interest to take possession of it and pay off the debts with which it is burdened [1].

Personal rights are of three kinds, as they arise from contract, quasi contract, or delinquency.

The foundation of contract is the reasonable expectation, which the person who promises raises in the person to whom he binds himself; of which the satisfaction may be extorted by force.

[1] The reference is to Roman or Scotch law, not English.

Quasi contract is the right which one has to a compensation for necessary trouble and expense about another man's affairs. If a person finds a watch in the highway he has a claim to a reward, and to the defraying of his expenses in finding out the owner. If a man lend[1] me a sum of money, he has a right not only to the sum, but to interest also.

Delinquency is founded upon damage done to any person, whether through malice or culpable negligence. A person has a right to claim these only from a certain person.

The objects of these seven rights make up the whole of a man's estate.

The origin of natural rights is quite evident. That a person has a right to have his body free from injury and his liberty free from infringement unless there be a proper cause, nobody doubts. But acquired rights such as property require more explanation. Property and civil government very much depend on one another. The preservation of property and the inequality of possession first formed it, and the state of property must always vary with the form of government. The civilians begin with considering government and then treat of property and other rights. Others[2] who have written on this subject begin with the latter and then consider family and civil government. There are several advantages peculiar to each of these methods, though that of the civil law seems upon the whole preferable.

[1] Scil. 'involuntarily,' i.e. if I find a man's money and keep it till I discover the owner. See Hutcheson, *Introduction to Moral Philosophy*, 1747, p. 224.

[2] E.g. Hutcheson, *Introduction to Moral Philosophy*.

[DIVISION I.] OF PUBLIC JURISPRUDENCE

[§ 1. *Of the Original Principles of Government.*]

THERE are two principles which induce men to enter into a civil society, which we shall call the principles of authority and utility. At the head of every small society or association of men, we find a person of superior abilities. In a warlike society he is a man of superior strength, and in a polished one of superior mental capacity. Age and a long possession of power have also a tendency to strengthen authority. Age is naturally in our imagination connected with wisdom and experience, and a continuance in power bestows a kind of right to the exercise of it. But superior wealth still more than any of these qualities contributes to confer authority. This proceeds not from any dependence that the poor have upon the rich, for in general the poor are independent, and support themselves by their labour, yet, though they expect no benefit from them, they have a strong propensity to pay them respect. This principle is fully explained in the Theory of Moral Sentiments [1], where it is shown that it arises from our sympathy with our superiors being greater than that with our equals or inferiors: we admire their

[1] *The Theory of Moral Sentiments by Adam Smith, Professor of Moral Philosophy in the University of Glasgow*, was published early in 1759 (see John Rae, *Life of Adam Smith*, 1895, pp. 141–146) in one octavo volume of 551 pages. This edition contains much less matter than the sixth (1790), which would occupy considerably more than 800 similar pages.

happy situation, enter into it with pleasure, and endeavour to promote it [1].

Among the great, as superior abilities of body and mind are not so easily judged of by others, it is more convenient, as it is more common, to give the preference to riches. It is evident that an old family, that is, one which has been long distinguished by its wealth, has more authority than any other. An upstart is always disagreeable, we envy his superiority over us and think ourselves [as] well entitled to wealth as he [2]. If I am told that a man's grandfather was very poor and dependent on my family, I will grudge very much to see his grandson in a station above me, and will not be much disposed to submit to his authority. Superior age, superior abilities of body and of mind, ancient family and superior wealth seem to be the four things that give one man authority over another [3].

The second principle which induces men to obey the civil magistrate is utility. Every one is sensible of the necessity of this principle to preserve justice and peace in the society. By civil institutions the poorest may get redress of injuries from the wealthiest and most powerful; and though there may be some irregularities in particular cases, as undoubtedly there are, yet we submit to them to avoid greater evils. It is the sense of public utility, more than of private, which influences men to obedience. It may sometimes be for my interest to disobey, and to wish government overturned, but I am sensible that other men are of a different opinion from me, and would not assist me

[1] *Moral Sentiments*, 1759, pt. i. sect. 4. ch. ii. 'Of the origin of ambition, and of the distinction of ranks.'

[2] 'An upstart, though of the greatest merit, is generally disagreeable, and a sentiment of envy commonly prevents us from heartily sympathizing with his joy.' *Moral Sentiments*, 1759, p. 86. 'Upstart greatness is everywhere less respected than ancient greatness.' *W. of N.* bk. v. ch. i. pt. 2, vol. ii. p. 296.

[3] The four things reappear in *W. of N.* bk. v. ch. i. pt. 2, vol. ii. pp. 294–6, and are there more fully treated.

in the enterprise. I therefore submit to its decision for the good of the whole.

If government has been of a long standing in a country, and if it be supported by proper revenues, and be at the same time in the hands of a man of great abilities, authority is then in perfection.

In all governments both these principles take place in some degree, but in a monarchy the principle of authority prevails, and in a democracy that of utility. In Britain, which is a mixed government, the factions formed some time ago, under the names of Whig and Tory, were influenced by these principles, the former submitted to government on account of its utility and the advantages which they derived from it, while the latter pretended that it was of divine institution, and to offend against it was equally criminal as for a child to rebel against its parent. Men in general follow these principles according to their natural dispositions. In a man of a bold, daring and bustling turn the principle of utility is predominant, and a peaceable easy turn of mind usually is pleased with a tame submission to superiority [1].

It has been a common doctrine in this country that contract is the foundation of allegiance to the civil magistrate [2]. But that this is not the case will appear from the following reasons.

In the first place the doctrine of an original contract is peculiar to Great Britain, yet government takes place where it was never thought of, which is even the case with the greater part of people in this country [3]. Ask a common

[1] Hume, 'Of the Parties of Great Britain,' ad init., *Essays*, 1741, pp. 119, 120.

[2] Adam Smith's master, Hutcheson, taught the doctrine. See his *Introduction to Moral Philosophy*, 1747, p. 285, and his posthumous *System of Moral Philosophy*, 1755, vol. ii. pp. 225 sqq.

[3] 'These connexions are always conceived to be equally independent of our consent, in Persia and China; in France and Spain; and even in Holland and England wherever the doctrines above mentioned have not been care-

porter or day-labourer why he obeys the civil magistrate, he will tell you that it is right to do so, that he sees others do it, that he would be punished if he refused to do it, or perhaps that it is a sin against God not to do it. But you will never hear him mention a contract as the foundation of his obedience.

Secondly, when certain powers of government were at first entrusted to certain persons upon certain conditions, it is true that the obedience of those who entrusted it might be founded on a contract, but their posterity have nothing to do with it, they are not conscious of it, and therefore cannot be bound by it. It may indeed be said that by remaining in the country you tacitly consent to the contract and are bound by it. But how can you avoid staying in it? You were not consulted whether you should be born in it or not. And how can you get out of it? Most people know no other language nor country, are poor, and obliged to stay not far from the place where they were born, to labour for a subsistence. They cannot, therefore, be said to give any consent to a contract, though they may have the strongest sense of obedience. To say that by staying in a country a man agrees to a contract of obedience to government is just the same with carrying a man into a ship and after he is at a distance from land to tell him that by being in the ship[1] he has contracted to obey the master[2]. The foundation of a duty cannot be a principle with which mankind is entirely unacquainted. They must have some idea, however confused, of the principle upon which they act.

fully inculcated,' Hume, 'Of the Original Contract,' *Essays*, 1748, p. 293.

[1] MS. reads 'shop.'

[2] 'Can we seriously say that a poor peasant or artisan has a free choice to leave his own country when he knows no foreign language or manners, and lives from day to day by the small wages he acquires? We may as well assert that a man by remaining in a vessel freely consents to the dominion of the master; though he was carried on board while asleep.' Hume, *Essays*, 1748, p. 299.

But again, upon the supposition of an original contract, by leaving the state you expressly declare that you will no longer continue a subject of it and are freed from the obligation which you owed it. Yet every state claims its own subjects and punishes them for such practices [1], which would be the highest injustice if their living in the country implies a consent to a former agreement. Again, if there be such a thing as an original contract, aliens who come into a country, preferring it to others, give the most express consent to it. Yet a state always suspects aliens as retaining a prejudice in favour of their mother country, and they are never so much depended upon as free-born subjects [2]. So much is the English law influenced by this principle that no alien can hold a place under the government, even though he should be naturalized by act of parliament [3]. Besides, if such a contract were supposed, why should the state require an oath of allegiance, whenever a man enters on any office? For if they supposed a previous contract, what occasion is there for renewing it? Breach of allegiance or high treason is a much greater crime, and more severely punished, in all nations, than breach of contract, in which no more but fulfilment is required. They must, therefore, be on a different footing, the less can by no means involve in it the greater contract. Contract is not therefore the principle of obedience to civil government, but the principles of authority and utility formerly explained.

[1] Viz. emigration coupled with renunciation of allegiance. Hume notices that colonists peopling an uninhabited region are still claimed by their sovereign. *Essays*, 1748, p. 300.

[2] 'Yet is his allegiance, though more voluntary, much less expected or depended on than that of a natural born subject.' Hume, *Essays*, 1748, p. 300.

[3] See below, p. 65, note 1.

[§ 2. *Of the Nature of Government and its Progress in the first Ages of Society.*]

We shall now endeavour to explain the nature of government, its different forms, what circumstances gave occasion for it, and by what it is maintained.

The forms of government, however various, may not improperly be reduced to these three, monarchical, aristocratical, and democratical. These may be blended in a great number of ways, and we usually denominate the government from that one which prevails.

Monarchical government is where the supreme power and authority is vested in one who can do what he pleases, make peace and war, impose taxes, and the like.

Aristocratical government is where a certain order of people in the state, either of the richest or of certain families, have it in their power to choose magistrates who are to have the management of the state.

Democratical government is where the management of affairs belongs to the whole body of the people together.

These two last forms may be called republican, and then the division of government is into monarchical and republican.

To acquire proper notions of government it is necessary to consider the first form of it, and observe how the other forms arose out of it.

In a nation of hunters there is properly no government at all[1]. The society consists of a few independent families

[1] 'In the first state of man, viz. that of hunting and fishing, there obviously is no place for government.' Lord Kames, *Historical Law Tracts*, 1758, vol. i. p. 78 note. 'Strictly speaking they [the aboriginal Americans] seem to have no government, no laws, and are only cemented by friendship and good neighbourhood.' William Douglass, *Summary, historical and political, of the first planting, progressive improvements, and present state of the British Settlements in North America*, 1760, vol. i. p. 160. See *W. of N.* bk. v. ch. i. pt. 2, vol. ii. p. 274.

who live in the same village and speak the same language, and have agreed among themselves to keep together for their mutual safety, but they have no authority one over another. The whole society interests itself in any offence; if possible they make it up between the parties, if not they banish from their society, kill or deliver up to the resentment of the injured him who has committed the crime[1]. But this is no regular government, for though there may be some among them who are much respected, and have great influence in their determinations, yet he never can do anything without the consent of the whole.

Thus among hunters there is no regular government, they live according to the laws of nature.

The appropriation of herds and flocks which introduced an inequality of fortune, was that which first gave rise to regular government[2]. Till there be property there can be no government, the very end of which is to secure wealth, and to defend the rich from the poor[3]. In this age of shepherds, if one man possessed 500 oxen, and another had none at all, unless there were some government to secure them to him, he would not be allowed to possess them. This inequality of fortune, making a distinction between the rich and the poor, gave the former much influence over the latter, for they who had no flocks or herds must have depended on those who had them, because they could not now gain a subsistence from hunting, as the rich had made the game, now become tame, their own property. They therefore who had appropriated a number of flocks and herds, necessarily

[1] Lafitau, *Mœurs des sauvages amériquains comparées aux mœurs des premiers temps*, 1724, 4to, tom. i. p. 490 sqq.

[2] *W. of N.* bk. v. ch. i. pt. 2, vol. ii. p. 297.

[3] 'Government has no other end but the preservation of property.' Locke, *Civil Government*, § 94. In *W. of N.* a qualification is introduced: 'Civil government, so far as it is instituted for the security of property, is in reality instituted for the defence of the rich against the poor' (bk. v. ch. i. pt. 2, vol. ii. p. 298).

came to have great influence over the rest; and accordingly we find in the Old Testament that Abraham, Lot, and the other patriarchs were like little petty princes. It is to [be] observed that this inequality of fortune in a nation of shepherds occasioned greater influence than in any period after that. Even at present, a man may spend a great estate, and yet acquire no dependents. Arts and manufactures are increased by it, but it may make very few persons dependent. In a nation of shepherds it is quite otherways. They have no possible means of spending their property, having no domestic luxury, but by giving it in presents to the poor, and by this means they attain such influence over them as to make them, in a manner, their slaves[1].

We come now to explain how one man came to have more authority than the rest, and how chieftains were introduced. A nation consists of many families who have met together, and agreed to live with one another. At their public meetings there will always be one of superior influence to the rest, who will in a great measure direct and govern their resolutions, which is all the authority of a chieftain in a barbarous country. As the chieftain is the leader of the nation, his son naturally becomes the chief of the young people, and on the death of his father succeeds to his authority. Thus chieftainship becomes hereditary. This power of chieftainship comes in the progress of society to be increased by a variety of circumstances. The number of presents which he receives, increase his fortune, and consequently his authority; for amongst barbarous nations nobody goes to the chieftain, or makes any application for his interest, without something in his hand. In a civilized nation the man who gives the present is superior to the person who receives it, but in a barbarous nation the case is directly opposite.

[1] *W. of N.* bk. v. ch. i. pt. 2, vol. ii. pp. 294, 295.

We shall now consider the different powers which naturally belong to government, how they are distributed, and what is their progress in the first periods of society.

The powers of government are three, to wit, the legislative, which makes laws for the public good: the judicial, or that which obliges private persons to obey these laws, and punishes those who disobey: the executive, or as some call it, the federal power, to which belongs the making war and peace[1].

All these powers in the original form of government belonged to the whole body of the people. It was indeed long before the legislative power was introduced, as it is the highest exertion of government to make laws and lay down rules to bind not only ourselves, but also our posterity, and those who never gave any consent to the making them. As for the judicial power, when two persons quarrelled between themselves, the whole society naturally interposed, and when they could not make up matters, turned them out of the society. During this early age crimes were few[2], and it was long before the punishment was made equal to the crime.

Cowardice and treason were the first crimes punished, for cowardice among hunters is considered as treason, because when they went out in small numbers, if their enemy attacked them, and some of their party deserted them, the rest might suffer by it, and therefore they who deserted were punished for treason.

The priest generally inflicted the punishment, as it were by command of the gods, so weak at that time was government. The power of making peace and war in like manner belonged to the people, and all the heads of families were consulted about it

Though the judicial power which concerns individuals

[1] 'La puissance législative'; 'la puissance exécutrice'; 'la puissance de juger.' Montesquieu, *Esprit des lois*, liv. xi. ch. vi.

[2] I.e. 'of few kinds,' not 'infrequent.' Cf. pp. 18, 19.

was long precarious, the society first interposing as friends and then as arbitrators, the executive power came very soon to be exerted absolutely. When any private quarrel happens concerning the property of this cow, or of that ox, society is not immediately concerned, but it is deeply interested in making peace and war. In the age of shepherds this power is absolutely exerted. In Great Britain we can observe vestiges of the precariousness of the judicial power, but none of the executive. When a criminal was brought to trial, he was asked how he would choose that his cause should be decided, whether by combat, the ordeal trial, or the laws of his country. The society only obliged him not to disturb them in the decision. In England the question still remains, though the answer is not now arbitrary[1]. It was very common in the ruder ages to demand a trial by dipping their hands in boiling water, by means of which almost every one was found innocent, though now scarce any one would escape by this means. When people were constantly exposed to the weather, boiling water could have little effect upon them, though now, when we are quite covered, it must have a contrary effect[2]. This choice of trial shows the weakness of the judicial laws. We find that the judicial combat continued in England as late as the days of Queen Elizabeth[3]. It has now worn out gradually and insensibly without so much as a law or a rule of court made against it.

In the periods of hunters and fishers, and in that of shepherds, as was before observed, crimes are few; small crimes passed without any notice. In those ages no controversies arose from interpretations of testaments, settlements, contracts, which render our law-suits so numerous,

[1] I.e. is not now dependent on the will of the accused.

[2] Montesquieu attributes success in passing the ordeal of fire or boiling water to the callous nature of the skin of people accustomed to arms and labour. *Esprit des lois*, liv. xxviii. ch. xvii.

[3] John Dalrymple, *Essay towards a General History of Feudal Property in Great Britain*, third edition, 1758, p. 312.

for these were unknown among them. When these took place and difficult trades began to be practised, controversies became more frequent, but as men were generally employed in some branch of trade or another, without great detriment to themselves they could not spare time to wait upon them. All causes must be left undecided, which would be productive of every inconvenience, or they must fall upon some other method more suitable to the several members of society. The natural means they would fall upon would be to choose some of their number to whom all causes should be referred. The chieftain who was before this distinguished by his superior influence, when this comes to be the case, would preserve his wonted precedence, and would naturally be one of those who were chosen for this purpose. A certain number would be chosen to sit along with him, and in the first ages of society this number was always considerable[1]. They would be afraid to trust matters of importance to a few, and accordingly we find that at Athens there were 500 judges at the same time[2]. By this means the chieftain would still further increase his authority, and the government would appear in some degree monarchical. But this is only in appearance, for the final decision is still in the whole body of the people, and the government is really democratical.

The power of making peace and war, as was before observed, was at first lodged in the whole body of the people. But when society advanced [and] towns were fortified, magazines prepared, stocks of money got together, generals and officers appointed, the whole body of the people could not attend to deliberations of this kind. This province would either fall to the court of justice, or

[1] Brady, quoting from Tacitus, *Germ.* cap. 12, says, 'Every one of these princes had a hundred of the common people their assessors, from whom they had advice and authority, which were called *comites*.' *Complete History of England*, 1685, p. 55.

[2] *W. of N.* bk. v. ch. i. pt. 3, art. 2, vol. ii. pp. 361, 362.

there would be another set of people appointed for this purpose, though it would naturally at first fall to the court of justice. This is properly called the senatorial power, which at Rome took care of the public revenue, public buildings, and the like. But afterwards at Rome, the court of justice and the senatorial one became quite distinct. The same may be said of the Areopagite court at Athens.

We shall now make some observations on nations in the two first periods of society. Those, viz. of hunters and shepherds.

In a nation of hunters and fishers few people can live together, for in a short time any considerable number would destroy all the game in the country, and consequently would want a means of subsistence. Twenty or thirty families are the most that can live together, and these make up a village. But as they live together for their mutual defence, and to assist one another, their villages are not far distant from each other. When any controversy happens between persons of different villages, it is decided by a general assembly of both villages. As each particular village has its own leader, so there is one who is the leader of the whole nation. The nation consists of an alliance of the different villages, and the chieftains have great influence on their resolutions, especially among shepherds. In no age is antiquity of family more respected than in this. The principle of authority operates very strongly, and they have the liveliest sense of utility in the maintenance of law and government.

The difference of the conduct of these nations in peace and war is worth our observation.

The exploits of hunters, though brave and gallant, are never very considerable. As few of them can march together, so their number seldom exceeds 200 men, and even these cannot be supported above fourteen days. There is therefore very little danger from a nation of hunters. Our colonies are much afraid of them without any just grounds.

They may indeed give them some trouble by their inroads and excursions, but can never be very formidable[1]. On the other hand a much greater number of shepherds can live together. There may be a thousand families in the same village. The Arabs and Tartars, who have always been shepherds, have on many occasions made the most dreadful havoc. A Tartar chief is extremely formidable, and when one of them gets the better of another, there always happens the most dreadful and violent revolutions. They take their whole flocks and herds into the field along with them, and whoever is overcome loses both his people and wealth. The victorious nation follows its flocks, and pursues its conquest, and if it comes into a cultivated country with such numbers of men, it is quite irresistible. It was in this manner that Mahomet ravaged all Asia[2].

There is a very great difference betwixt barbarous nations and those that are a little civilized. Where the land is not divided, and the people live in huts which they carry about with them, they can have no attachment to the soil, as all their property consists in living goods which they can easily carry about with them. On this account barbarous nations are always disposed to quit their country. Thus we find such migrations among the Helvetii, Teutones, and Cimbrians. The Huns, who dwelt for a long time on the north side of the Chinese wall, drove out the Astrogoths on the other side of the Palus Maeotis, they again the Wisigoths, &c.

[§ 3. *How Republican Governments were introduced.*]

Having considered the original principles of government, and its progress in the first ages of society, having found

[1] Douglass, *British Settlements in North America*, vol. i. p. 183, note.

[2] Probably a reporter's or copyist's mistake for 'Arabia.' This paragraph reappears without important alteration in *W. of N.* bk. v. ch. i. pt. 1, vol. ii. pp. 275, 276.

it in general to be democratical, we come now to consider how republic[an] governments were introduced.

It is to be observed in general that the situation of a country, and the degree of improvement of which it is susceptible, not only in the cultivation of the land, but in other branches of trade, is favourable to the introduction of a republican government. There is little probability that any such government will ever be introduced into Tartary or Arabia, because the situation of their country is such that it cannot be improved. The most part of these is hills and deserts which cannot be cultivated, and is only fit for pasturage. Besides, they are generally dry, and have not any considerable rivers[1]. The contrary of this is the case in those countries where republican governments have been established, and particularly in Greece. Two-thirds of Attica are surrounded by sea, and the other side by a ridge of high mountains. By this means they have a communication with their neighbouring countries by sea, and at the same [time] are secured from the inroads of their neighbours. Most of the European countries have most part of the same advantages. They are divided by rivers and branches of the sea, and are naturally fit for the cultivation of the soil and other arts. We shall now see how favourable this is to the reception of a republican government. We may suppose the progress of government in Attica in the infancy of the society to have been much the same with that in Tartary and the other countries we have mentioned, and we find in reality that at the time of the Trojan war it was much in the same situation, for then there was little or no cultivation of the ground, and cattle was the principal part of their property. All the contests about property in Homer regard cattle[2]. Here, as in every other country in the same period, the

[1] Different reasons for the same proposition are given by Montesquieu, *Esprit des lois*, liv. xvii. ch. vi.

[2] E.g. *Iliad*, I. 154, XI. 670.

influence of the chieftain over his own vassals was very considerable. A people inhabiting such a country, when the division of land came to take place and the cultivation of it to be generally practised, would naturally dispose of the surplus of their product among their neighbours, and this would be a spur to their industry. But at the same time it would be a temptation to their neighbours to make inroads upon them. They must therefore fall upon some method to secure themselves from danger, and to preserve what it formerly cost them so much trouble to procure. It would be more easy to fortify a town in a convenient place than to fortify the frontiers of the whole country, and accordingly this was the method they fell upon. They built fortified towns in the most convenient places, and whenever they were invaded took shelter in them with their flocks and moveable goods, and here they cultivated the arts and sciences. Agreeable to this, we find that Theseus fortified Athens and made the people of Attica carry into it all their goods[1], which not only increased his power over them, but also the authority of that state above others. When people agreed in this manner to live in towns, the chieftains of the several clans would soon lose their authority, and the government would turn republican, because their revenue was small, and could not make them so conspicuous and distinguished above others as to retain them in dependence. The citizens gradually increase in riches, and coming nearer the level of the chieftain, become[2] jealous of his authority. Accordingly we find that Theseus himself was turned out. After this nine regents were set up who were at first to have authority for life, but were afterwards continued only for ten years[3]. Thus Athens, and in

[1] The reporter may have omitted some qualifying phrase such as 'to market' or 'in time of war.'

[2] MS. reads 'his' after 'become.'

[3] It was the single 'regent' or archon who held office at first for life and afterwards for ten years;

like manner all the Greek states, came from a chieftainship to something like monarchy, and from thence to aristocracy. In general, as was before observed, the revenue becomes insufficient to support the authority of a number of chieftains, but a few, getting into their hands superior wealth, form an aristocracy.

It is to be observed that there is a considerable difference between the ancient and modern aristocracies. In the modern republics of Venice, Milan, &c., the government of the state is entirely in the hands of the hereditary nobility, who are possessed of all the three powers of government. Both in modern and ancient aristocracies the people had the choice of those in authority, but the difference is this, that only the nobility could be elected in modern times. The institution of slavery is the cause of this difference. When the free men had all their work done by slaves, they had it in their power to attend on public deliberations, but when the ground came to be cultivated by free men, the lower sort could not have it in their power to attend, but, consulting their interest, they would endeavour to avoid it. Agreeable to this we find that at Venice the populace desired to be free of it. In the same manner the towns in Holland voluntarily gave it up to the town council, which was, in consequence of this, vested with the whole power.

Nothing like this happened in the republics of Greece and Rome. In the early ages of these states, though the populace had the whole power, they were called aristocracies, because they always chose their magistrate from among the nobility. They were not indeed hindered by any express law to do otherwise, but it was customary

when his duties were divided among nine archons, the office became an annual one. The confusion in the text might easily be made by any one trying to follow John Potter, *Archaeologia Graeca*, 1706. The phrase 'continued them in their government only for ten years' occurs in that work, vol. i. p. 13.

to do so, because the lower classes were maintained by the fortunes of the rich, and thereby became dependent on them, and gave their vote for him whose bounty they shared. The nobility might differ among themselves about elections, but would never propose the election of plebeians. Thus the influence of the nobility was the law, and not any express prohibition.

At Athens Solon enacted that none of the lower of the four classes into which the people were divided should be elected; but afterwards magistrates were elected out of all classes, and the government became democratical[1].

At Rome it was long before the power of being elected extended to the whole body of the people. After decemvirs were appointed, the power of the people began to encroach more and more upon the nobles, and still more when they got military tribunes elected. The cause of this was the improvement of arts and manufactures. When a man becomes capable of spending on domestic luxury what formerly supported an hundred retainers, his power and influence naturally decrease. Besides, the great usually had every trade exercised by their own slaves, and therefore the tailors and shoemakers, being no longer dependent on them, would not give them their votes. The popular leaders then endeavoured to get laws passed by which they might be allowed to be elected magistrates. It was long before the generality even of the plebeians would consent to this, because they thought it disagreeable to have their equals so far above them[2]. In process of time, however, they got it enacted that there should be in authority an equal number of patricians and plebeians, viz., a consul chosen out of each.

[1] Potter, *Archaeologia Graeca*, vol. i. pp. 14, 16.

[2] Livy, *Hist.*, lib. iv. cap. 25.

[§ 4. *How Liberty was lost.*]

We have shown how republics arose, and how they again became democratical; we are next to show how this liberty was lost, and monarchy or something like it was introduced.

Considering these states in the situation above described, as possessed of their towns and a small territory in the adjacent country, they must either confine themselves within their ancient boundaries, or enlarge their territory by conquest. They must either be what may not improperly be called a defensive republic or a conquering one. The Grecian states are a good example of the former, and Rome and Carthage of the latter. We are to show how each of these lost their liberty: and first how the defensive states lost theirs.

When a country arrives at a certain degree of refinement it becomes less fit for war. When the arts arrive at a certain degree of improvement, the number of the people increases, yet that of fighting men becomes less. In a state of shepherds the whole nation can go out to war; and even when it becomes more refined, and the division of labour takes place, and everyone is possessed of a small farm, they can send out a great number. In such an age their campaigns are always in summer, and from seed time till harvest their young men have nothing ado but to serve in them. The whole business at home can be performed by the old men and women, and even these have sometimes beat the enemy in the absence of their soldiers. In a state where arts are carried on, and which consists chiefly of manufacturers[1], there cannot be sent out such numbers,

[1] The word is used (as always by Adam Smith) in its old and more literal sense, not in its modern sense of 'persons who employ others to make things by machinery.'

because if a weaver or tailor be called away, nothing is done in his absence. Scarce one in an hundred can be spared from Britain and Holland[1]. Of an hundred inhabitants fifty are women, and of fifty men twenty-five are unfit for war. In the last war Britain could not spare so many, as any one almost may be convinced, if he reflect whether among his acquaintances he missed one out of twenty-five. According to this principle Athens, though a small state, could once send out 30,000 fighting men, which made a very considerable figure; but after the improvement of arts, they could not send out more than 10,000, which was quite inconsiderable. Britain, notwithstanding the politeness and refinement at which it has arrived, on account of the largeness of its territories[2], can still send out a very formidable army, but a small state necessarily declines. However, there is one advantage attending slavery in a small republic, which seems to be its only advantage, that it retards their declension. At Rome and Athens the arts were carried on by slaves, and the Lacedaemonians went so far as not to allow any freeman to be brought up to mechanic employments, because they imagined that they hurt the body. Accordingly we find that at the battle of Chaeronea, when the Athenians were come to a considerable degree of politeness, they were able to send out great numbers of men purely on this account, that all trades were carried on by slaves. We may observe that in the Italian republics, where slavery did not take place, they soon lost their liberty. When, in consequence of the improvement of arts, a state has become opulent, it must be reckoned a great hardship to go out to war, whereas among our ancestors it was thought no inconvenience to take the field. A knight (*eques*) was no more than a horseman, and a foot-soldier was a gentleman. They were inured to hardships at home, and therefore a campaign

[1] *W. of N.* bk. v. ch. i. pt. 1, vol. ii. pp. 276-279.

[2] Scil. 'compared with those of Greek states.'

appeared no way dreadful. But when opulence and luxury increased, the rich would not take the field but on the most urgent account, and therefore it became necessary to employ mercenaries and the dregs of the people to serve in war. Such persons could never be trusted in war unless reduced to the form of a standing army, and subjected to rigid discipline, because their private interest was but little concerned, and therefore without such treatment they could not be expected to be very resolute in their undertakings. Gentlemen may carry on a war without much discipline, but this a mob can never do. As the citizens in Greece thought it below them to bear arms, and entrusted the republic to mercenaries, their military force was diminished, and consequently a means was provided for the fall of the government. Another cause of their declension was the improvement of the art of war, which rendered everything precarious. In early ages it was very difficult to take a city, as it could only be done by a long blockade. The siege of Troy lasted ten years, and Athens once could withstand for two years[1] a siege both by land and sea. In modern times the besiegers have an advantage over the besieged, and a good engineer can force almost any town to surrender in six weeks. But it was not so once. Philip of Macedon made great improvements in this art, which at last occasioned the dissolution of all the Greek governments and their subjection to foreign powers. Rome stood out much longer than Greece because the number of its citizens was daily increasing. At Rome any person might be made a citizen, as this was of little advantage. But at Athens the right of citizenship was given to very few, as it was itself a little estate. However, Rome itself after opulence and luxury increased, shared the fate of other republics, though the event was brought about in a different manner. Till the time of Marius, the better sort of free men went out

[1] No siege of Athens of such long duration appears to be known to historians.

to the field. Marius was the first that recruited [slaves]. He gathered the freed slaves into his army, and established a rigid military discipline. That army which before had consisted of gentlemen was now made up of runaway slaves and the lowest of the people. With such an army Marius conquered and kept in awe the provinces. He had the disposal of all offices and posts in this army. Every one among them owed his rise to him, and was consequently dependent upon him.

Whenever such a general was affronted he would naturally apply to his army for relief, who would easily be induced to side with their general against their own nation. This was the very expedient that Marius fell upon. By the influence of Sylla he was, in his absence, banished from Rome, and a price set upon him. Marius applied to his army, who were determined at all events to follow him, marched to Rome when Sylla was abroad on an expedition against Mithridates, took possession of the government and vanquished Sylla's party. Marius died soon after, and Sylla, having conquered Mithridates, returned to Rome, and in his turn beat the Marian party, changed the government into a monarchy, and made himself perpetual Dictator, though he afterwards had the generosity and magnanimity to resign it. About thirty or forty years afterwards the same thing happened between Caesar and Pompey. Caesar as well as Sylla got himself made perpetual Dictator, but had not enough of public spirit to resign it. His veteran troops which were settled in Italy, mindful of the favours which he conferred upon them, after his death gathered about Octavius, his adopted son, and invested him with the supreme authority. Much the same thing happened in our own country with respect to Oliver Cromwell. When the Parliament became jealous of this man, and disbanded the army, he applied to them in a manner indeed more canting than that of the Roman generals, and got the Parliament turned out and a new one appointed more suitable to his mind, with the whole authority vested in himself[1].

Thus we have seen how small republics, whether conquering or defensive, came at length to a dissolution from the improvements in mechanic arts, commerce, and the arts of war.

[§ 5. *Of Military Monarchy.*]

We are next to consider what form of government succeeded the republican.

When small republics were conquered by another state, monarchy, or whatever other government pleased the conquerors, was established, though they generally followed the model of their own country. The Athenians always established democracy, and the Spartans aristocracy. The Romans indeed more prudently divided their conquests into provinces which were governed pretty absolutely by persons appointed by [the] Senate for that purpose. The case is somewhat different when a state is conquered by its own subjects. Both the nature of the action and the instruments by which it is performed require a military monarchy, or a monarchy supported by military force, because it is as necessary to keep them in awe as to conquer them. This was the form of government that was established in Rome during the time of the emperors. These emperors took the whole executive power into their own hands, they made peace and war as they thought proper, and even named the magistrates either immediately themselves, or by means of a Senate of their own appointment. They did not, however, alter any institutions of the civil law; right and wrong were decided as formerly. Cromwell did the same in our own country, he kept the State in awe by an insignificant army, but he allowed the

[1] The facts are more shortly dealt with in *W. of N.* bk. v. ch. i. pt. 1, vol. ii. p. 290.

judge to determine right and wrong as formerly. Nay, he made such improvement in the civil law by taking away wardships, &c., that the first thing the Parliament of Charles II did was to confirm many of Cromwell's laws.

The Roman authors tell us that justice was never better administered than under the worst of the emperors, Domitian and Nero[1]. It is the interest of all new administrators to make few alterations in what the generality of people are much concerned and have been long accustomed to. They will more easily go into anything else, when they are indulged in this. It was particularly the interest of the emperors to keep up the ancient system of laws, and accordingly we find that all consuls who misbehaved in their respective provinces were severely punished. It was not so under the republic; the most scandalous crimes were committed by governors, as we learn from Cicero's Orations. A military government allows the strictest administration of justice. Nobody indeed can have a fair trial where the Emperor is immediately concerned: then he will do as he pleases; but where he is in no way interested it is his interest to adhere to the ancient laws.

It is to be observed that there was a very great difference between the military government established at Rome and those that were established in Asia. At Rome the conquerors and conquered were the same people. The conquerors themselves were sensible of the good effects of these laws, and were so far from being willing to abrogate them, that they made improvements upon them. It is not so with the Asiatic governments, though they are purely military. Turkey, Persia, and the other countries were conquered by Tartars, Arabians, and other barbarous nations who had no regular system of laws, and were entirely ignorant of their good effects. They established in all public offices their own people, who were entirely ignorant

[1] Suetonius, *Nero*, 15, sqq.; *Domitianus*, 8.

of all the duties of them. A Turkish bashaw or other inferior officer is decisive judge of everything, and is as absolute in his own jurisdiction as the Signior. Life and fortune are altogether precarious, when they thus depend on the caprice of the lowest magistrate. A more miserable and oppressive government cannot be imagined.

[§ 6. *How Military Monarchy was dissolved.*]

We have considered how the dissolution of small states was brought about, and what form of government succeeded them, by what means an imperial government was introduced into conquering republics, and what kind of administration this was. We come now to show how this military monarchy came to share that fated dissolution that awaits every state and constitution whatever.

In the time of the imperial governments at Rome they had arrived at a considerable degree of improvement both in arts and commerce. In proportion as people become acquainted with these and their consequence, domestic luxury, they become less fond of going out to war; and besides, the government finds that it would hurt its revenue [to call out] those employed in manufactures. If barbarous nations be in the neighbourhood, they can employ them as soldiers at an easier rate, and at the same time not hurt their own industry. Sensible of these things, the Romans recruited their armies in Germany, Britain, and the northern barbarous countries which bordered on the Roman Empire. They had the liberty of recruiting in these countries in the same manner that the Dutch did in Scotland before the beginning of the last war[1]. After they had gone

[1] Enlistment or recruiting without leave or licence from the crown was felony under 9 Geo. II, cap. 30. In 1756, at the beginning of the Seven Years' War, an act (29 Geo. II, cap. 17) was passed to prevent his Majesty's subjects from serving as officers under the French king; for the better enforcing of the act 9 Geo. II, cap. 30; 'and for obliging such of his Majesty's subjects as shall accept

on for some time in this practice, they would find for several reasons that it would be much easier to make a bargain with the chieftains of these barbarous nations whom they employed, and give him so much money to lead out a number of men to this or that expedition.

Supposing then an institution of this kind, the barbarous chieftain, at the head of his own men, possessed the whole military authority of the people for whom he fought, and whenever the government in the least offended him, he could turn his arms against those who employed him, and make himself master of their country. We find that all the western provinces were taken possession of much in this manner. After they had by their practice given such invitations to the inroad of barbarians, we find that most of the Roman provinces were infested by them. In this country the Romans built a wall and kept garrisons to secure their province from the pillagers of the north. The garrisons which secured this station were called away to the defence of Gaul, which at that time was also infested. The historians tell us that the Britons then got leave to shake off the Roman yoke, but it could be no advantage to the Romans to give any country in Britain its liberty, and it was no favour done it to have no protection from Rome, which the province in reality wanted to have continued. The Romans undoubtedly meant that they should take the trouble of defending themselves, as they were, for some time, to be otherwise employed. The Britons, however, did not like the proposal, but resolved to invite over a body of Saxons to their relief. Accordingly Hengist and Hursa came over with a considerable army which was frequently recruited, entirely drove out the Romans [1], and

commissions in the Scotch Brigade, in the service of the States General of the United Provinces, to take the oaths of allegiance and abjuration.'

[1] The term 'Romans' might be correctly applied to the Romanized population of Britain, but it is probably used here merely by mistake for 'Britons,' since a little lower down we find the phrase 'the old inhabitants' employed

finding themselves masters of the whole country, took possession of it and founded the Saxon Heptarchy. In this manner fell the Western Empire of Europe, and military monarchy came to ruin. We find in the last hundred and fifty years of the Roman Empire this custom of recruiting in barbarous nations carried on, and many of their chieftains had greatly raised themselves. Patricius Ælias[1] under Honorius, and many others, acquired great power. In the same manner all the Asiatic governments were dissolved. Their soldiers were hired from Tartary, arts and manufactures were carried on, the people made more by their trades than by going to war. The East India trade which Italy and some other nations carried on by the Red Sea had rendered them very opulent. Every nation as well as Rome was willing to make a bargain with the neighbouring barbarous princes to defend them, and this proved the ruin of the government.

[§ 7. *Of the Allodial Government.*]

Having now considered all the ancient forms of government of which we have any distinct accounts, we show next what form succeeded the fall of the Roman Empire, and give an account of the origin of the modern governments of Europe.

The government which succeeded this period was

in the case of Gaul in order to avoid the ambiguity of 'Romans.'

[1] A mistake for 'the patrician Aetius.' An easily-made error in transcription will account for 'Ælias.' 'Patricius' may possibly be due to phrases in Jornandes *De Getarum origine*, such as 'Ætius ergo Patricius tunc praeerat militibus fortissimorum Moesiorum stirpe progenitus' (cap. 34), 'tanta Patricii Ætii providentia fuit' (cap. 36). Patricius, thus printed with a capital initial letter, as it is in Muratori, *Rerum Italicarum scriptores*, tom. i. pars i, might easily mislead any one who did not happen to be very familiar with the technical use of the term in the later Roman Empire. Aetius was later than Honorius. The influential barbarian under Honorius was Stilicho, whose name was very probably mentioned in the lecture and omitted by the reporter.

not altogether unlike the Tartar constitution formerly mentioned, though the Germans and others who, upon the fall of the Roman Empire, took possession of the western countries, had better notions of property, and were a little more accustomed to the division of lands. The king and the other chieftains, after they had become conquerors of the country, would naturally for their own purposes take possession of a great part of it. They would distribute it among their vassals and dependents, as they thought proper, and would leave but a very inconsiderable share to the ancient inhabitants. They did not, however, extirpate them entirely, but still paid them some little regard. Among the Franks who took possession of Gaul, the person who killed a Frank paid only five times the fine which was payable for killing one of the old inhabitants [1]. As these nations were almost lawless, and under no authority, depredations were continually committed up and down the country, and all kinds of commerce stopped.

In consequence of this arose the allodial government, which introduced an inequality of fortune. All these chieftains held their lands allodially without any burden of cess, wardship, &c. One of these great lords was possessed of almost a county, but as he was unable himself to reap any advantage from so much of it, he found it necessary to parcel it out among vassals, who either paid a certain annuity, attended him in war, or performed some service of this nature. By this means his incomes became so great that, as there was then no domestic luxury, he could not consume them in any way but by maintaining a great number of retainers about his house. These were another species of dependents, who increased his authority and secured domestic peace, for they kept the tenants in awe and were kept in awe by the tenants. So great was the authority of these lords, that if any one claimed a debt from

[1] For a Frank 200 sous, for a Roman serf 45; Montesquieu, *Esprit des lois*, liv. xxviii. ch. iii ; liv. xxx. ch. xxv.

any of their vassals the king had no power to send a messenger into the lord's dominions to force payment[1]. He could only apply to the lord, and desire him to do justice. To them also lay the last resort[2] in judging of all manner of property under their own jurisdiction, the power of life and death, of coining money, and of making bye-laws and regulations in their own territories. But besides this power of government, which in a great measure was betwixt the king and the great lords, if there had been no other the balance would not have been properly kept. But besides the allodial lords there was a great number of free people who were allowed to consult about justice in their own spheres. Every county was divided into hundreds and subdivided into tens. Each of these had their respective court, viz:—the decennary court, the hundred court. Over those was placed the Wittenagemot or assembly of the whole people[3]. Appeals were brought from the ten to the hundred, and from it to [the] county court. An appeal could be brought to the king's court in case the inferior court denied justice by refusing to hear a cause, or if it was protracted by unreasonable delays[4]. Appeals were also sometimes carried to the Wittenagemot, which was made up of the king, allodial lords, aldermen or earls, bishops, abbots, &c. This was the first form of government in the West of Europe, after the downfall of the Roman Empire.

[§ 8. *Of the Feudal System.*]

We are next to show how the allodial government was overturned and the feudal system introduced.

As these great lords were continually making war upon

[1] *W. of N.* bk. iii. ch. iv. vol. i. p. 413.

[2] MS. reads 'result.'

[3] I.e. commune concilium totius regni (Spelman, *English Works*, 1723, pt. ii. p. 61), not 'assembly composed of the whole people.'

[4] Hume, *History of England from Julius Caesar to Henry VII*, 1762, vol. i. pp. 151, 152.

one another, in order to secure the attendance of their tenants, they gave them leases of the lands which they possessed from year to year, which afterwards, for the same reasons, came to be held for life[1].

When they were about to engage in any very hazardous enterprise, that, in case of the worst consequences, the families of their vassals who went along with them might not be left destitute, and that they might still be more encouraged to follow them, they extended this right to the life of the son and grandson: as it was thought cruel to turn out an old possessor, the right became at last hereditary, and was called *feuda*[2]. The feudal tenant was bound to certain offices, but service in war was the chief thing required, and if the heir was not able to perform it, he was obliged to appoint one in his place. It was in this manner that wardships were introduced[3]. When the heir female succeeded, the feudal baron had a right to marry her to whomever he pleased, because it was thought reasonable that he should have a vassal of his own choosing[4]. The prima seizin was another emolument of the master. When the father died the son had no right to the estate till he publicly declared his willingness to accept of it; and on this account the lord sometimes had the estate in his own

[1] Hume, *History of England from Julius Caesar to Henry VII*, 1762, vol. i. p. 399.

[2] Reference to Smith's authority shows that the plural 'feuda' is correct in spite of the context properly requiring the singular. Dalrymple, in his *Feudal Property*, pp. 198, 199, says that when the grants of land were held at will they 'were properly called *Munera*. . . . Soon afterwards they were granted for life, and they were then called *Beneficia*. . . . But . . . it was accounted hard, after the father's death, that the sons should not have the possession of what they had formerly had a share in the enjoyment of; it occurred likewise readily to superiors that a man would venture himself less in battle, when the loss of his life was to be attended with the ruin of his family; from these considerations the grants were extended to the vassal and his sons; and they were then, and not till then, properly styled *Feuda*.'

[3] Dalrymple, *Feudal Property*, pp. 44, 45.

[4] *Ibid.* pp. 45–47.

hand, and enjoyed the profits of it for some time. The heir paid a sum to get it back, which was called relief[1]. There was still another emolument belonging to the lord, called escheat; that is, after the estate became hereditary, if there was no heir of the family to succeed, it returned to the lord. The same thing happened if the heir failed of performing the services for which he had the tenure[2]. There were besides these some small sums due to the superior on redeeming his son when taken prisoner, or on knighting him[3], and on the marriage of his daughter, and some such occasions[4].

The same causes that made allodial lords give away their lands to their vassals on leases which afterwards became hereditary, made the king give away the greater part of his lands to be held feudally: and what a tenant possessed in feu was much the same with real property. They were indeed subject to the above-mentioned emoluments, but they possessed their lands for themselves and posterity. Feudal property may in some respects be inferior to allodial, but the difference is so inconsiderable that allodial lordships soon become to be held feudally. About the tenth century all estates came to be held feudally, and the allodial lords, that they might enjoy the king's protection, exchanged their rights for a feudal tenure[5].

It is to be observed that those historians who give an account of the origin of feudal laws from the usurpation of the nobility are quite mistaken[6]. They say that the nobility wanted to have those lands which they held at pleasure of the king to be hereditary, that it might not be in his power to turn them out, and that the feudal law was introduced

[1] Dalrymple, *Feudal Property*, pp. 49-59.

[2] *Ibid.* pp. 66-67.

[3] This should, of course, read 'for redeeming him when taken prisoner, or on the knighting of his eldest son.'

[4] Dalrymple, *Feudal Property*, p. 61.

[5] Hume, *History of England* (*Caesar to Henry VII*), vol. i. p. 400.

[6] *W. of N.* bk. iii. ch. iv. vol. i. p. 414.

on account of the diminution of the king's power. But it was actually the contrary; it was on account of the increase of his power, and it required great influence in the king to make the lords hold their lands feudally. The best proof of this is that William the Conqueror changed all the allodial lordships in England into feudal tenures and Malcolm Kenmure[1] did the same in Scotland[2].

The introduction of the feudal system into all Europe took away everything like popular government. The popular courts were all removed. Neither decennary, hundred, nor county courts were allowed. All public affairs were managed by the king and the great feudal lords. No commoners, none but hereditary lords had a right to sit in parliament. Those great lords who held immediately of the king were considered as his companions, *pares convivii comites*. They advised concerning public affairs, and nothing of importance could be done without them. The consent of the majority was to be obtained before any law could be passed, and it was necessary to have them called together. The barons or inferior lords observed the same method in their jurisdictions, and they who held[3] of them were called *pares curiae baronis*. It was likewise necessary that they should be consulted, as they too were in arms. The baron could neither go to war, nor make a law, without the consent of the majority. Nothing could be done in the kingdom without almost universal consent, and thus they fell into a kind of aristocracy with the king at the head of it.

Besides these orders of men of which we have taken notice, there were two others which in that period were held in the utmost contempt[4]. The first was that of the villains (*villani*) who ploughed the ground and were

[1] Canmore.

[2] Lord Kames, *Essays upon British Antiquities*, 1747, pp. 11–17; Dalrymple, *Feudal Property*, p. 25.

[3] MS. reads 'them' between 'held' and 'of them.'

[4] Hume, *History of England (Caesar to Henry VII)*, vol. i. p. 404.

adscripti glebae. The second order was the inhabitants of boroughs, who were much in the same state of villainage with the former, or but a little beyond it. As the boroughs were much under the influence of the lord who gave them protection, it was the king's interest to weaken as much as possible this interest and to favour their liberty. Henry II carried this so far that if a slave escaped to a borough and lived there peaceably a year and day, he became free [1]. He gave them many other privileges, but what secured them most was the power of forming themselves into corporations upon paying a certain sum to the king. They held of him *in capite* [2], and at first every man paid his proportion to the king [3]; but afterwards the borough paid the sum and levied it as it seemed proper to itself. By this means, as the number of inhabitants increased, the burden became lighter, and the boroughs became opulent and very considerable. In the reign of King John a law was made that if a lord married his ward to a burgher he only forfeited his wardship [4].

[§ 9. *Of the English Parliament.*]

Thus we have considered the several orders of men of which the whole kingdom then consisted. We shall next show how each of them got a share in the government, and what share of it was allotted to each of them. Every person who had an estate great or small, had a right to sit

[1] This is ascribed to Henry II, probably only because it is mentioned in Glanvill, *De legibus Angliae*, lib. v. cap. 5. Brady, *Complete History of England*, pref. p. xxvii, quotes from Glanvill. In *W. of N.* bk. iii. ch. iii. vol. i. p. 405, the phrase is 'at that time.'

[2] Madox, *Firma burgi*, ch. i. § 8, pp. 21-23.

[3] *W. of N.* bk. iii. ch. iii. vol. i. p. 400.

[4] 'King John' appears to be a mistake for 'Henry III,' the reference apparently being to the Statute of Merton, 20 Hen. III, cap. 6, 'As touching lords which marry those that they have in ward to villains or other, as burgesses, where they be disparaged . . . the lord shall lose the wardship.'

in the king's court, and to consult and advise with him about public matters. In the reign of William Rufus 700 sat in parliament[1]. In Henry III's time it was enacted that the smaller barons, who could not afford to attend in parliament, should send a representative. These representatives were considered as lords, and sat in the same house with them[2]. In the same manner boroughs came to have representatives in parliament, because they themselves were become opulent and powerful, and the king found it his interest to give them some weight so as to lessen the authority of the peers[3]. It became necessary to have their consent as well as that of the barons before any law was passed. These representatives of the boroughs sat in a house by themselves, and the smaller barons, being far from the level of the great lords with whom they sat, and not much superior to the commons, soon joined them[4]. The king's revenues were then on many occasions insufficient for his demands. They consisted chiefly, first, of the royal demesnes; secondly, knights' services; thirdly, feudal emoluments such as wardships; fourthly, fines, amercements, compositions for crimes, &c.; fifthly, all waff[5] goods, res nullius, &c. These were the principal sources of the king's revenue. But these were by no means sufficient to supply the increasing expenses of government. The two bodies of the commoners when joined made a very considerable figure, and the greater part of the subsidies came from them. The king excused the smaller barons from a constant attendance, and called

[1] Dalrymple, *Feudal Property*, pp. 325, 326, says that Domesday shows that there were 700 immediate vassals of the crown in the time of the Conqueror, and then mentions that 'all who held of the king in capite sat in parliament.' Cp. Hume, *History of England* (*Caesar to Henry VII*), vol. i. p. 407.

[2] Hume, *History of England* (*Caesar to Henry VII*), vol. ii. p. 88.

[3] *W. of N.* bk. iii. ch. iii. vol. i. p. 404.

[4] Hume, *History of England* (*Caesar to Henry VII*), vol. ii. pp. 92, 93; Carte, *History of England*, 1750, vol. ii. p. 451.

[5] I.e. ownerless; a Scotch form of 'waif.'

them or not as he pleased[1]. When he did call them he issued a writ summoning them, and from this was the origin of creating peers by writ or patent, which is the only way of doing it at present.

[§ 10. *How the Government of England became Absolute.*]

Having shown how the House of Commons became considerable, we shall next show how the nobility's power decreased and the government turned arbitrary.

In all the courts of Europe the power of the nobility declined from the common causes, the improvements in arts and commerce. When a man could spend his fortune in domestic luxury he was obliged to dismiss his retainers. By their ancient rustic hospitality they could more easily maintain 1000 retainers than at present lodge one lord for a night. Richard, Earl of Warwick, who was styled Make-King, maintained every day forty thousand people besides tenants[2]. But when luxury took place he was unable to do this[3]. Thus the power of the nobility was diminished, and that too before the House of Commons had established its authority, and thus the king became arbitrary. Under the House of Tudor the government was quite arbitrary, the nobility were ruined, and the boroughs lost their power.

It might be expected that the sovereign also should have lost his authority by the improvement of arts and commerce, but a little attention will convince us that the case must have been quite opposite. A man possessed of forty thousand pounds a year, while no other body

[1] Hume, *History of England* (*Caesar to Henry VII*), vol. ii. p. 88.

[2] 'Forty thousand' is probably a mistake for the thirty thousand mentioned in *W. of N.* bk. iii. ch. iv. vol. i. p. 411. See Hume, *History of England* (*Caesar to Henry VII*), vol. ii. pp. 361, 362.

[3] Andrew Fletcher, *Political Works*, 1737, pp. 11–16; Hume, *History of England under the House of Tudor*, 1759, vol. i. p. 63.

can spend above a hundred, cannot be affected by the increase of luxury. This is precisely the case of the king. He is possessed of a million, while none of his subjects can spend above thirty or forty thousand pounds, and therefore he can spend it in no other way, but by maintaining a great number of people[1]. Luxury must therefore sink the authority of the nobility, whose estates are small in proportion to that of the king; and as his continues unaffected, his power must become absolute. Though this was the case in most nations of Europe, yet in Germany it was quite otherways. The monarchy there was elective, and consequently never could have so much authority. The country is much larger than any other in Europe, and at the dissolution of the feudal government the nobility, who were possessed of considerable fortunes already, got more in proportion than the rest; thus their estates rose so high above those that were immediately below them, that it was impossible for them to spend them in luxury, and therefore they were able to keep a considerable number of retainers. Thus in Germany the power of the nobility was preserved, while in England it was utterly destroyed, and the king rendered absolute.

[§ 11. *How Liberty was restored.*]

We have now shown how the government of England turned absolute: we shall next consider how liberty was restored, and what security the British have for the possession of it.

The act of Henry VII allowing the nobility to dispose of their estates[2] had already placed them entirely on a level with the commons. Elizabeth, who always affected

[1] In *W. of N.* bk. v. ch. iii. vol. ii. p. 508, the whole of this argument is rather contemptuously rejected.

[2] 4 Hen. VII. c. 24; Dalrymple, *Feudal Property*, p. 166; Hume, *History of England under the House of Tudor*, vol. i. p. 63.

popularity, was continually unwilling to impose taxes on her subjects. In order to supply her exigencies she sold the royal demesnes, as she knew that none of her offspring was to succeed her[1]. Her successors therefore, standing in need of frequent supplies, were obliged to make application to parliaments. The Commons were now become very considerable, as they represented the whole body of the people; and as they knew the king could not want, they never granted him anything without in some degree infringing his privileges. At one time they obtained freedom of speech, at another they got it enacted that their concurrence should be necessary to every law. The king, on account of his urgent necessities, was forced to grant whatever they asked, and thus the authority of the parliament established itself. A peculiar advantage which Britain enjoyed after the accession of James I was that as the dominions of Britain were every way bounded by the sea, there was no need for a standing army, and consequently the king had no power by which he could overawe either people or parliament. The 1,200,000[2] pounds a year which was settled upon the king at that time[3] might have secured his independency, had not the bad economy of Charles II rendered him as indigent as any of his predecessors. His successor was still more dependent, and was forced to quit the throne and the kingdom altogether. This brought in a new family, which, as the royal demesnes were entirely alienated, depended wholly upon taxes, and were obliged to court the people for them. Ever since, the king's revenue, though much greater than it was then, depends so much on the concurrence of the parliament that it never can endanger the liberty of the nation.

[1] Dalrymple, *Feudal Property*, p. 168; Hume, *History of England under the House of Tudor*, vol. ii. p. 729.

[2] MS. reads '120,000.'

[3] At the Restoration, Rapin, *History of England*, translated by Tindal, 1743, vol. ii. p. 621.

The revenues at present consist chiefly of three branches, to wit, first, the civil list, which is entirely consumed in the maintenance of the royal family, and can give the king no influence, nor hurt the liberty of the subject; secondly, the annual land and malt taxes, which depend entirely on the parliament; thirdly, the funds mortgaged for paying off the public debts, such as the taxes on salt, beer, malt[1], &c., levied by the officers of custom and excise. These the king can by no means touch: they are paid to the court of exchequer, which is generally managed by people of interest and integrity, who possess their offices for life and are quite independent of the king. Even they can pay nothing but to those appointed by parliament, and must have the discharge of the public creditor. The surplus of the mortgages[2] goes into what is called the sinking fund for paying the public debt, [which] secures the government in the present family, because if a revolution were to happen, the public creditors, who are men of interest, would lose both principal and interest. Thus the nation is quite secure in the management of the public revenue, and in this manner a rational system of liberty has been introduced into Britain. The parliament consists of about 200 peers and 500 commoners. The Commons in a great measure manage all public affairs, as no money bill can take its rise except in that House. Here is a happy mixture of all the different forms of government properly restrained, and a perfect security to liberty and property.

There are still some other securities to liberty. The judges appointed for the administration of justice are fixed for life, and quite independent of the king. Again,

[1] In addition to the annual malt-tax mentioned under the second head, there was a perpetual malt-tax.

[2] I.e. the surplus remaining after the interest on the debt has been paid out of the produce of the mortgaged taxes. See Thos. Mortimer, *Every Man his own Broker*, fifth edition, 1762, pp. 205-207.

the king's ministers are liable to impeachment by the House of Commons for maladministration, and the king cannot pardon them[1]. The Habeas Corpus Act, by which the arbitrary measures of the king to detain a person in prison as long as he pleased is restrained, and by which the judge who refuses to bring a prisoner to his trial if desired within forty[2] days is rendered incapable of any office, is another security to the liberty of the subject. The method of election, and placing the power of judging concerning all elections into the hands of the Commons, are also securities to liberty. All these established customs render it impossible for the king to attempt anything absolute.

Besides all these, the establishment of the courts of justice is another security to liberty. We shall therefore consider the origin of these courts, the history of them, and their present state.

[§ 12. *Of the English Courts of Justice.*]

In England, and indeed in all Europe, after the feudal law was introduced, the kingdom was governed and justice administered in the same manner as by a baron in his jurisdiction; as a steward managed all affairs in the county belonging to the lord, so the grand justiciary had the management of all in the kingdom. He appointed sheriffs and other inferior officers. He was himself a great lord, and, by the authority of his office, in every country but England he became as powerful as the king. But Edward I saw the danger and got it prevented. All kinds of law, criminal or civil, were determined by the justiciary or king's court which always attended the king: those delays and adjournments in civil suits to which this court

[1] This should read, 'cannot stay the proceedings by pardoning them.'

[2] Twenty days is the outside limit. The same mistake occurs again below, Div. iii. § 11.

always attending the king must have been liable, gave occasion for separating common causes from the king's court, and fixing for them at Westminster a court of common pleas. Criminal causes have always a more speedy determination[1]. One would indeed think that when a person's life is at stake, the debate should be longer than in any other case: but resentment is roused in these cases and precipitates to punish. It is a matter of no moment to the spectator how a trifling matter of cash be determined, but it is by no means so in criminal cases. When common pleas were taken away the criminal and fiscal powers were connected, and the power and authority of the great justiciary little diminished. Afterwards Edward I divided the business of the justiciary into three different courts, viz:—

The court of king's bench.

The court of exchequer.

The court of common pleas.

In the last all civil suits were tried. In the first all criminal ones, and to it lay the appeal from the court of common pleas. It was called king's bench, because the king then frequently sat upon it, though this cannot now be done, as it is improper that the king should judge of breaches of the king's peace. The court of exchequer judged in all affairs between the king and his subjects, the debts due by either of them to the other, and whatever regarded the revenue. The court of chancery was originally no court at all. The chancellor was no more than a keeper of briefs or writs according to which justice was done. What gave occasion to the keeping of these briefs shall now be considered.

Edward I abolished the power of the grand justiciary[2]. He employed mean persons to be judges, generally clergy-

[1] It was the rule to finish every criminal trial on the day on which it began; Lecky, *History of England*, vol. vi. 1887, p. 252.

[2] Hume, *History of England* (*Caesar to Henry VII*), vol. ii. p. 122.

men. As the decision depended on such persons, their jurisdictions would be exercised very precariously, and accordingly we find that both in criminal and civil cases they interposed with hesitation, in the former as mediators, and in the latter as arbitrators, and accordingly they would be unwilling to give justice in those cases where they had no precedent from the court of justiciary. On this account all the briefs by which the court of justiciary determined were kept. To keep these seems to have been originally the office of chancellor. If a person had a law-suit he went to the clerk of the court of chancery, who examined the briefs, and if he found one that comprehended your case, justice was done accordingly; but if one could not be found, you could not have justice. Thus we find that the chancellor was not a judge originally. In Scotland the office of the English chancellor is lodged in the court of session. In England a brief was sent from the chancellor to the sheriff by which he was obliged to appear before the king's judges. Judges then, from the irregularity and inaccuracy of their proceedings, gave great jealousy to the king, and on this account many severe sentences went out against them; £10,000 has at one time been levied from the judges on account of corruption[1]. They were therefore tied down strictly to the chancery briefs, and always bound by their records in such a manner that they could not be in the least amended, not so much as a word wrong spelled rectified. This precision still remains in some cases where not taken away by the statutes of amendment; a mere orthographical blunder, though evidently so, has in many cases made the whole of no effect. The judges were therefore tied down to the precise words of the brief, or if there was a statute, to the words of it. This was the origin and jurisdiction of the court of chancery.

[1] Hume, *History of England* (*Caesar to Henry VII*), vol. ii. p. 68; but the amount should be 100,000 marks.

During the improvement of the law of England there arose rivalships among the several courts. We shall therefore show how each of them began to extend its power and encroach [on] the privileges of another, and how the court of chancery increased its influence. The court of king's bench, which judged criminal causes and every breach of the king's peace, was the first that assumed immediately, and previously to an appeal, to judge in civil causes, and to encroach on the jurisdiction of the court of common pleas, by what is called a writ of error, that is, they supposed the person to be guilty of a trespass. For example, when a man owed £10, and did not come to pay it at the time appointed, an order went out from the king's bench to examine and find him out, supposing that he intended to conceal himself, and they punished him for this trespass[1]. At present an action on contract can come immediately before the king's bench. In this manner it was that this court extended its power, and, being supreme over all, none could encroach upon it.

The court of exchequer brought in civil causes to be tried immediately by them in the following manner: suppose a man owed a sum of money to the king, which it is the business of the court to take care of, and the man cannot pay unless his debtors first pay him, the court took upon them to sue this other man by what is called the *quo minus*, that is, by what he is rendered less able to pay the king. As the debts of the king were many, and as the profits of the judges arose from sentence money, which was more or less according to the business of the court, they eagerly grasped at this extension of their power. All the courts endeavoured, by the speediness of their determinations and accuracy of their proceedings, to encourage prosecutors to come before them[2].

[1] There is some confusion or omission, as the process described is that followed under a 'bill of Middlesex,' not a 'writ of error.'

[2] *W. of N.* bk. v. ch. i. pt. 2, vol. ii. pp. 302, 303.

In what manner the chancellor came to attain his equitable jurisdiction shall be taken notice of in the next place. After the improvement of arts and commerce, which gave occasion to many law-suits unheard of before, people suffered a great deal by the imperfections of law. Edward III[1] found that there were a great many injuries to which no brief nor court statute extended; and therefore the parliament allowed that if a person applied to the clerk of chancery and found there was no brief that could give him any remedy, the clerk should look for some briefs of a similar nature and out of them compose a new one by which the complainer might have redress[2]. In this manner the chancery prescribed rules to the other courts; but as they appointed the briefs and manner of proceeding, this was putting an end to the affair, for there was no occasion to go to any other court, and the chancery got these affairs into its own hands. There could be no appeal brought from the courts of king's bench or of common pleas to that of chancery, but they applied to it for what the common law could not redress. The chancellor in this manner obtained the power of judging in all cases of equity, and is applied to in the greater part of civil cases, the chief of which are, first, the specific performance of contracts. By the common law if a person was bound by contract to deliver a piece of ground, and afterwards refused to do it, he was only obliged to pay damages, but not to perform it specifically. The chancery, which was now considered as a court of conscience, enjoined the specific performance of it. Secondly, the chancery gave redress for all incests[3] and frauds in trust when the common law could not. As the leaving lands to the church deprived the king of the emoluments arising from

[1] This should be 'Edward I.'

[2] Stat. Westm. II, 13 Ed. I. cap. 24; Dalrymple, *Feudal Property*, p. 316.

[3] The reporter's or copyist's mistake for some other word, possibly 'deceits.'

them, an act was passed against it. The clergy ordered that they should be left to certain persons who would dispose of them for the benefit of the church, and if they did not perform it, then, as it was a fraud in trust, the chancellor allowed the bishop to see it done. In like manner, when persons in the state of affairs at that time were obliged to alienate their estates to persons that had no concern in them, the chancellor caused them to be restored. Wills, legacies, and things of this sort also fell under the equitable decision of the chancellor.

It will be proper when we are treating of courts to inquire into the origin of juries. In the beginning of the allodial government when the several courts had arrived at a very small degree of improvement, and before they had experience to examine thoroughly into matters, when any person was brought before them on an action depending on his oath, he was obliged to bring twelve compurgators to swear that the oath was just. There are remains of this at present in actions of debt, where, if the person can bring in a certain number of persons to swear that his oath is just, he gains the suit. It is to be observed that the imperfection of this way of trying was one of the great causes that gave origin to the judicial combat. A nobleman, or indeed any man of spirit, who was eluded of his right by a set of perjured fellows, would rather choose to combat it in the field and appeal to the judgement of God than leave his cause to them. Henry II first instituted that the sheriff and a certain number of persons who had opportunity to be best acquainted with the crime should have the whole affair laid before them, and that the person should be judged by their sentence. The law of England, always the friend of liberty, deserves praise in no instance more than in the careful provision of impartial juries. They who are chosen must be near the place where the crime was committed that they may have an opportunity of being acquainted with it. A great part of the jury may be laid aside by the panel[1]. He can lay aside thirty of their number, and he can challenge them either *per capita*, that is, any single juryman, or any number of them, if he suspect the sheriff of partiality. There may be many small causes for suspicion of partiality, and of the relevancy of these the court is judge. Nothing can be a greater security for life, liberty, and property than this institution; the judges are men of integrity, quite independent, holding their offices for life but are tied down by the law. The jurymen are your neighbours who are to judge of a fact upon which your life depends. They too can be laid aside for several reasons.

The laws of England with regard to juries are only defective in one point, in which they differ from the laws of Scotland. In England the whole jury must be unanimous, which renders the office of a juryman a very disagreeable service. A case may appear to you more clear than it does to me, and may really be different from what it appears to either of us, and yet there is a necessity for our agreement, and of consequence a necessity that one of us should swear contrary to our conscience. In criminal causes there is little danger, people are generally disposed to favour innocence and to preserve life. But in civil cases people are not so much troubled, they are not so much disposed to favour, and many of them are exceedingly doubtful. People of fashion are not fond of meddling in a jury attended with such inconveniences, and therefore only the meaner sort of people attend the judge. A great man would not choose to be so often called and returned, and perhaps treated in such a manner as no gentleman would choose to be. In this case the law providing for security has done too much. In this country, where unanimity is not required, the service is not so disagreeable. Though a person differ from the majority he may stand by his opinion and is not forced to comply, and the

[1] Scotch term for the accused.

people of the highest rank are willing to be jurors. In the actions which come before the court of chancery no jury is required, and the court of session in Scotland has taken them away in civil causes.

Besides the courts that have been mentioned there were several others erected by the king's patent. Henry VIII erected three. The court of high commission which sat upon ecclesiastics, the court of star chamber which takes in anything less than death, and the court of wardship which took care of the king's interest in these emoluments. This last was taken away by Charles II, who accepted a sum for the whole. It is now understood that the king cannot erect a court without consent of parliament. In no other country of Europe is the law so accurate as in England, because it has not been of so long standing. The parliament of Paris was only erected about the time of Henry VIII of England. The British parliament consists of a great number of men, and these of great dignity [1]. All new courts disdain to follow the rules that were formerly established. All new courts are a great evil, because their power at first is not precisely determined, and therefore their decisions must be loose and inaccurate.

Thus we have considered the origin of government

1. Among a nation of savages;

2. Among a nation of shepherds;

3. The government of small clans with chieftains; the manner in which aristocracies arose; the fall of little republics, conquering or defensive, and, lastly, the different forms of government that arose in Europe after the dissolution of arbitrary government.

[§ 13. *Of the little Republics in Europe.*]

We shall next consider the origin of the little republics in Europe, and consider the rights of sovereign and subject.

[1] This and the preceding sentence appear hopelessly corrupt.

First, of the origin of these republics. In some countries the provinces which were far from the seat of government sometimes became independent, as was the case in a good part of Germany and France during the time of Charlemagne. Hugh Capet, who was chief justiciary[1], got the government into his hands, but took only the title of the King of France. The Pope, by raising disturbances in Germany, for a long time hindered the Emperor Otho from taking possession of Italy. But when he got possession of it, on account of its distance, he could not retain it. Every little town formed itself into a republic, with a council of its own choosing at its head. Some towns in Germany being well fortified, such as Hamburgh, assumed the same privileges, and still in some measure retain[2] them. The Italian towns are governed by a hereditary nobility, though the ancient republics were perfectly democratical. In Venice the people freely gave up the government, as they also did in Holland, because they could not support the trouble which it gave them. The Dutch and Swiss republics are formed into a *respublica foederata*, and on this depends their strength.

We shall make some remarks on the manner of voting in these republics. When there are 100 votes and three candidates, it is possible that the person who is most odious may be elected. If *A*, *B* and *C* be candidates, there may be 34 votes for *A*, and 33 for *B*, and as many for *C*. Thus though there are 66 votes against *A*, he carries it. This must be still more the case when a criminal is brought before this assembly, for 34 may think him guilty of murder, 33 of manslaughter, and 33 of chance medley, yet he must suffer for murder[3]. To prevent this, in some of these republics they always bring the question

[1] Gilbert, *Treatise on the Court of Exchequer*, 1758, p. 8.

[2] MS. reads 'retains.'

[3] Hutcheson, *System of Moral Philosophy*, vol. ii. p. 241; Grotius, *De iure belli et pacis*, lib. ii. cap. v. § 19; Pufendorf, *De iure naturae et gentium*, lib. vii. cap. ii. § 18.

to a simple state. Is he guilty of murder or not? If there be three candidates, they put a previous vote, by which they exclude one of the candidates. In their senates the president never has a deliberative vote, but only a decisive one, because they will allow no member to have two votes. When there is an equality on both sides, nothing can be done, and therefore the business is not rejected, but referred to another meeting.

[§ 14. *Of the Rights of Sovereigns.*]

We shall now consider what duty is owing to the sovereign, and what is the proper punishment of disobedience. Every attempt to overturn this power is in every nation considered as the greatest crime, and is called high treason. It is to be observed that there is a great difference between treason in monarchies and treason in republics. In the one it is an attempt on the king's person, and in the other on the liberties of the people, from whence we may see how the maxim of assassination came to be established in republics, and not in monarchies. It is the interest of monarchies that the person in authority be defended, whatever his title or conduct be, and that no person be allowed to enquire into them. The laws of monarchy are therefore unfavourable to the assassination of tyrants. In a republic the definition of a tyrant is quite clear. He is one who deprives the people of their liberty, levies armies and taxes, and puts the citizens to death as he pleases. This man cannot be brought to a court of justice, and therefore assassination is reckoned just and equitable. The present republican governments in Europe, indeed, do not encourage this maxim, because monarchies now set the fashion, and [other] government[s] copy their pattern. According to our present notions Oliver Cromwell's assassination is most opprobrious, but it would have appeared otherwise when the republics of Greece and Rome set the fashion.

Having thus taken notice of this difference between monarchical and republican governments, we shall next consider the crimes reckoned treason. There are three kinds of treason or attacks upon the essence of government. First, *perduellio*, or an attempt to subvert the established government by force or rebellion. Secondly, *proditio*, or the joining of the enemy, delivering up to him forts, hostages, &c., or the refusing to deliver up garrisons, &c., to the government when they demand them. This is called high treason. Thirdly, *laesa maiestas*, or an insult on the authority of the magistrate, which is not so heinous a crime as the two former. These were the kinds of treason among the Romans. Under the emperors these were blended, and a breach of the smallest, even in so trifling a manner as throwing a stone at the emperor's statue, was punished with death [1]. Under Honorius, a conspiracy against any of the emperor's ministers was high treason [2].

The crimes accounted treason by the English law [3] are the following. First, killing the king, wishing his death [4], or providing arms against him, with every attempt of this kind are punished capitally. The gunpowder plot was never executed, yet the conspirators were put to death. Had they intended only the death of some other person, they would not have been executed. Secondly, corrupting the king's wife or oldest daughter [5], because these are

[1] According to Marcianus (in *Digest.* lib. xlviii. tit. iv. 5), 'non contrahit crimen maiestatis qui statuas Caesaris vetustate corruptas reficit, nec qui, lapide iactato incerto, fortuito statuam attigerit, crimen maiestatis commisit; et ita Severus et Antoninus Iulio Cassiano rescripserunt.' It is natural to infer that it was treason to throw a stone at the emperor's statue on purpose.

[2] *Cod.* lib. ix. tit. viii. 5.

[3] I.e. by 25 Ed. III. st. 5. cap. 2.

[4] Compassing or imagining the death of the king or queen, or of their eldest son.

[5] Eldest daughter unmarried, or the wife of the king's eldest son.

affronts to the king, and may introduce a spurious offspring to the crown. If it be a younger daughter, the crime is not so great. Thirdly, levying a force against the king, aiding his enemies, &c. Fourthly, attempting the life of the chancellor or [judge of] assize when sitting in court; at another time it is only felony. Edward I, however, made the mere wounding of them not treason[1]. Fifthly, counterfeiting the king's great or privy seal, which is accounted an usurpation of the government, because by them the acts of government are carried on. Sixthly, counterfeiting of the king's coin, though this should not properly be treason, because it is no attempt on the essence of government. This crime is no more than forgery, and is usually punished as such[2]. These were the branches of treason before the reformation. At this period Henry VIII declared himself head of the Church, assumed the sovereignty in ecclesiastical affairs as a part of his prerogative, and established for this purpose the court of high commission to judge of ecclesiastics, which was abolished by Mary and restored by Elizabeth. As there was some danger then from the Popish party, the Catholic religion was considered as influencing the being of government, and therefore it was declared high treason to bring in any bull of the Pope, *agnus dei*, or whatever might support his authority[3], to support popish seminaries[4], or conceal

[1] Under 25 Ed. III, st. 5. cap. 2, it was high treason to take, not merely to attempt, the life of a judge on the bench. Adam Smith may have had authority for believing that before that statute an attempt was high treason, in which case 'taking' should be read for 'attempting' and 'Edward III' for 'Edward I, however.'

[2] Men convicted were drawn and hanged, but not disembowelled and quartered. Hawkins, *Pleas of the Crown*, 3rd ed. 1762, bk. ii. ch. xlviii. § 4.

[3] Under 13 Eliz. cap. 2, it was high treason to introduce a bull, but to bring in or receive an agnus dei only subjected offenders to the pains of praemunire. Hawkins, *P. C.* bk. i. ch. xvii. § 75; ch. xix. § 24.

[4] It was treason under 27 Eliz. cap. 2, for a lay person to remain at a foreign popish seminary in

popish priests[1]. This law, however proper then, should now be repealed, as there is no more occasion for it; no notice would now be taken of entertaining a popish priest.

During the civil war and usurpation of Cromwell it became a question how far it is lawful to resist the power of government. The court party believed the king to be absolute, and the popular doctrine was that the king is only a steward, and may be turned out at the pleasure of the people. After the restoration the court party got the better, and the other party became odious. At the Revolution the Stewart family were set aside for excellent reasons, and the succession established in the present family. By this the court party was turned out, and began to influence the dispositions of the people. It was therefore enacted that whoever should speak against the present succession should be guilty of treason[2]. This is now altogether unnecessary, because the government is now so well established that there is no reason to take notice of those who write or speak against it.

In Scotland the laws were very confused with regard to treason. Prejudicing the people against the king, or the king against the people, were made high treason. But by the Union they are made the same with those of England[3]. These are the laws of Britain with respect to treason, and they subject the person who breaks them to the highest penalties. He is half hanged, and then his entrails are taken out, he forfeits his estate, his wife's dowry[4], &c.,

defiance of a proclamation; but only praemunire to send money to such seminaries. Hawkins, *P. C.* bk. i. ch. xvii. § 80; ch. xix. § 26.

[1] Concealment of popish priests was only punishable by fine and imprisonment under 27 Eliz. cap. 2; but the offence is dealt with in Hawkins' chapter on high treason, *P. C.* bk. i. ch. xvii. § 81.

[2] 'Speak' should be 'write or print.' Mere speaking was only praemunire (4 Ann. cap. 8; and 6 Ann. cap. 7). Both offences are dealt with in Hawkins' chapter on high treason, § 85.

[3] 7 Ann. cap. 21, § 3.

[4] A mistake for 'his wife her dower.'

and corrupts his blood, so that his children cannot succeed.

Besides these there are other offences against the crown which do not subject to the pains of high treason, but to those of felony[1]. First, the making of coin below the standard[2] and the exportation of coin[3]. From the notion that opulence consists in money, the parliament resolved that every one might have bullion coined without any expense of mintage[4]. Thus coined money was never below the value of bullion, and therefore there was a temptation to melt it down. This occasioned the act declaring this practice felony[5]. Secondly, any attempt to increase the coin, as by the philosopher's stone, was made felony[6]. Thirdly, destroying the king's armour is also felony[7]. Fourthly, any attempt against the king's officers is also felony[8], and in general whatever is felony against another person is felony against the king. If his pocket were picked it would be felony against him, as it is against any private gentleman, but the former offences are committed against him as king. There are some other small offences which may be done to the king which do not amount to felony, but incur what is called a praemunire. This is necessary to explain. In the reigns of King John and Henry III,

[1] Hawkins, *P. C.* bk. i. ch. xviii.

[2] 7 Ann. cap. 25.

[3] An erroneous inference from an incorrect statement in Hawkins, *P. C.* bk. i. ch. xviii. § 2. Though still prohibited, exportation had not been felony since 1573. See Hale, *History of the Pleas of the Crown*, 1736, vol. i. pp. 654-656.

[4] 18 & 19 Car. II. cap. 5.

[5] By 15 Car. II. cap. 7, exportation of foreign bullion was permitted. English coin was then melted down into ingots resembling Spanish ingots. This practice was forbidden under a penalty of £500, by 6 & 7 Will. III. cap. 17, which is probably the act referred to. It does not declare the practice felony, but it is included in Hawkins' chapter on 'Felonies against the King,' *P. C.* bk. i. ch. xviii. §§ 1-3.

[6] 5 Hen. IV. c. 4; repealed however by 1 W. & M. cap. 30.

[7] 31 Eliz. cap. 4.

[8] 3 Hen. VII. cap. 14, and 9 Ann. cap. 16.

England was entirely under the dominion of the Pope. His legate brought over bulls, and raised contributions as he pleased, and long before the Reformation it was necessary to defend the king's liberty against the Pope. The king sometimes appointed one to a benefice, and the Pope another, and the Pope's candidate was often preferred. A law was therefore made forbidding any bull to be brought from Rome, or any appeal to be carried thither, and subjecting every person who refused to ordain the king's presentee, to the penalties of *praemunire regem*, i. e. to fortify the king against the Pope[1]; the penalty was forfeiture of goods and outlawry. After Henry VIII was declared head of the Church by the Pope, it was made a praemunire to attack the king's prerogative with regard to ecclesiastical matters[2].

Beside these there are other offences called misprisions of treason, and are either positive or negative. Positive[3] misprision of treason is the not revealing an attempt against the king's person, his oldest daughter, or the

[1] 'Touching the etymology of this word (*Praemunire*) thus affirmeth Sir Tho. Smith, "that it is so-called of *Praemuniting* and fortifying and strengthening the Crown by the former statutes, against the usurpation of foreign and unnatural power:" which opinion may receive some ground from the statute an. 25 Ed. III, Stat. 6. c. 1; or to grow from the verb *praemonere*, that is to forewarn, as it were a forewarning to any, lest he fall by such attempt into a *Praemunire*, being barbarously turned for *praemonere*, which corruption is taken from the rude interpreters of the civil and canon laws, who indeed do use the effect (*Praemunire*) many times for the efficient cause (*Praemonere*) according to our proverb: He that is well warned, is half armed. And of this I gather reason from the form of a writ, which is thus conceived in the *Old Nat. Br.* fol. 143. Praemunire facias praedictum praepositum, et I. R. procuratorem, &c., quod tunc sint coram nobis, &c. For these words can be referred to none but parties charged with the offence.' Minshaeus, *The Guide into Tongues*, 1626, p. 572. Coke, *Inst.* pt. iii. ch. 53 says he that is praemonitus is praemunitus.'

[2] Hawkins, *P. C.* bk. i. ch. xix. § 23; cf. ch. xvii. § 72.

[3] A mistake for 'negative.' Hawkins, *P. C.* bk. i. ch. xx. §§ 1-6.

heir of the kingdom. In like manner it is felony if you do not reveal any notice you receive of conspiracies and rebellions. Negative[1] misprision is the counterfeiting of foreign coin current in the kingdom, such as Portuguese gold, but it is not felony to counterfeit French or Dutch money, because they are not current here[2].

In the last place there are offences against the king called contempts, which are fourfold[3]. First, contempt of the king's court or palaces. A riot committed in any of these is a great indignity offered to the sovereign. Riots in courts of justice are also severely punished, because there persons are often provoked, and if the law were not strict they would disturb the court[4]. Secondly, contempt of the king's prerogative, such as disobeying the king when lawfully called, going out of the kingdom, when in office, without his leave, refusing to come after a summons under the privy seal, accepting a pension from a foreign prince without the king's permission[5], even in a man of letters Thirdly, contempt of the king's person and government (of which many are guilty), as by saying he is indolent or cowardly, that he has broken the coronation oath, or to speak disrespectfully of his ministers[6]. These are never regarded at present, because the government is so well established that writing and speaking cannot affect it. Fourthly, contempt of the king's title, by denying it, or preferring the Pretender's to it, by drinking the Pretender's health, or refusing the oath of allegiance and abjuration[7]; all these subject to imprison-

[1] A mistake for 'positive.' Hawkins, *P. C.* bk. i. ch. xx. § 7.

[2] This is altogether erroneous. Under 1 Mar. sess. 2. cap. 6, it was high treason to forge any foreign coin current by consent of the crown; and under 14 Eliz. cap. 3, it was misprision of treason to forge foreign coin which was not current. Hawkins, *P. C.* bk. i. ch. xvii. § 59; ch. xx. § 7.

[3] Hawkins, *P. C.* bk. i. ch. xxi. ad init.

[4] *Ibid.* bk. i. ch. xxi. §§ 1–15.

[5] *Ibid.* bk. i. ch. xxii.

[6] *Ibid.* bk. i. ch. xxiii.

[7] *Ibid.* bk. i. ch. xxiv.

ment or fining, but not to the penalties of treason, felony, praemunire, nor outlawry.

Having considered the offences of the subject against the sovereign, we shall next treat of the crimes which the sovereign may commit against the subject. But first it is proper to consider who are subjects of a state.

[§ 15. *Of Citizenship.*]

The laws of different countries vary much with regard to those to whom the right of citizenship belongs. In most of the Swiss republics nothing gives the right of citizenship, but to be born of a citizen. In Rome a family might be *peregrina* for four or five generations. At Athens no man was a citizen unless both father and mother were Athenians. It is to be observed that the Athenians were particularly sparing in giving the right of citizenship, because it entitled them to very great privileges. Even kings were denied that honour; all they did when they wanted to bestow a favour on a neighbouring king was to free him from taxes on imports. This they did to Amyntas, father of Philip, king of Macedon. As aliens paid higher duties than natives, it was no small privilege to have these removed. After the defeat of the Persians their forces amounted to 25,000 men: their country was well cultivated: many cities in Asia paid them tribute. In consequence of this the people were entitled to attendance on the court of justice, to have their children educated at the public expense, to have certain distributions of money among them, with many other emoluments. If the number of citizens increased, these privileges would not be so valuable, and therefore they were very jealous of it. As whoever comes into a parish in England must give a bond not to be burdensome to it[1], so [in] all little

[1] Either 'sufficient security' (13 & 14 Car. II. cap. 12) or a certificate from the parish where he was last legally settled (8 & 9 W. III. cap. 30), *W. of N.* bk. i. ch. x. vol. i. pp. 146, 147.

republics where the number of freemen are small and election in the hands of a few, citizenship is of great importance, but in a large city such as Rome it was a very small compliment, and accordingly they made whole provinces citizens at once. In Britain one born within the kingdom is under the protection of the laws, can purchase lands, and if of the established religion, can be elected to any office. In great states[1] the place of birth makes a citizen, and in small ones the being born of parents who are citizens. In like manner the incapacity of being a citizen is different in different countries. By the old laws of Rome, and of every barbarous nation, the goods of every person who came within their territories were confiscated, and he himself became a slave to the first person who happened upon him. By a law of Pomponius, if he came from a nation at peace with Rome, he was treated as the law prescribed[2]. In barbarous countries they have but one word to signify a stranger and an enemy. At Rome every stranger was *hostis*[3], as they considered all nations as their enemies, and the person who came from them as a spy. The Litchfield man of war was shipwrecked on the Emperor of Morocco's dominions, and because we had no league with him, the whole crew were made slaves. Our sovereign so far complied with

[1] MS. reads 'estates.'

[2] 'Si cum gente aliqua neque amicitiam, neque hospitium, neque foedus amicitiae causa factum habemus, hi hostes quidem non sunt; quod autem ex nostro ad eos pervenit, illorum fit, et liber homo noster ab iis captus servus fit et eorum. Idemque est, si ab illis ad nos aliquid perveniat.' Pomponius in *Digest.* lib. xlix. tit. xv. 5. The words are quoted in Grotius, *De iure belli et pacis*, lib. ii. cap. xv. § 5, but neither Grotius nor Cocceius mention Pomponius or give the reference to the *Digest.* Montesquieu (*Esprit des lois*, liv. xxi. chap. 14) however, in quoting the passage, attributes it to Pomponius, and gives the reference as 'Leg. 5, § 2, ff. *de capitivis*,' which may account for the phrase 'a law of Pomponius.'

[3] 'Ipsa vox hostis veteri Latio nihil nisi externum significabat.' Grotius, *De iure belli et pacis*, lib. ii. cap. xv. § 15.

the custom of the place as to ransom them[1]. When they[2] found the advantage of exporting their own goods, and importing those of others, they would naturally allow those who trafficked with them to be in a state of safety, both with respect to his person and goods, and would allow him an action if injured in either. This is the state of aliens in most of the countries of Europe at present. In Britain an alien cannot purchase nor inherit land property, nor maintain a real action. He cannot make a will because it is the greatest extension of property, and is founded on piety and affection to the dead, which an alien can have but few opportunities of deserving. By a particular statute an alien merchant, but not a tradesman, may have a lease of a house. This arises from a whimsical principle that it would discourage our own tradesmen to allow foreigners to settle among them[3]. This is the state of aliens in most countries.

In Britain the manner of obtaining citizenship is twofold. First, by letters of denization, which is a part of the king's prerogative. Secondly, by a bill of naturalization, which is an act of parliament. By the former an alien is capacitated to purchase lands and to transmit them to posterity if subjects of Great Britain, but he cannot inherit, because

[1] The Litchfield was wrecked on 29 Nov. 1758, and the crew were ransomed for 225,000 hard dollars in April 1760. See *Gentleman's Magazine*, 1760, pp. 200, 391; and 1761, pp. 359-63.

[2] I.e. the nations mentioned a few lines higher up.

[3] The judges decided that a merchant might hold a lease of a house. Coke, *Littleton*, 2 b. The 'particular statute' is 32 Hen. VIII. c. 16, which prohibits a 'tradesman' (i.e., as usual in Adam Smith, an artificer or handicraftsman) from holding a lease of a house. The 'whimsical principle' is enunciated in the preamble, which denounces the 'infinite number of strangers and aliens of foreign countries and nations which daily do increase and multiply within his grace's realm and dominions in excessive numbers, to the great detriment, hindrance, loss and impoverishment of his grace's natural true lieges and subjects of this his realm, and to the great decay of the same.'

as the king is heir of aliens he may transfer his own right, but cannot take away the right of the person who ought to succeed. A denizen alien may inherit an estate bequeathed to him, but to be capable of inheriting in all respects, an act of naturalization is necessary, by which he has a right to all the privileges of a freeborn subject. When king William came to the throne, naturalized aliens were made peers. As many Dutch families came over with him, it was natural to suppose that he would favour them with every privilege. The English, offended at this partiality, made an act declaring that there should be no act of parliament for the future by which they should be allowed such emoluments[1]. As in most countries they are [not] allowed the right of transmitting lands, it was [un]necessary that they should have an action for it. Neither in England nor in Germany are aliens allowed to make a will[2]. In Saxony there was made a very equitable law that aliens from countries where they were allowed no privileges, should be allowed

[1] The act, which has been already somewhat obscurely referred to on p. 13 above, is 1 Geo. I. cap. 4, which provides that 'no person shall hereafter be naturalised unless in the bill exhibited for that purpose there be a clause or particular words inserted to declare that such person shall not thereby be enabled to be of the privy council, or a member of either house of parliament, or to take any office or place of trust either civil or military, or to have any grant of lands, tenements, or hereditaments from the crown to himself or to any other person in trust for him; and that no bill of naturalisation shall hereafter be received in either house of parliament, unless such clause or words be first inserted or contained therein.' The provision was often repealed by special act (see Hargrave's *Coke upon Littleton*, 1788, p. 129 a, note).

[2] A mistake as regards alien friends in England (see Blackstone, *Commentaries*, vol. i. p. 372). Matthew Bacon in his *New Abridgement of the Law*, 1736, which Adam Smith possibly followed in this account of aliens, says nothing about the matter, s. v. 'aliens.' As to Germany, Vattel, *Droit des gens*, 1758, liv. ii. ch. viii. § 112, does not clearly decide the point.

none among them[1]. In Rome it was the right of citizens only to make a will.

It is to be observed with respect to aliens, that they are aliens amis, or aliens ennemie[2]. If a number of the latter should make war upon the king, or injure him, they cannot be prosecuted for high treason, because he is not their lawful sovereign, and they owe no allegiance to him. If the laws of nations do not protect them, they must be dealt with by martial law. Aliens, however, who live in the country, are protected by the laws, and as they thus own allegiance to the king, they may be prosecuted for treason, and punished accordingly. Whatever makes a freeborn subject guilty of treason makes an alien ami guilty of it. An alien ennemie, that is one who comes from a country at war with us, if he give information to his natural sovereign, is also guilty of treason.

[§ 16. *Of the Rights of Subjects.*]

Having thus considered who are properly the subjects of a state, we come now to treat of the crimes of the sovereign against the subject, or the limitations of his power.

On this branch of public law it is impossible to speak with any degree of precision. The duties of one subject to another are sufficiently ascertained by the laws of every country and the courts of justice, but there are no judges to determine when sovereigns do wrong. To suppose a sovereign subject to judgement, supposes another sovereign. In England it can be exactly as-

[1] 'Le droit d'aubaine est établi en Saxe; mais le souverain juste et équitable n'en fait usage que contre les nations qui y assujetissent les Saxons.' Vattel, *Droit des gens*, liv. ii. ch. viii. § 112.

[2] The spelling of the MS. is preserved here and ten lines lower down, as it apparently represents a careful though unsuccessful attempt to reproduce law-French. Elsewhere in the MS., 'enemy' is spelt in the ordinary way.

certained when the king encroaches on the privileges of the people, or they on that of the king, but none can say how far the supreme power of king and parliament may go. In like manner where the absolute power of sovereignty is lodged in a single person, none can tell what he may not do, with accuracy. God is the only judge of sovereigns, and we cannot say how he will determine. All decisions on this subject have been made by the prevailing party, and never coolly by a court of justice, and can give us no light into the subject. Our best notions of it will arise from considering the several powers of government and their progress.

In the beginning of society all the powers of government are exercised precariously. The majority may make war, but cannot force the minority to it, though this power was the first that was exerted absolutely. The judicial power was much longer executed precariously than the federative. In every country the judges once only interposed as mediators, and sometimes the panel had his choice to refer his cause to the judge or to God, by combat, hot water, and, nay, if the sentence of the judge did not please the panel, he might challenge the judge to fight him in the court[1]. In time, however, it became absolute. The legislative power was absolute whenever it was introduced, but it did not exist in the beginnings of society, it arose from the growth of judicial power. When the judicial power became absolute, the very sight of a judge was terrible, as life, liberty, and property depended on him. Tacitus tells us that Quintilius Varus, having conquered a part of the Germans, wanted to civilize them by erecting courts of justice, but this so irritated them that they massacred him and his whole army[2]. To a rude

[1] Montesquieu, *Esprit des lois*, liv. xxviii. ch. xxvii.

[2] The particular information contained in this sentence appears to be taken from Florus, *Epitome rerum Romanarum*, lib. iv. cap. xii. 30–38. It is not all to be found either in Tacitus or in Montes-

people a judge is the most terrible sight in the world. When property was extended, it therefore became necessary to restrain their arbitrary decisions by appointing strict rules which they must follow. Thus the legislative power was introduced as a restraint upon the judicial. In Britain the king has the absolute executive and judicial power. However, the Commons may impeach his ministers, and the judges, whom he appoints, are afterwards independent of him. The legislative power is absolute in the king and parliament. There are, however, certain abuses which no doubt make resistance in some cases lawful, on whatever principle government be founded.

Suppose that government is founded on contract, and that these powers are entrusted to persons who grossly abuse them, it is evident that resistance is lawful, because the original contract is now broken. But we showed before that government was founded on the principles of utility and authority. We also showed that the principle of authority is more prevalent in a monarchy, and that of utility in a democracy, from their frequent attendance on public meetings and courts of justice. In such a government as this last, as the principle of authority is, as it were, proscribed, popular leaders are prevented from acquiring too great power, because they are not allowed to continue in office till they acquire any great ascendency; but, still, there is a respect paid to certain offices, whoever be the person that exercises them. In Britain both principles take place. Whatever be the principle of allegiance, a right of resistance must undoubtedly be lawful, because no authority is altogether unlimited. Absurdity of conduct may deprive an assembly of its influence as well as a private person, an[d] imprudent conduct will take away all sense of authority. The folly and cruelty

quieu, *Esprit des lois*, liv. xix. ch. ii, where the Germans' saying to the Roman advocates, 'Viper, cease to hiss,' is erroneously attributed to Tacitus instead of Florus.

of the Roman emperors make the impartial reader go along with the conspiracies formed against them.

It is to be observed that the right of resistance is more frequently exerted in absolute monarchies than in any other, because one man is more apt to fall into imprudent measures than a number. In Turkey eight or ten years seldom pass without a change of government. The same degree of ill usage will justify resistance to a senate or body of men. It must be allowed that resistance is in some cases lawful, but it's excessively difficult to say what an absolute sovereign may do or may not do, and there are different opinions concerning it. Mr. Locke says that when a sovereign raises taxes against the will of the people resistance is lawful[1], but there is no country besides England where the people have any vote in the matter. In France the king's edict is all that is necessary, and even in Britain it is but a very figurative consent that we have, for the number of voters is nothing to that of the people. Exorbitant taxes no doubt justify resistance, for no people will allow the half of their property to be taken from them; but though the highest propriety be not observed, if they have any degree of moderation, people will not complain. No government is quite perfect, but it is better to submit to some inconveniences than make attempts against it.

Some other writers allege that the king cannot alienate any part of his dominions[2]. This notion is founded on the principle of the original contract, by which indeed, though a people were willing to submit to one government, they will not have one of another's choosing. This doctrine is, however, groundless. In France and Spain great part of

[1] Locke, *Civil Government*, §§ 138-140, as quoted by Hume, 'Of the Original Contract,' *Essays*, 1748, p. 307.

[2] E.g. Pufendorf, *De iure naturae et gentium*, lib. viii. cap. v. § 9; Cocceius on Grotius, *De iure belli et pacis*, lib. i. cap. iii. § 12; Vattel, *Droit des gens*, liv. i. ch. i. § 17; Hutcheson, *System of Moral Philosophy*, vol. ii. pp. 297-299.

the dominions have been given to the king's children as a portion without any complaint; when Florida was put into our hands, they never made any opposition. The King of Spain and Czar of Moscovy can even alter the succession as they please. This was in general the case in all feudal jurisdictions, they were divisible[1] at the pleasure of the lord. It was but lately that the right of primogeniture took place in the principalities of Germany. It is alleged that the King of France cannot alter the Salic law, by which daughters cannot succeed to the crown. This law was owing to the power of the princes of the blood, who would not allow the succession to go past themselves. But if France had been as destitute of nobility as Britain was at the accession of the present family, the Salic law might have been altered as easily as any other law.

It is hard to determine what a monarch may or may not do. But when the *summa potestas* is divided as it is in Britain, if the king do anything which ought to be consented to by the parliament, without their permission, they have a right to oppose him. The nature of a parliamentary right supposes that it may be defended by force, else it is no right at all. If the king impose taxes or continue them after the time is expired, he is guilty of breach of privilege. James II attempted some impositions of this sort upon importation. In the petition of right[2] it is expressly appointed that the taxes shall not continue a moment after the time determined by act of parliament.

When the parliament saw the crown going to James II, who was a Roman Catholic, they appointed two tests, to wit, an abjuration of the Pope and the oath of supremacy, and that every person within three months after his acceptance of any office should take the sacrament after the form prescribed by the Church of England. King James employed Roman Catholics both in the army and

[1] See below, p. 118. [2] A slip for 'Bill of Rights.'

privy council, and besides, appointed persons entirely unqualified to the treasury, and broke in upon the privileges of the Universities. He also assumed a power of dispensing with the law in cases where he himself was no way concerned. Some of the bishops, merely for doing what every British subject has a right to do, to wit, remonstrating against such proceedings, were sent to the Tower. Nothing could more alarm the nation than this attack upon the bishops. One Sharp preached against popery, the religion of the king, upon which the bishop of London was ordered to suspend him, but he only cautioned him against such practices. The king, not pleased with this, created a court of high commission, which had been long abrogated and discharged ever after to be erected, and summoned both the bishop and Sharp to appear before it. The king, perceiving the disgust of the people, and thinking it proceeded from the fear of those possessed of abbey lands, lest they should be taken from them, and from a fear of a change in the religion of the country, he declared that he would grant liberty of conscience to all, and retain every one in the possession of the Church lands. This plainly showed his intention to change the religion of the country, which is the most difficult thing in the world. It is necessary before a religion be changed that the opinions of the people be changed, as was done by Luther, Calvin, John Knox, and others before the Reformation. King James then applied to the army, but found they by no means sympathized with him. He, in return, told them that he would never any more bring down his sentiments to theirs, nor consult them on any occasion[1]. It was no wonder that by such practices

[1] He 'sullenly told them that for the future he would not do them the honour to ask their advice.' Rapin, *History of England*, transl. by Tindal, vol. ii. p. 768. But the rest of the account of the causes of the Revolution appears to be founded on Burnet, *History of his Own Time*, vol. i. pp. 621–714, rather than Rapin.

the Revolution was brought about, and the family set aside, for the whole nation was disposed to favour the Prince of Orange. They might justly have passed by the whole family, but they generously dispensed with the rigorous law which corrupts the blood with the forfeiture of the estate, and bestowed the crown on his two Protestant daughters. Their brother, on account of the suspicions of his being a Papist, as he had been educated in that religion, was rejected. The present family, being the nearest Protestant heirs, was by an act of parliament settled in the government, and it was enacted that no prince, unless a Protestant, shall sit on the throne of Britain. Thus King James, on account of his encroachments on the body politic, was with all justice and equity in the world opposed and rejected.

Thus we have considered man as a member of a state.

As ecclesiastics and laymen are two grand divisions of men in a state, under this head too might be considered ecclesiastic law and the respective rights of these two bodies of men. Here too we might consider military law, which arises from considering the state as divided into two bodies, civil and military. But these are foreign to our purpose.

[DIVISION II.] DOMESTIC LAW

[§ 1. *Husband and Wife.*]

WE come now to consider man as a member of a family, and in doing this we must consider the threefold relation which subsists in a family. These, to wit, between husband and wife, parent and child, master and servant [1].

First of these we shall consider husband and wife. In every species of animals the connexion between the sexes is just as much as is necessary for the propagation and support of the species. Quadrupeds, whenever the female impregnates, have no farther desire for each other; the support of the young is no burden to the female, and there is no occasion for the assistance of the male. Among birds some such thing as marriage seems to take place, they continue the objects of desire to each other, their connexion remains for a considerable time, and they jointly support the young; but whenever the young can shift for themselves all further inclination ceases [2]. In the human species women by their milk are not capable of providing long for their children. The assistance of the husband is therefore necessary for their sustenance, and this ought to make marriage perpetual [3]. In countries, however, where Christianity is not established, the husband possesses an

[1] Hutcheson, *System of Moral Philosophy*, vol. ii. p. 149.

[2] Locke, *Civil Government*, §§ 79, 80; Hume, 'Of Polygamy and Divorces,' *Essays*, 1748, p. 249.

[3] Hutcheson, *Introduction to Moral Philosophy*, p. 257; *System of Moral Philosophy*, vol. ii. pp. 150, 161.

unlimited power of divorce, and is not accountable for his conduct. In ancient Rome, though they had the power of doing it, yet it was thought contrary to good manners [1]. We may observe an utility in this constitution of our nature that children have so long a dependence upon their parents, to bring down their passions to theirs, and thus be trained up at length to become useful members of society. Every child gets this piece of education, even under the most worthless parent.

On this subject it is proposed to consider the duties of each of the two parties during their union, how this union should [be] begun and ended, and what are the particular rights and privileges of each.

The first duty is fidelity of the wife to the husband; breach of chastity is the greatest of offences. Spurious children may be introduced into the family, and come to the succession instead of lawful ones. This real utility, however, is not the proper foundation of the crime. The indignation of the public against the wife arises from their sympathy with the jealousy of the husband, and accordingly they are disposed to resent and punish it. The sentiment of jealousy is not chiefly founded, or rather not at all, upon the idea of a spurious offspring. It is not from the particular act that the jealousy arises, but he considers her infidelity as an entire alienation of that preference to all other persons which she owes him. This is the real idea he has of it, as may appear from the following consideration. The idea we have of a father does not arise from the voluptuous act which gave occasion to our existence, for this idea is partly loathsome, partly ridiculous. The real idea that a son has of a father is the director of his infancy, the supporter of his helplessness, his

[1] Scil. 'to exercise the power of divorce.' Heineccius, *Antiquitatum Romanarum iurisprudentiam illustrantium syntagma* (in *Opera omnia*, 1744-8, vol. iv), lib. i. adp. § 45; Montesquieu, *Esprit des lois*, liv. xvi. ch. xvi.

guardian, pattern and protector. These are the proper filial sentiments. The father's idea of a son is of one that depends upon him, and was bred up in his house or at his expense, by which connexion there should grow up an affection towards him; but a spurious offspring is disagreeable from the resentment that arises against the mother's infidelity.

In those countries where the manners of the people are rude and uncultivated, there is no such thing as jealousy, every child that is born is considered as their own. The foundation of jealousy is that delicacy which attends the sentiment of love, and it is more or less in different countries, in proportion to the rudeness of their manners. In general, wherever there is little regard paid to the sex, infidelity is little regarded, and there will be the greatest looseness of manners. Agreeable to this we find that Menelaus expressed his resentment against Paris, not against Helen, and this not for debauching her, but for carrying her away. In the Odyssey she talks before her husband of that action without reserve. In Sparta it was common for them to borrow and lend their wives. When manners became more refined, jealousy began, and rose at length to such a height that wives were shut up, as they are among the Turks at this day. As mankind became more refined, the same fondness which made them shut up women made them allow them liberties. In the latter ages of Greece women were allowed to go anywhere. This same fondness, carried to a high degree, gives as great a licence as when infidelity was disregarded. In no barbarous country is there more licentiousness than in France. Thus we may observe the prejudice of manners, with respect to women, in the different periods of society.

Though there was little or no regard paid to women in the first state of society as objects of pleasure, yet there never was more regard paid them as rational creatures. In North America the women are consulted concerning the carrying on of war, and in every important undertaking[1]. The respect paid to women in modern times is very small; they are only put to no trouble for spoiling of their beauty. A man will not exempt his friend from a laborious piece of business, but he will spare his mistress. When the infidelity of the wife is considered as an injury to the husband, it is necessary that unmarried women should be laid under restraints, that when married they may be accustomed to them. Hence the origin of punishment for fornication.

We come now to consider how this union is begun. As the duty after marriage is quite different from what it was before, it is necessary that there should be some ceremony at the commencement of it. This differs in different countries, but in general is connected with religion, as it is supposed to make the greatest impression. In the infancy of society, though marriage seemed intended to be perpetual, yet the husband had an unlimited power of divorce, though it was reckoned indecent to exercise it unless for an enormous crime. The reason was that the government durst intermeddle little with private affairs, and far less with matters in private families. For the security of government they endeavoured by all means to strengthen the power of the husband and make him as absolute as possible. In ancient Rome the husband was sovereign lord of life and death in all matters belonging to his own family.

In Rome three kinds of marriages took place[2]:

First, by confarreation, a religious ceremony;

Secondly, by coemption[3], when the husband bought his wife;

Thirdly, by use. If he had lived with her a year and day, she was his by prescription, and he could divorce her.

[1] Lafitau, *Mœurs des sauvages amériquains*, tom. i. p. 477.

[2] Heineccius, *Antiq. Rom.* lib. i. tit. x. § 1.

[3] MS. reads 'exemption' here and below, p. 79.

The power of divorce extended to the wife after female succession took place. A woman possessed of a great fortune, who lived happily before marriage and had so much in her own power, would not incline to give it all to her husband. The lawyers therefore invented a new kind of marriage in favour of heiresses, which was called the *deductio domi*, or marriage by contract; certain terms were agreed on between the parties, and then the husband came and carried her home. To prevent prescription taking place, she went away three or four days every year, which, according to the form of the contract, secured her fortune [1]. Thus the wife became equally independent with the husband, and had equally the power of divorce. As the marriage was founded upon the consent of both parties, it was reasonable that the dissent of either party should dissolve it.

This form of marriage is pretty similar to the present, with this material difference however, that it did not legitimate the children nor preserve the honour of the women [2]. The Roman form caused great disorders. When the parties separated, which was often the case, they married others, and very often the women went through five or six husbands [3]. This so corrupted their morals that about the end of the monarchy there was scarce a great man that was not cuckolded. The disorder came to such a height

[1] 'Deductio domi' should be 'deductio in domum.' This was an incident of all kinds of marriage. The 'new kind of marriage' is thus described by Heineccius: 'Si itaque uxor nollet in manum convenire: instrumenta quidem dotalia conficiebantur, et domum deducebatur, sed dabat illa operam ut saltim tres noctes a marito abesset.' *Antiq. Rom.* lib. i. tit. x. § 14.

[2] Perhaps a rash inference from Heineccius' statement, 'Contracto sine uno horum rituum matrimonio, uxor non conveniebat in manum mariti, neque adeo fiebat materfamilias, sed matrona.' *Antiq. Rom.* lib. i. tit. x. § 14.

[3] 'Nobiles feminae non consulum numero sed maritorum annos suos computant.' Seneca, *De benef.* lib. iii. cap. xvi, quoted in Heineccius, *Antiq. Rom.* lib. i. adp. § 46.

that, after the establishment of Christianity, the power of divorce was restrained unless for certain causes. Among the Scythian nations, which settled in the West of Europe, divorce was taken away altogether. In Burgundy, however, the power of the husband was very great. By a law there, if a man abused his wife he was liable to a fine, but if the wife misbehaved she was put to death.

As in general only flagrant crimes were taken notice of by the civil court, small ones went into the hands of the ecclesiastics, and that first gave occasion to their great power. When the civil court gave no redress for breach of contract, the ecclesiastics punished the offender for perjury, and when any difference happened betwixt man and wife, they made them suffer penance for it. Afterwards the power of divorce was taken away unless for adultery, and when the one was afraid of bodily harm from the other. Even this last was not a perfect divorce, for neither of the parties was allowed to marry again, but only a separation *a mensa et toro*.

The causes of a perfect divorce, after which they were allowed to marry again, were these three. First, if they were within the degrees of consanguinity, the marriage was made null unless they had a dispensation from the Pope. Secondly, precontract with any other woman. Thirdly, frigidity in a man, and incapacity in a woman. The ecclesiastics brought in other alterations besides these with regard to marriage. It is to be observed that the laws made by men are not altogether favourable to women. They considered the infidelity of the husband and wife were equally punished, he had no more power to divorce than she [1]. Adultery, *saevitia*, and *metus* were considered as causes of separation, but not of divorce.

[1] The text appears to be corrupt. It should perhaps read, 'It is to be observed that the laws made by clergymen are not altogether unfavourable to women. They considered the infidelity of the husband and wife were to be equally punished; he had no

The canon law, when it took place, was dictated by ecclesiastics, who on most occasions copied the Roman law, as they were the only persons that understood Latin, and among whom the remains of literature were preserved. At first even the ecclesiastic law required no ceremonies at marriage. As the ceremonies of confarreation and coemption[1] had gone into desuetude in the latter times of the Roman law, when the only thing that was required was the *deductio domi*[2]; so by the ecclesiastic law for a long time, a contract of any kind made a marriage, whether a contract *in praesenti* or *in futuro*. Contract *in praesenti* is when I say, I take you for a wife, or, I take you for a husband. Contract *in futuro* is when they say, I will do it. Either of these contracts might be proved either by evidence or by oath, if they declared themselves married persons, or that they were to be so. Pope Innocent III enacted that all marriages should be performed *in facie ecclesiae*, but though this was considered as the only decent marriage, yet others were often in use and in some cases were valid. If a person was married *in futuro*, and afterwards *in facie ecclesiae*, and the first wife made no opposition till after the banns were out, the first marriage was null. If it was contract *in praesenti* the second was null[3]. This was the case in England till the late Marriage Act[4]. If a contract *in futuro* can be proved, or if the man refuse his oath, the marriage is in some countries considered as valid. The contract *in praesenti* is everywhere valid, especially if they cohabit afterwards. All these institutions are derived from the canon law, which made the breach of them liable to church censures as ours does.

more power to divorce than she.' Cp. Montesquieu, *Esprit des lois*, liv. xxvi. ch. viii.

[1] MS. reads 'exemption' as on p. 76 above.

[2] See above, p. 77, note 1.

[3] MS. reads 'contractu presenti.'

[4] The report is unduly condensed. What 'the late Marriage Act' (26 Geo. II. cap. 33) did was to make contracts of matrimony no longer enforceable in the ecclesiastical courts.

An act of parliament only makes a divorce in England, the infidelity of the wife will not do it. In Scotland it is much more easily done. Protestants never carried matters so far as the canon law, for the clergy married themselves. Besides, love, which was formerly a ridiculous passion, became more grave and respectable. As a proof of this, it is worth our observation that no ancient tragedy turned on love, whereas now it is more respectable and influences all the public entertainments. This can be accounted for only by the changes of mankind.

The species of marriage of which we have been treating took place only in Rome and in the Christian countries with a few others, for in many countries they took as many wives as they were able to maintain. This naturally leads us to consider the origin of polygamy. It is to [be] observed that though voluntary divorce be attended with inconveniences, yet it is not altogether contrary to the principle of justice that a man should put away his wife and take another for less reasons than adultery, because they make them quite unhappy together, though either of them might live very well elsewhere. The same is the case with polygamy. If a woman consents to be one of five, or twenty, or more wives, and the law[1] allows it, there is no injury done her, she meets with the treatment which she might naturally expect. The ancient Jewish and oriental laws tolerated polygamy, but though it and voluntary divorce be not altogether contrary to justice, it must always be a very bad policy where they are established or allowed.

Polygamy excites the most violent jealousy, by which domestic peace is destroyed. The wives are all rivals and enemies, besides, the children are ill taken care of, and the wife complains that her children are not used as they ought; because she measures the affection of the father by her own, between which there is no proportion, as his[2] is divided among forty or fifty children, and hers

[1] MS. reads 'laws.' [2] MS. reads 'he.'

only among four or five. Where polygamy takes place there must both be a jealousy of love and a jealousy of interest, and consequently a want of tranquillity. It may be said that in the seraglios of the Eastern monarchs there is the greatest peace, but this is owing to the most imperious discipline: when rebels are subdued their humility is remarkable. In Africa we find the most horrid disorders, their discipline not being severe enough. It is the greatest misery to the women that they are entirely shut up and can enjoy no company but that of the eunuchs, which they detest.

The man too who has the seraglio is by no means happy, though apparently so. He too must be jealous, and on account of the inequality betwixt him and them he can have no entertainment at his own house, no opportunity of social improvements; you must never mention his wife to a Turk, she can never be seen by men, not even by her physician, as Tournefort tells us[1]. This gravity and reserve of the husband must have a bad effect upon the manners of the country. As the men have no trust nor dependence upon each other, they cannot form into parties, and therefore the government must always be arbitrary, of which they have a model in their own houses, where there is little parental and less conjugal affection. Besides all this it tends to depopulate the species, the greater part of men can get no wives, and many of them are castrated to take care of the seraglio. It is indeed alleged that there are more women born than men. Montesquieu says that at Bantam in the East Indies there are ten women born for one man[2]. Dutch authors say that on the coast of Guinea there are fifty to one. The account from Japan is better attested, where it is said there are eleven women to nine

[1] *Relation d'un voyage du Levant*, 1718, tom. ii. pp. 27, 28, quoted in Hume, 'Of Polygamy and Divorces,' *Essays*, 1748, p. 253.

[2] *Esprit des lois*, liv. xvi. ch. iv; liv. xxiii. ch. xii.

men[1]. Where this is the case, if the fact be true, it would be an inconvenience if polygamy did not take place.

By strict examination we find that in Europe there is little difference. The general computation is that there are thirteen men to twelve women, or seventeen to sixteen, which, as men are more exposed to dangers than women, makes the number about equal[2]. Now if there be no difference in Europe, we have reason to conclude that

[1] Montesquieu, *Esprit des lois*, liv. xvi. ch. iv. note (b), quotes from Kaempfer, *History of Japan* (transl. by J. G. Scheuchzer, 1727, p. 199), an enumeration of 182,072 males and 223,573 females, and gives 'le voyage de Guinée de M. Smith, partie seconde, sur le pays d'Anté' as his authority for the statement that more girls than boys are born in Africa. He does not refer to 'Dutch authors' nor give the figures 50 to 1. But, as is remarked by J. Green, the editor of *A new general collection of Voyages and Travels*, 1745-7, vol. ii. p. 464, much of William Smith's *New Voyage to Guinea*, 1744, is taken from Bosman, *New and accurate description of the Coast of Guinea*, 1705, a work originally written in Dutch. Bosman (pp. 211, 344) and Smith (pp. 200, 224) following him, say that the women continue longest unmarried because their number greatly exceeds that of the men, and also that men commonly have forty or fifty wives. These two statements taken together would justify any one in concluding that there must be about fifty women to one man. It is true that they do not apply to exactly the same part of the Gold Coast; but minute accuracy in ridiculing travellers' tales would not appear necessary to Adam Smith.

[2] Montesquieu fails to distinguish between the proportion of males to females born, and the proportion of males to females living. In the text above the two things are kept separate. The remarks about Guinea and Japan refer to persons living, the 'thirteen men to twelve women, or seventeen to sixteen' refer to persons born, and 'the number' to the number living. Dr. John Arbuthnot, whom Montesquieu quotes as an authority for the statement that the number of boys born in England exceeds that of girls, gave some London statistics on the subject in *Philosophical Transactions*, 1710, pp. 186-90, and remarked that the greater number of boys was necessary in order to make up for their greater liability to 'external accidents' in consequence of their having to 'seek their food with danger.'

there is not any difference in any other place. The laws of nature are the same everywhere, the laws of gravity and attraction the same, and why not the laws of generation? In some of the fore-mentioned places there may indeed be more women than men. In places where the seat of religion is, and where the court sits, and consequently the opulent live, there must be more women, because the rich only have seraglios, and they purchase the women from other places, so that there is a constant import of women from those countries in which polygamy does not take place.

Polygamy takes place under despotic governments. When a country is conquered by savages, they indulge themselves in all manner of brutality, and this among the rest, as there is no established law to the contrary. It never took place in ancient Carthage or Rome, though it takes place in Turkey. In every country freedom puts out polygamy; there is nothing that free men will less submit to than a monopoly of this kind, but despotism is always favourable to polygamy.

Montesquieu observes still further in favour of polygamy, that in some countries women are marriageable at eight or nine, and are old and withered at twenty[1]. When they have their beauty they cannot have much understanding, and when it increases their beauty is gone, and consequently they cannot long be agreeable companions, and therefore a husband had need of more than one[2]. It may be their custom[3] indeed to deflower infants, but the fact is not well attested. Cleopatra was

[1] MS. reads '30,' which is inconsistent with the context and *Esprit des lois*, liv. xvi. ch. ii: 'Les femmes sont nubiles dans les climats chauds à huit, neuf et dix ans: ainsi l'enfance et le mariage y vont presque toujours ensemble. Elles sont vieilles à vingt: la raison ne se trouve jamais chez elles avec la beauté.'

[2] A free translation from the first paragraph of *Esprit des lois*, liv. xvi. ch. ii.

[3] I. e. the custom of the people in the warm climates spoken of by Montesquieu.

thirty-six when taken by Augustus, yet she was with child. Constantia bore a child at fifty-four[1]. But though the fact were true[2], it is not reasonable that polygamy should take place, but only voluntary divorce. If women were only useful ten or twelve years, it might be reasonable to take another, but not a number at the same time.

Wherever polygamy takes place there can be no hereditary nobility. It is difficult to make the right of primogeniture take place where there are so many wives, several of whom bring forth nearly at the same time. Where there are so many children, they cannot all have the affection of the parent, and it is only by this means that any of them can establish themselves. Where the children are numerous affection diminishes. I may regard four or five children who are connected with my friend, but if there are a hundred in the same relation they are little regarded. Now hereditary nobility is the great security of the people's liberty. Being in every corner of the country, whenever the subjects are oppressed they fly to him as their head. In Eastern countries there is no such thing. Every man is almost an upstart, and the royal family alone is regarded. The families of the Bashaws after their death mix with the vulgar. Wherever there is a hereditary nobility, the country cannot easily be conquered, or rather not at all. They may be beat once or twice, but they still recover under their natural heads. Eastern countries, for this very reason that they want these, make feeble resistance against foreign invaders.

Polygamy is exceedingly hurtful to the populousness

[1] Villani says that Constance of Sicily was 'd' anni 50 o più' at the birth of Frederick II (*Historie Fiorentine*, lib. v. cap. xvi. in Muratori, *Rerum Italicarum scriptores*, tom. xiii. p. 140 B). Possibly 'fifty-four' is a reporter's mistake for 'fifty or more.'

[2] That girls are married at an early age, and become old and withered at twenty.

of a nation. An hundred women married to an hundred men will have more children than the same number married to two or three. It may indeed be said that in China, about the mouth of the Ganges, and in Egypt, they are populous notwithstanding polygamy. In those countries there are regulations regarding populousness, and some other circumstances contribute to it, such as the remarkable fertility of the soil.

Thus we see marriage is of two kinds, viz. polygamy or monogamy, of which the latter is of three kinds: first, when the husband can divorce the wife at pleasure; secondly, when the power of divorce is equally in their power[1]; and thirdly, when it is in the power of the civil magistrate entirely. Where polygamy is allowed, the wife is entirely in the power of the husband, he may divorce her or dispose of her as he pleases.

The laws concerning monogamy differ according to the species of it. That kind where the contract or agreement is indissoluble but by the civil magistrate, is the most convenient. By this indeed nothing but what is very disagreeable to society is the occasion of divorce. But it is always better that the marriage tie should be too strait, than that it should be too loose. The unlimited power of divorce in the latter ages of the Republic[2] was productive of the most disorderly consequences, the prevention of which sufficiently atones for any hardships it may occasion. When both parties have the power of divorce, they can have no mutual trust nor dependence upon each other, but their interests are quite separate.

We come now to consider what interest the husband has in the property of the wife, or the wife in that of the husband, according to the different species of marriage. Where polygamy takes place, the wife, being in absolute

[1] This should obviously read either 'in her power' or 'in the power of each.'

[2] Of Rome.

slavery, has no interest at all in the husband's property, and is only entitled to an aliment after his death. When the husband only has the power of divorce, the property of the wife becomes his as much as his own. When they have the power of divorce in the hands of both, whatever portion the wife brings is secured, and the husband can have no more ado with it but to manage it. When he dies, the wife has no more share of the husband's property than was agreed upon by the contract. In the species of monogamy when divorce is in the hand of the magistrate, the right of the husband extends not so far as formerly; but that of the wife extends further, as she is more independent of him than in any other species. If a wife has a land estate, the husband receives the rents, which are at his absolute disposal. If the wife die and leave a son, the husband is the natural guardian of it, and is entitled to a courtesy of the life-rent of his wife's estate. In England the husband can dispose of all [his wife's] chattels real in his lifetime, but if he do not dispose of them in his lifetime, they go to the wife, not to the heir at his death. All [her] chattels personal he can dispose of as he pleases. Debts on bonds are the same with chattels real. If the husband demands payment of the debt, he can dispose of the money as he pleases, but if he do not claim it in his lifetime, it goes to his wife after his death. If the wife die first, all chattels real and debts on bond go to her relations, if the husband have not already disposed of them. If the husband die first, the wife has a third part of his land estate[1], whether there be children or not. This is considered as her dowry[2]. In England she has a complete third of all[3], but in Scotland she has only a third of all

[1] Scil. 'for her life.'

[2] A mistake for 'dower.'

[3] Of course with the qualification indicated in note 1 above as regards land, and with the qualification 'if there be children' as regards personal estate, since if there are no children the widow takes half.

bills, money, moveables, and bygone rents; bonds bearing interest go to the children. In Scotland the husband can sell his wife's land with her own consent, but she must first be examined before a court, and declare that it was with her own consent, and then her executors [1] cannot claim it. Both in Scotland and in England, no bond granted by the wife is binding upon the husband unless it be granted for the necessaries of life. In this respect she is considered as a servant, for if a servant buys provision in his name, he is obliged to pay [for] them. In Scotland the husband may have a writ of inhibition to prevent the wife from contracting debts in his name. In England any verbal notice that he will not be accountable for them is sufficient. If they be separated he is not even obliged to pay [for] what she purchases for her aliment.

We come now to consider what persons are capable of contracting marriage. Betwixt ascendants and descendants marriage is prohibited *in infinitum*. Nothing can be more shocking to nature than for a mother to marry her son. By this the mother becomes inferior to her son, and on account of the inequality of their ages the ends of marriage are seldom accomplished. Therefore it is never tolerated unless where superstition takes place. In like manner a marriage between a father and a daughter is incestuous. It is, however, to be observed that this is not so contrary to nature as the former, because the father still is superior when he is husband, and accordingly we find that many barbarous nations tolerated this [2]. But still it is unnatural that the father, the guardian and instructor of the daughter, should turn her lover and marry her. Besides, a mother can never look agreeably on a daughter who will probably supply her place. Nothing can be more destructive of domestic happiness. For the same reasons, the uncle and

[1] Rather, 'heirs.'

[2] The argument is the same as that of Montesquieu, *Esprit des lois*, liv. xxvi. ch. xiv.

niece, or the aunt and nephew, never marry. At Rome and Carthage indeed, they used sometimes to give a dispensation to the uncle and niece, but never to the aunt and nephew.

The marriage of collaterals, such as brother and sister, seems to have been prohibited chiefly from political views, because they are bred up together, and would be in danger of mutual corruption, unless properly restrained. The same reason lay against a marriage between cousins in those ages when they were brought up in the same house. At Athens a man might marry his sister *consanguinea* but not his sister *uteral*[1]. Many eminent men married in this manner, thus Cimon married his father's daughter Elpinice [2]. By the law of England the wife of the deceased grand-uncle can marry her husband's grand-nephew, it being above four degrees [3].

Affinity by the Christian law is considered as the same with consanguinity. The wife's sister is considered as the husband's sister, and the wife's aunt as the husband's aunt. It is to be observed that the rules of affinity are rather rules of police than of nature, for it is not contrary to nature that a man should marry his wife's sister. In many countries of the East Indies this kind of marriage takes place, because they think that the wife's sister will probably make the best mother-in-law to her sister's children. But it may be answered to this that it entirely hinders all intercourse between the sister and her brother-in-law's family, and that it might be expected that she would answer this purpose by living in his house unmarried with no children of her own. The canon and

[1] Uterine.

[2] 'Habebat in matrimonio sororem suam germanam nomine Elpinicem, non magis amore quam patria more ductus, nam Atheniensibus licet eodem patre natas uxores ducere.' Cornelius Nepos, *Cimon.*

[3] This was decided in 1669 in the case of Thomas Harrison and Jane Abbot. Vaughan, *Reports*, pp. 206–250.

civil law reckoned affinity[1] differently. The civil law counted brothers and sisters as one degree removed from the common stock, and cousins german two. The canon law counted how far the persons were asunder. Brothers were two degrees, the father being one, and either of the brothers another. In the same manner cousins german were four degrees. The canon counted both sides from the stock, and the civil law only one[2]. When the one says the second degree was prohibited from marriage, and the other the fourth, they both mean cousins german. The Pope often dispensed with these laws, and by that means extended his authority and promoted his interest.

Having now considered all the different species of marriage, we come to consider the effects of the want of it. The effect of marriage is to legitimate the children. We must therefore consider the difference of legitimate and illegitimate. Legitimation gives the children inheritable blood, so that they can succeed to their father and his relations. An illegitimate child has no inheritable blood, and therefore cannot succeed to his father *intestato*, because it is unknown who is his father, nor to his mother, because no child succeeds that is not lawfully begotten. As a bastard can succeed to nobody, so nobody can succeed to him[3], as he is not related to any human creature. If he die intestate without children, his wife has one half of his moveables and one third of his land estate, and the rest goes to the king; but if he has children, the wife has a third of all[4]. The king is still considered as *ultimus heres*. In Scotland there is a further inconvenience attending it. As the king is the heir of bastards, a bastard

[1] A mistake for 'consanguinity' or 'consanguinity and affinity.'

[2] Doubtless owing to a slip on the part of the lecturer, 'canon' and 'civil' have changed places throughout this exposition of the two different methods of computing the degrees of relationship. The case is exactly the opposite of what is stated in the text.

[3] Scil. 'if he die childless.'

[4] See above, p. 86 and notes.

is incapable of making a testament, because it would cut the king out of his right. The king can, however, grant him letters of legitimation which make him capable of testating, because, as the right of succession belongs to the king, he may dispose of it as he pleases. However, this, or anything less than an act of parliament, cannot give him inheritable blood, but an act of the whole legislature can do anything.

The canon and civil law restore to blood a person born out of wedlock in the following ways[1]:—

First, *per subsequens matrimonium*, or marrying the woman that had the children. As concubines were numerous, it was enacted that whoever married his concubine legitimated her children. This Justinian afterwards made perpetual.

Secondly, *per oblationem curiae*. When the children were willing to execute certain parish offices, as deacons[2], &c., though this entitled them only to succeed to the father, and not to his relations.

Thirdly, *per adrogationem*. As for example, one Roman could adopt the son of another, and the son accept of him as a father. They had it in their power to adrogate any free man. Bastards were considered as free men, and if they were willing to accept might be adrogated as such[3].

Fourthly, *per [re]scriptum principis*, which was much the same with letters of legitimation.

Fifthly, *per testamentum*, by which they probably succeeded only to their father's estate.

The canon law introduced the *subsequens matrimonium* into all countries but England. The English clergy were

[1] Heineccius, *Antiq. Rom.* lib. i. tit. x. §§ 23-28.

[2] A free rendering of 'decuriones.'

[3] 'Quum enim naturales liberi non essent in patria potestate sed sui iuris, poterant profecto a parente naturali adrogari.' Heineccius, *Antiq. Rom.* lib. i. tit. x. § 27.

then[1] unpopular by joining with the king against the barons, and therefore in England the *subsequens matrimonium* never could legitimate. That *subsequens matrimonium* might legitimate, the canon law made some restrictions which did not take place at Rome. Bastards of adulterous persons could not succeed, those, to wit, of a woman who has a husband alive, or of a concubine to a man whose wife is alive, though they should marry afterwards. Incestuous children also could not succeed, unless legitimated by a dispensation from the Pope.

Thus we have seen the disabilities and incapacities of illegitimate children, which can only have an effect where monogamy prevails; and indeed, these alone hinder polygamy from gaining ground in any country, because, if bastards were allowed to succeed, men would hardly subject themselves to the inconveniences of lawful marriage. To have a wife entirely in their power, and to take others when they please, would be more convenient.

[§ 2. *Parent and Child.*]

We come now to consider the history of parentage, being the second relation in which we were to consider man as a member of a family. The authority of the father over his children, both with respect to liberty and property, was at first absolute. He was at liberty to choose whether he would bring up his children or not, and it was accounted no injustice to refuse to do it. The law hinders the doing injuries to others, but there can be no fixed laws for acts of benevolence. All that the law prohibited was immediately putting them to death; but he might expose them if he pleased. Even with us a father is not obliged to ransom a son who is taken captive, but may do it or not

[1] Presumably in 1235-6, when the earls and barons refused the request of the bishops that the law should be altered. Statute of Merton, 20 Hen. III. cap. 9.

as he pleases. In the same manner anciently a father might choose whether he would ransom his son from starving, from wild beasts, and the like. Though some regulations were made in Rome concerning this, they were never well kept, and the practice was not abolished till the establishment of Christianity. In China, at present, where polygamy takes place, they are often obliged to expose them and generally drown them[1]. As the father had it entirely in his power to bring up his son or not, he had an absolute jurisdiction over him if he did bring him up. At Rome the father had the *ius vitae et necis et vendendi*. Besides, whatever the son acquired belonged to the father, and if he married, his children were considered as members of the grandfather's family. This power of the father over his son was very soon lessened. The son was connected with the mother's relations, and the uncle, whom on some occasions he was to succeed, would naturally look after the person who was to be his heir. By a law of Numa Pompilius, if a son was married, it was no longer in the father's power to sell him [2]. The twelve tables indeed mention this privilege of the father, but it is probable it was only those who married without their father's consent. In like manner the *ius vitae et necis* went out. The father only put in execution the laws of his country for capital crimes. He could take the power out of the hands of the magistrate, and condemn his son to punishment himself, but he could not free his son if he was accused by the laws of his country. This shows that the *patria potestas* was not altogether absolute. This power of the father weakened by degrees, and at last went out altogether. The father only pronounced the sentence as it was dictated to him by the civil magistrate, as he himself might have gone wrong in some forms, and by that means rendered

[1] *W. of N.* bk. i. ch. viii. vol. i. p. 76.

[2] Dion. Hal. *Antiq. Rom.* lib. ii. cap. xxvii. quoted in Heineccius, *Antiq. Rom.* lib. i. tit. ix. § 6.

the whole null. It is much the same with the gentlemen in this country, who have it in their power to seize the goods of their tenants when in debt, without any form of law. As they are ignorant how it ought to be done, they are obliged as well as others to apply for authority to the civil court, though they are vested with the power of doing it themselves.

The power of the father with respect to the property of the son soon went out likewise. We find that very early, by a law of Marcianus, the fathers were obliged to provide proper wives for their sons, and to bestow proper portions upon [them]; and if they refused, the government was to see it done[1]. This shows that the property after marriage must have been their own. The law seems to have[2] been made because the wife brought a fortune along with her, and therefore it was but reasonable the husband should also have some property independent of his father. It must therefore only have been the property of unmarried children over which the parent had any power, and this is not unreasonable. The authority of the father was not arbitrary at Rome, for we often find men accused there for not taking proper care of their children, which could hardly have been the case if they could have put them to death.

Julius Caesar, and after him Augustus, were the first that gave to sons property independent of their fathers. At first they kept as their own whatever they took in war, or the *peculium castrense*, afterwards whatever they acquired by the liberal and mechanic arts. This was extended by Adrian and afterwards by Justinian to everything unless what they got from their fathers. All donations and legacies were entirely at their own disposal. We also find the power of the father in disinheriting them limited. There were only certain cases in which it was in his power.

[1] *Digest.* lib. xxiii. tit. ii. cap. 19.

[2] MS. reads '& has' for 'to have,' but 'has' is written over 'have.'

After the fall of the Roman Empire the power of the father over the son, as well as over the wife, was softened. The father came to have over the son, while he continued in the family with him, an authority much the same with that a father has among us, that, to wit, of taking care of his morals. But when out of the family he was not so immediately concerned about him. The father has this particular privilege with respect to his son, that he can become tutor to him without surety, and is not accountable, as every other tutor is, for negligence and omission. This is the natural authority the father has over the son. The father is obliged to bring up his children, and the children, in case of old age or infirmity, to maintain the father.

[§ 3. *Master and Servant.*]

We now come to consider the history of law with regard to masters and servants, which was the third relation in which we proposed to consider family. We have found that the same principle which gave the husband authority over the wife, also gave the father authority over the son. As the power of the husband was softened by means of his wife's friends, with whom she was connected, and to whom she could complain, so that of the father was softened by the same means. But it was not so with the servants; they had nobody to whom they could complain, they had no connexion with any person, and having none to take their part they necessarily fell into a state of slavery. Accordingly we find that the master had the power of life and death over them, quite different from the *ius vitae et necis* over the wife and children, which was restricted to criminal cases: the power over the servants was perfectly arbitrary. Besides, as the master had the disposal of his liberty, a slave could have no property. Whatever he has or can acquire belongs to his master. No contract of the slave could bind the master, however, unless the laws found a tacit consent of the master implied. A slave can only acquire for his master. If I promised a slave £10, I am obliged to pay it to the master. But besides these disadvantages, there are many others, to which the ancient Greek and Roman slaves as well as our negroes were liable, though less attended to.

First. They were hindered from marriage. They may cohabit with a woman, but cannot marry, because the union between two slaves subsists no longer than the master pleases. If the female slave does not breed, he may give her to another or sell her. Among our slaves in the West Indies there is no such thing as a lasting union, the female slaves are all prostitutes, and suffer no degradation by it.

Second. But slavery is attended with still greater evils than these ; for a slave who is a polytheist is properly under the protection of no religion. He has no God any more than liberty and property. The polytheistic religion consists of a great number of local deities. Every place has its own divinity. The slaves belong not to the country, and therefore its gods are no way concerned about them. Besides, a heathen can never approach a deity empty-handed. The slaves had nothing to offer, and therefore could expect no favour from them. Those slaves who were employed about the temples were the only ones who could have any title to the protection of the gods. The master prayed for them, but it was in the same manner that he prayed for his cattle. Every person is superstitious in proportion to the precariousness of his life, liberty, or property, and to their ignorance. Gamesters and savages are remarkably so. It is then a very great hardship that a slave, who is addicted to superstition from both these causes, should be deprived of that which is so well fitted to soothe the natural feelings of the human breast. The religion therefore which discovered one God who governed all things, would naturally be very acceptable to slaves. Accordingly we find that the Jewish religion, which, though well fitted for defending itself, is, of all others, the worst adapted to the making of converts, because they could never be of the stock of Abraham, from whom the Messiah was to come, could not be on a level with the Jews, but only proselytes of the gate, and were obliged to abstain from many kinds of food, with all these disadvantages made great progress among the Roman slaves. When Christianity was introduced, which was attended with none of these disadvantages, it made the most rapid progress among the slaves.

We are apt to imagine that slavery is quite extirpated, because we know nothing of it in this part of the world; but even at present it is almost universal. A small part of the West of Europe is the only portion of the globe that is free from it, and is nothing in comparison with the vast continents where it still prevails. We shall endeavour to show how it was abolished in this quarter, and for what reasons it has continued in other parts, and probably will continue.

It is to be observed that slavery takes place in all societies at their beginning, and proceeds from that tyrannic disposition which may almost be said to be natural to mankind. Whatever form of government was established, it was a part of its constitution that slavery should be continued. In a free government the members would never make a law so hurtful to their interest, as they might think the abolishing of slavery would be [1]. In [a] monarchy there is a better chance for its being abolished, because one single person is lawgiver, and the law will not extend to him, nor diminish his power, though it may diminish that of his vassals. In a despotic government slaves may be better treated than in a free government, where every law is made by their masters, who will never pass anything prejudicial to them-

[1] 'The late resolution of the quakers in Pennsylvania to set at liberty all their negro slaves may satisfy us that their number cannot be very great.' *W. of N.* bk. iii. ch. ii. vol. i. p. 391.

selves. A monarch is more ready to be influenced to do something humanely for them. When Augustus was visiting Vedius Pollio, one of the slaves, who had accidentally broken a platter, threw himself down before Augustus imploring his protection, that he might not be cut in pieces and thrown into the fish pond. Augustus was so shocked with this, that he immediately manumitted all Pollio's slaves, though Pollio, no doubt, relished not the behaviour of his guest[1]. In the reigns of Adrian and Antoninus, when monarchy had taken place, there were several laws made in favour of slaves, but never one in the times of the Republic. Slavery, then, may be gradually softened under a monarch, but not entirely abolished, because no one person whatever can have so much authority as to take away at once the most considerable part of the nation's property, because this would occasion a general insurrection.

In an opulent country the slaves are always ill-treated, because the number of slaves exceeds the number of free men, and it requires the most rigid discipline to keep them in order. If a free man was killed in a house all the slaves

[1] This story is to be found in Seneca, *De ira*, lib. iii. cap. 40, and in Dio Cassius, *Hist.* lib. liv. cap. 23, but neither of these authorities says that all Pollio's slaves were manumitted. Seneca says, 'Motus est novitate crudelitatis Caesar et illum quidem mitti, crystallina autem omnia coram se fringi iussit, complerique piscinam.' Dio Cassius says nothing of manumission. After describing the destruction of Pollio's valuable goblets, his account of the matter, in the words of the Latin translation probably used by Adam Smith (ed. H. S. Reimarus, 2 vols. fol. Hamburg, 1750-2), proceeds, 'Quod visum etsi indigne ferebat Vedius, quia tamen neque propter unicum poculum, respectu tantae eorum, quae perierant, multitudinis, amplius irasci, neque poenas eius rei quam et Augustus fecisset, a servo exigere poterat, vel invitus conquievit.' In *W. of N.* bk. iv. chap. vii. pt. 2, vol. ii. p. 168, Vedius is said to have been commanded 'to emancipate immediately not only that slave, but all the others that belonged to him,' so that the mistake cannot be ascribed to the reporter.

were put to death[1]. Several authors tell us that in the night-time at Rome, nothing was to be heard but the cries of slaves whom their masters were punishing[2]. Ovid tells us that the slave who kept the gate was chained to it[3], and the slaves who manured the ground were chained together lest they should run away[4]; and what was more cruel, when an old slave was incapable for work he was turned out to die on an island, near the city[5], kept for that purpose. Slavery is more tolerable in a barbarous than in a civilized society. In an uncultivated country the poverty of the people makes the number of the slaves anyone can keep quite inconsiderable, and therefore their discipline will not be so rigid as when they are numerous[6]. Besides, in a barbarous country, the master labours himself as well as the slave, and therefore they are more nearly on a level. In the early periods of Rome the slave worked with his master and ate with him, and the only punishment in case of misbehaviour was the carrying a cross stick through the

[1] Scil. 'at Rome'; 'a house' should be 'his house.' Hume, 'Of the Populousness of Ancient Nations,' *Political Discourses*, 1752, p. 174, quotes a case from Tacitus, *Ann.* lib. xiv. cap. 42-45, where four hundred slaves were put to death.

[2] Seneca, as quoted by Hume, 'Of the Populousness of Ancient Nations,' *Political Discourses*, 1752, pp. 164, 165, mentions the case of a man who turns night into day, so that regularly about the third hour of the night, his neighbours hear the noise of whips and lashes. 'This is not remarked,' says Hume, 'as an instance of cruelty, but only of disorder, which, even in actions the most usual and methodical, changes the fixed hours that an established custom had assigned for them.'

[3] 'A chained slave for a porter was usual in Rome, as appears from Ovid and other authors:' Hume, 'Of the Populousness of Ancient Nations,' *Political Discourses*, 1752, p. 164. The reference is to *Amor.* lib. i. eleg. 6, 'Ianitor (indignum!) dura religate catena.'

[4] Heineccius, *Antiq. Rom.* lib. i. tit. iii. § 8 n: 'Sic et ruri quidam vincti faciebant opus; Columella, *De re rust.* I. ult.; Plin. *Hist. nat.* xviii. 3; Seneca, *De benef.* vii. 10'. 'Manured' is of course used in its old sense of 'cultivated.'

[5] In the Tiber: Hume, 'Of the Populousness of Ancient Nations,' *Political Discourses*, 1752, p. 163.

[6] *Ibid.* p. 223.

town or village. In Jamaica and Barbadoes, where slaves are numerous and objects of jealousy, punishments even for slight offences are very shocking; but in North America they are treated with the greatest mildness and humanity [1].

Thus we have shown that slavery is more severe in proportion to the culture of society. Freedom and opulence contribute to the misery of the slaves. The perfection of freedom is their greatest bondage; and, as they are the most numerous part of mankind, no human [2] person will wish for liberty in a country where this institution is established.

It is almost needless to prove that slavery is a bad institution even for free men. A free man who works for day's wages will work far more in proportion than a slave in proportion to the expense that is necessary for maintaining and bringing him up [3]. In ancient Italy an estate managed by slaves, in the most fertile country, yielded to the master only one-sixth of the produce, whereas a landlord even in our barren country receives a third, and the tenants live much better. Slaves cultivate only for themselves; the surplus goes to the master, and therefore they are careless about cultivating the ground to the best advantage. A free man keeps as his own whatever is above his rent, and therefore has a motive to industry. Our colonies would be much better cultivated by free men. That slavery is a disadvantage appears from the state of colliers and salters in our own country. They have indeed privileges which slaves have not. Their property after maintenance is their own, they cannot be sold but along with the work, they enjoy marriage and religion, but they have not their liberty altogether, and it would certainly be an advantage

[1] Kalm, *En Resa til Norra America*, 1753-61, tom. ii. (1756), p. 480, makes a statement to this effect, but his work was not translated into English till 1770-71. Adam Smith may however have come across a quotation from the German version (1754-1764).

[2] Humane.

[3] *W. of N.* bk. i. ch. viii. vol. i. p. 85.

to the master that they were free. The common wages of a day labourer is between six and eight pence, that of a collier is half-a-crown. If they were free their prices would fall. At Newcastle the wages exceed not tenpence or a shilling, yet colliers often leave our coal-works, where they have half-a-crown a day, and run there, though they have less wages, where they have liberty.

There is still one inconvenience more that attends slavery, that it diminishes the number of free men even to a degree beyond imagination, for every slave takes up the room of a free man. The inequality of fortune seemed at first a misfortune, and laws were made against it. £10 per annum is reckoned the necessary expense of one man. A landed gentleman who has £10,000 per annum spends what would maintain a thousand men. At first sight we are apt to conceive him a monster who eats up the food of so many, but if we attend to it he is really useful, and he eats or wears no more than the rest. £10 serves him too, and his £10,000 maintains a thousand people who are employed in refining his £10 by an infinity of ways so as to make it worth the whole. This gives room for all kinds of manufactures. When slaves are employed to sift, as it were, this £10 out of the £10,000, one must be a tailor, another a weaver, a third a smith, and thus each takes up a free man's place.

We come now to account for the abolition of slavery in this part of the world. The slaves in this and the neighbouring countries were those who cultivated the ground, and were what was called *adscripti glebae*, and could only be sold along with the land. As they had nothing but their maintenance for their labour, the ground was but badly cultivated. To remedy this disadvantage, tenants by steelbow were introduced[1]. They had no stock themselves, and therefore the landlord gave them cattle and the implements for ploughing, which they resigned at the

[1] *W. of N.* bk. iii. ch. ii. vol. i. p. 393.

end of the lease. At harvest the crop was equally divided between the landlord and tenant. This was the first species of free tenants, who were plainly emancipated villains. After this custom had continued for a long time the tenants picked up so much as enabled them to make a bargain with the landlord to give him a certain sum for a lease of so many years; and whatever the ground should produce they would take their venture. This is plainly an advantage to the landlord; the ground every year is better cultivated, he is at no expense, and the half of the product was better to the tenants than any sum they would give[1]. By the feudal law the lord had an absolute sway over his vassals. In peace he was the administrator of justice, and they were obliged to follow him in war. When government became a little better established, the sovereign did all he could to lessen this influence, which on some occasions was dangerous to himself, and hindered people from applying to him for justice. As therefore the ancient villains were tenants at will, were obliged to perform certain duties to their master, and were entirely at his disposal, a law was made taking away all their burdens but that of being tenants at will, and at last their privilege was extended and they became copyholders.

Another cause of the abolition of slavery was the influence of the clergy, but by no means the spirit of Christianity, for our planters are all Christians. Whatever diminished the power of the nobles over their inferiors increased the power of the ecclesiastics. As the clergy are generally more in favour with the common people than the nobility, they would do all they could to have their privileges extended, especially as they might have expectations of reaping benefit by it. Accordingly we

[1] I.e. the half of the product which the tenants used to hand over to the landlord, and now kept for themselves in addition to the other half, was of more value to them than any money rent they were likely to pay instead of it.

find that Pope Innocent III encouraged all landlords to emancipate their slaves[1]. Thus the influence of the clergy, combining with that of the king, hastened the abolition of slavery in the West of Europe. Agreeable to this we find that, in countries where neither the king nor the church were very powerful, slavery still prevails. In Bohemia, Hungary, and those countries where the sovereign is elective, and consequently never could have great authority, and besides, where the church never had any great influence, servitude still remains, because the court is by no means powerful enough to emancipate the slaves of the nobility.

To show by what means slaves are acquired, to consider the state of domestic servants in our own country, together with mentioning a certain particular state of families, will be all that is to be said on this head respecting man as a member of a family.

Slaves may be acquired five different ways. First, captives in war, in almost every country, are slaves. If the conqueror does not kill them, he has a right to make them slaves. Secondly, as captives become slaves, having nobody to deliver them, so their children become slaves also. Thirdly, persons guilty of certain crimes were made slaves, sometimes to the person injured, sometimes to the public. Fourthly, debtors in the ancient state of the Roman Republic were made slaves. If they could not pay their debt it was thought reasonable they should work for it. This still takes place in all countries where slavery is established. Fifthly, there is a sort of voluntary slavery when an indigent citizen sells himself to be the slave of another person. When a person sells himself to another for any sum, by the laws of slavery this very sum becomes the property of the person who bought

[1] In *W. of N.* bk. iii. ch. ii. vol. i. p. 393, Alexander III is mentioned as the author of a bull for the general emancipation of slaves.

him. But when a person was in debt and obliged to become a slave for it, he would not perhaps choose to be his creditor's slave for fear of ill-usage, and would therefore sell himself to another person, on condition that he would pay his debt. The citizens of Rome were often in debt, and by that means became entirely dependent upon their superiors. Many of them had no means of subsistence but what they received from candidates for their votes, and, as this was by no means sufficient for that purpose, they often borrowed from them to whom they gave their votes, who were ready enough to lend that they might secure them entirely to their interest. By this means they could not give their vote to any other person unless he paid what they owed to their creditors, which few would be willing to do, as for the most part they owed more than the value of their votes.

In the middle age of the Republic these two last methods of acquiring slaves were prohibited by express laws, the first by what was called *cessio bonorum*, and the latter by a law prohibiting any free man to sell himself.

The slavery in the West Indies took place contrary to law. When that country was conquered by Spain, Isabella and Ferdinand were at the greatest pains to prevent the Indians from falling into a state of servitude, their intention being to make settlements, to trade with them, and to instruct them. But Columbus and Cortez were far from the law, and obeyed not their orders, but reduced them to slavery, which in a manner instituted itself among them.

We come now to consider the state of servants. A negro in this country is a [free] man. If you have a negro servant stolen from you, you can have no action for the price, but only for damages sustained by the loss of your servant. In like manner if a negro is killed, the person who does it is guilty of murder; but though a negro servant is entitled to the privileges of a free man while here, you can oblige him to return to America and keep him as formerly. It is not from Christianity, but from the laws of this country that he enjoys freedom, because there is no such thing as slavery among us.

The greatest dependents among us are menial servants (*inter moenia*) who are bound from one term to another. They have almost the same privileges with their master, liberty, wages, &c. The master has a right to correct his servant moderately, and if he should die under his correction it is not murder, unless it was done with an offensive weapon, or with forethought and without provocation. A servant can acquire property for his master either when he acts by his express authority, or when a tacit consent is implied. If a servant buys or sells goods in his master's name, his master has room for an action in case of non-payment or of non-delivery. As there is a peculiar connexion between master and servant, they can be vindicated in many cases where any other person would be found guilty. If either master or servant kill any other person in defence of each other, it is justifiable homicide. If a master dies before the term, the executors are obliged to pay up the whole of the servant's wages and to maintain him besides.

Apprentices are much in the same way with servants, only with this difference, that the master receives a fee with the apprentice, and is obliged to teach him a trade; and if he refuse to do it he may be pursued for damages and loss of time.

[§ 4. *Guardian and Ward.*]

We come now to consider the particular state of families. When a father dies leaving his children young, it is necessary that they should be taken care of. Even in the times of exposition, when an infant was some time kept, it was thought cruel to put him to death: the child was destitute, there were then no hospitals or places of charity: it must therefore be put into the custody of some person. The nearest relation by the father's side was he whom the law fixed upon. In an early age the maintenance of the child was all that was to be taken care of, for there were no estates to manage, and the mother went back to her father's family. This guardianship terminated when the child was about thirteen or fourteen years of age, at which time it was capable in that age to shift for itself. But when men came to be possessed of estates, though he might be supposed capable of shifting for himself about that age, yet he could not be capable of managing an estate. Now it became necessary to retain him in pupillarity more than fourteen years. By praetorian law, at that age he was allowed to choose his guardians or curators. A curator can do nothing without the consent of the pupil; a guardian can act without his consent, but is accountable to his pupil for whatever he does during his minority. At first lunatics and idiots were almost the only persons who had guardians; and, on account of its being disgraceful to have one, it was generally declined. Afterwards the law made invalid all acts of the pupil, till he was twenty-one, without the consent of his curators. As the nearest relation by the father's side is often next heir, it was reckoned improper to trust the person of the son with him. The English law carried this so far that if an estate was left to the son in [his] father's lifetime he was not trusted with him. By our law the care of an estate is entrusted to the next heir, as he will probably take best care of it; and the heir to a more remote relation, who will take best care of him, as he cannot be benefited by his death.

[§ 5. *Domestic Offences and their Punishments.*]

We will now mention some offences in families with their peculiar punishments. Infidelity of the wife to the husband is punished with the greatest ignominy. In the husband, it never was punished with death, nor in the woman unless where the greatest jealousy prevails. It would be thought ridiculous in our country to bring a woman to the scaffold for adultery. Forcible marriages and rapes are generally punished with death [1]. Bigamy, as it dishonours the former wife, is punished capitally [2]. As there is the closest connexion betwixt persons in a family, if the wife kills [3] the husband, it is considered as a sort of petty treason, and the punishment by the English law is burning alive [4]. The same is the punishment if a servant kills his master or makes an attempt upon him [5]. Thus we have finished all that is to be said with regard to man, considered as a member of a family.

[1] Hawkins, *Pleas of the Crown*, bk. i. chs. xli, xlii.

[2] *Ibid.* ch. xliii, under 1 Jac. I. cap. 11.

[3] MS. reads 'punishes.'

[4] Hawkins, *P.C.* bk. i. ch. xxxii, bk. ii. ch. xlviii. § 6. This was nominally the woman's punishment in all cases of treason, but the practice was to strangle her before burning her. See Lecky, *History of England*, vol. i. p. 506.

[5] 'His' should be 'her,' since 'the same is the punishment' would of course only be true if the servant was a woman. A man-servant's punishment was to be drawn and hanged (see Hawkins, *P. C.* bk. ii. ch. xlviii. § 5). 'Or makes an attempt' is simply erroneous. Hawkins, *P. C.* bk. i. ch. xxxii.

[DIVISION III.] PRIVATE LAW

[§ 1. *First way of acquiring Property: Occupation.*]

WE formerly explained the nature of rights, and divided them into natural and acquired. The former need no explanation; the latter are divided into real and personal. Real rights are property, servitude, pledge, and exclusive privilege. We are first to treat of property.

Property is acquired five ways. First, by occupation, or the taking possession of what formerly belonged to nobody. Second, by accession, when a man has a right to one thing in consequence of another, as of a horse's shoes along with the horse. Third, by prescription, which is a right to a thing belonging to another arising from long and uninterrupted possession. Fourth, by succession to our ancestors or any other person, whether by a will or without one. Fifth, by voluntary transference, when one man delivers over his right to another.

We shall first treat of occupation, the laws of which vary according to the periods of human society. The four stages of society are hunting, pasturage, farming, and commerce. If a number of persons were shipwrecked on a desert island their first sustenance would be from the fruits which the soil naturally produced, and the wild beasts which they could kill. As these could not at all times be sufficient, they came at last to tame some of the wild beasts that they might always have them at hand. In process of time even these would not be sufficient; and as they saw the earth naturally produce considerable quantities of vegetables of its own accord, they would think of cultivating it so that it might produce more of them. Hence agriculture, which requires a good deal of refinement before it could become the prevailing employment of a country. There is only one exception to this order, to wit, some North American nations cultivate a little piece of ground, though they have no notion of keeping flocks. The age of commerce naturally succeeds that of agriculture. As men could now confine themselves to one species of labour, they would naturally exchange the surplus of their own commodity for that of another of which they stood in need. According to these stages occupation must vary. Occupation seems to be well founded when the spectator can go along with my possession of the object, and approve me when I defend my possession by force. If I have gathered some wild fruit, it will appear reasonable to the spectator that I should dispose of it as I please.

The first thing that requires notice in occupation among hunters is what constitutes it, and when it begins, whether it be on the discovery of the wild beast or after it is actually in possession. Lawyers have varied on this head, some give a part to the person who has formerly wounded a wild beast, though [he] have given up the chase, and others do not. All agree that it is a breach of property to break in on the chase of a wild beast which another has started, though some are of opinion that if another should wound the beast in its flight he is entitled to a share, as he rendered the taking of it more easy upon the whole[1]. Among savages property begins and ends with possession, and they seem scarce to have any idea

[1] *Instit.* lib. ii. tit. i. § 13. Cp Hutcheson, *Introduction to Moral Philosophy*, p. 154; Locke, *Civil Government*, § 30; Pufendorf, *De iure naturae et gentium*, lib. iv. cap. vi. § 10.

of anything as their own which is not about their own bodies.

Among shepherds the idea of property is further extended. Not only what they carry about with them, but also what they have deposited in their hovels, is their own. They consider their cattle as their own while they have a habit of returning to them [1]. When the generality of beasts are occupied, they consider them as their own even after they have lost the habit of returning home, and they may be claimed for a certain time after they have strayed. But property receives its greatest extension from agriculture. When it first became necessary to cultivate the earth, no person had any property in it, and the little plot which was dressed near their hovels would be common to the whole village, and the fruits would be equally divided among the individuals. There are the remains of a common land property in our own country at this day. In many places there is a piece of ground belonging equally to several persons, and after harvest, cattle are, in many places, allowed to feed where they please. Private property in land never begins till a division be made from common agreement, which is generally when cities begin to be built, as every one would choose that his house, which is a permanent object, should be entirely his own [2]. Moveable property may be occupied in the very first beginnings of society, but lands cannot be occupied without an actual division. An Arab or a Tartar will drive his flocks over an immense country without supposing a single grain of sand in it his own [3]. By the laws of many countries there are some things, however, that cannot be occupied by any private person. Treasure and derelict goods, by the laws of Britain, belong to the king. This arises from that natural influence of superiors

[1] *Instit.* lib. ii. tit. i. § 15.

[2] Pufendorf, *De iure naturae et gentium*, lib. iv. cap. iv. § 6.

[3] Locke, *Civil Government*, § 38, of Abraham: Dalrymple, *Feudal Property*, p. 91, of North America.

which draws everything to itself that it can without a violation of the most manifest rules of justice. In like manner seas and rivers cannot be occupied by any private person: unless [it is] particularly specified in your charter, you cannot take large fishes in a river running through your own estate[1]. A sea surrounded by several nations cannot be occupied by any one, but all must have a part of the jurisdiction, but any nation may hinder another from fishing in its bays, or approaching its coasts with vessels of war.

[§ 2. *Second way of acquiring Property: Accession.*]

The right of accession is not so much founded in its utility as in the impropriety of not joining it to that object on which it has a dependence. The milk of a cow I have purchased may not be of great value, but it is very improper that another person should have a right to bring up his calf upon it. The most important accessions are in land property. Land property is founded on division or an assignation by the society to a particular person of a right to sow and plant a certain piece of ground. In consequence of this right he must also have a right to whatever it produces, trees, fruit, minerals, &c. Alluvions made by any river naturally belong to the proprietor of the adjacent territory; but when the additions are very large, as is often the case in low countries, the government claims them, and the proprietor of the adjacent estate must purchase it before he possess it[2].

The principal dispute concerning accession is, when does the principal belong to me, and the accession to another, or, if they be mixed, to whom does the whole belong? It is a maxim in law that no person be a gainer

[1] The reference is to salmon fishing in Scotland: MacDouall, *Institute of the Laws of Scotland*, 1751-3, vol. i. p. 574.

[2] Pufendorf, *De iure naturae et gentium*, lib. iv. cap. vii. § 12.

by another's loss[1]. If a man build a house by mistake upon my ground, though the materials be his, it is but reasonable that I should have the house, or be indemnified for my loss. In general the accession follows the principal, though in some cases, as where the workmanship is of more value than the materials, *substantia cedet formae*. The lawyers were, however, unwilling directly to contradict their general and established maxim, and therefore evaded it by giving the principal to the proprietor of the accession when it became a new species, that is, when it received a new form and a new name. This, however, was liable to exceptions. A picture and the board on which it was painted were in Latin of the same species; each was a *tabula*, and therefore the picture by this amendment still belonged to the proprietor of an insignificant board. The most general rule with regard to accessions is this, when the thing can be reduced to its primitive form without lessening its value or without any great loss to the proprietor of the accession, the proprietor of the principal may justly claim it, but when this cannot be done, the law justly favours the proprietor of the accession, and obliges him only to content the original proprietor for his property.

[§ 3. *Third way of acquiring Property: Prescription.*]

Prescription is founded on the supposed attachment of the possessor to what he has long been possessed of, and the supposed detachment of affection in the old possessor to what has been long out of his possession. There are four things requisite to form a right by prescription. First, *bona fides*, for if a person be sensible that his right to a thing is bad, it is no injury to deprive him of it, and

[1] 'Nihil tritius ea sententia nemo debet ex alterius damno lucrum capere.' Pufendorf, *De iure naturae et gentium*, lib. iv. cap. xiii. § 6.

the indifferent spectator can easily go along with the depriving him of the possession. Second, *iustus titulus*, by which is not meant a title just in all respects, for this is of itself sufficient without anything else, but a *iustus titulus* signifies some reasonable foundation that the person has to think a thing his own, such as [a] charter of some kind. If he claims a right without any such title, no impartial spectator can enter into his sentiments. Third, uninterrupted possession is also necessary to prescription, for if the property have often been claimed of him, the former possessor has not derelinquished his right. Fourth, the time is only to be reckoned when there was a person to claim the property; and therefore the longest uninterrupted possession when the proprietor was a minor, a lunatic, or in banishment, can give no right.

A *iustus titulus* is a proof of *bona fides*, and *bona fides* is requisite to a *iustus titulus*. By the Roman law, *bona fides* was only required at the first taking possession, and, though afterwards you found a fault in your title, prescription took place. Nature has fixed no period for prescription, and accordingly it varies according to the stability of property in a country. At Rome, [im]moveables once prescribed in two years, but afterwards more was required[1]. In our country a feudal lord, who continually had claims upon his neighbour, could scarce be brought to admit any law of this nature. He was willing to revive a claim though as old as the days of Noah, and when at last they fixed on a period, they made it as long as possible, to wit, forty years. Among the Romans, it is to [be] observed, that if anyone's possession was interrupted during the time required for prescription, by an enemy coming into the country, he had to begin anew again. By

[1] 'Res ergo immobiles Romae biennio, mobiles anno usucapiebantur. Sed Iustinianus . . . res . . . immobiles inter praesentes decennio, inter absentes vicennio usucapi voluit.' Heineccius, *Antiq. Rom.* lib. ii. tit. vi. §§ 2, 9.

the English law nothing can interrupt prescription but a claim of the old possessor. Kings seldom ever allow their claims to prescribe[1], at least they account no length of uninterrupted possession sufficient to do it. However, immemorial possession will ever carry this along with it.

[§ 4. *Fourth way of acquiring Property: Succession.*]

Succession is either legal or testamentary. By legal succession is meant that the law should distribute the goods of the deceased to those [to] whom it is to be presumed the person himself would have chosen that they should be given, according to some lawyers[2]. But this supposes that testamentary succession, or a distribution of the goods according to the will of the deceased, was previous to legal succession, which is contrary to experience. In a rude period a man had scarce the full property of his goods during his lifetime, and therefore it cannot be supposed that then he should have had a power to dispose of them after his death. In all nations the relations of the dead person succeeded long before there was any such thing as a testament. The twelve tables at Rome, and the laws of Solon at Athens, seem first to have introduced testamentary succession[3]; but long before this there was legal succession in both countries. The claim of the heir of blood is always thought the preferable one, but this claim is never founded on the presumed will of the deceased. If we consider succession in the earliest times, we shall find that it is more founded on the connexion of goods than of persons[4]. As the father and sons lived

[1] I.e. kings seldom allow their claims ever to prescribe.

[2] E.g. Grotius, *De iure belli et pacis*, lib. ii. cap. vii. § 3, and Pufendorf, *De iure naturae et gentium*, lib. iv. cap. xi. § 1.

[3] Heineccius, *Antiq. Rom.* lib. ii. tit. x. § 5.

[4] 'Veteres Romani in successione intestatorum non id agebant ut heredes essent, quos defunctus reliquis cariores habuisse vide-

together, and were joint acquirers of any property they had, when the father died the children had a joint right to the goods, not so much on account of their relation to the father as on account of the labour they had bestowed on acquiring them. The mother and the children would therefore continue in possession. Among the Romans the wife was considered as a daughter, and had her share accordingly. If any of the children were settled out of the family or were emancipated, they had no share in the succession [1], because they ceased to co-operate with the rest in acquiring the goods. It may be observed that when families in this manner lived together it was necessary to prohibit marriages of cousins. When men's [2] sons and grandsons lived in the same house, if all succeeded equally it was called *successio secundum capita*, but if the grandson succeeded only to his father's part it was *secundum stirpes.* If a man had three sons who were all dead, but the oldest had left behind him one son, the second two, and [the] third three, by the former rule, on the death of their grandfather, each would have a sixth; but by the latter, the son of the oldest would have a third alone, the two sons of the second a third between them, and the three sons of the third a third among them. The grandsons were as it were the representatives of their father. The right of representation is the same with the *successio secundum stirpes.* Among the Romans the right of representation was introduced in favour of the strong, and in prejudice of the weak, but in Britain [it] is the contrary [3].

Among the Romans a son could not succeed to the mother when she died, because, as she was considered

retur, (quod principium postea Iustiniano placuit) sed ut facultates penes familiam manerent.' Heineccius, *Antiq. Rom.* lib. iii. tit. i. § 1.

[1] *Ibid.* § 6.

[2] MS. reads 'wives.'

[3] The meaning of this possibly corrupt passage is not easy to conjecture.

as a daughter of the family, everything she had belonged to the husband; if the husband died first, the wife shared with her children, and then went home to her father's house, and succeeded anew to her father. But in times of more refinement under the emperors, the mother could succeed to the son, and the son to the mother [1]. Anciently, when a son died, no person succeeded to him, because he and everything he had belonged to his father. Caesar first made a law that a son might possess as his own whatever he got in war, or acquired by the liberal arts [2].

Three classes of men may succeed, ascendants, descendants, and collaterals, as those in an upper line may succeed to those in a lower, those in a lower to those in an upper line, or those of the same line to one another. Collateral succession at first extended only to the nearest in blood [3], and if he refused it the goods belonged to the public [4], but afterwards the praetor extended it to the seventh in blood [5]. When a brother died and another succeeded, it was in consequence of their connexion with the father, who is the common stock, and therefore succession of ascendants must have been prior to that of collaterals. But the right of descendants is stronger than either of these, because the son's claim on the father is evidently more strong than that of the father on the son. The principles of succession then in moveables are founded on the community of goods which took place anciently in families.

The different state of families in our country makes a considerable difference betwixt our [6] law and that of the Romans. The wife is among us a much more considerable person than a daughter, and accordingly succeeds to more.

[1] Heineccius, *Antiq. Rom.* lib. iii. tit. iii.

[2] *Ibid.* lib. ii. tit. ix. § 2.

[3] *Ibid.* lib. iii. tit. ii. § 3.

[4] To the 'gentiles' or members of the clan; *ibid.* § 7.

[5] *Ibid* tit. v. § 5.

[6] I.e. Scotch.

When the husband dies, the goods are supposed to be divided into three equal parts, one of which is supposed to belong to the deceased husband, one to the wife and one to the children: there is however this difference, that the husband can dispose of his part by testament, which the wife cannot. A forisfamiliated son is not in the same condition with an emancipated son among the Romans. He can succeed with his brothers; only if he has got a portion he must bring it into the common stock at his father's death. Grandchildren do not succeed in place of their deceased father, as among the Romans. The English law, however, admits of representation, and it prefers ascendants, if males, to collaterals.

We come now to treat of indivisible inheritance, which was introduced by the feudal law. When the nations that conquered the Roman Empire settled in the West of Europe, an inequality of fortune necessarily ensued. As the great had no way of spending their fortunes but by hospitality, they necessarily acquired prodigious influence over their vassals[1]. They gave out their lands merely as a maintenance to their dependents; and it is observable that the Saxon word farm signifies victuals[2].

The chieftains, from their influence, were the sole administrators of justice in their own territories. It was the interest of government to authorize this jurisdiction, as it was the only method of preserving peace, and as the superior was the leader both in peace and war. So lately as in the year 1745 this power remained in the Highlands of Scotland, and some gentlemen could bring several hundreds of men into the field[3]. As these lords had no other way to dispose of their lands, they gave some of them as *munera*, which were revocable at their pleasure, and

[1] Cp. above, p. 35.

[2] Dalrymple, *Feudal Property*, p. 33.

[3] *W. of N.* bk. iii. ch. iv. vol. i. pp. 413, 414, where, however, the jurisdiction is said to be allodial, not feudal.

others they gave as *beneficia*, which continued during life and returned to the lord after their decease [1].

The benefices of the clergy seem to have been on this foundation and have retained the name. By this means the lords secured the fidelity of their vassals. As benefices were for life, the property of them naturally came to be extended to the son of the deceased tenant, and by degrees the tenures became hereditary and were called feudal; thus the tenant became more independent. When any chieftain died and left his son a minor, the king appointed a leader to the vassals during the minority, and appropriated the profits and emoluments arising from the lands to his own use. When a female succeeded, the lord had the power of disposing of her in marriage, as it was reasonable that he should name the husband who was to be his own vassal. As the lord was guardian of the heir male, it was also thought unreasonable that he should marry without his consent. As the feudal lord possessed the lands during a minority, before the minor could recover his estate, he was obliged to pay what is called a relief. This was introduced by the court of the king or lord, before which the minor was obliged to swear fealty before he could recover his estate. He was also obliged to promise homage to his superior before he could enter on possession. Thus they held their lands of the superior for military service, homage, fealty, wardship, marriage, relief, &c. Allodial estates were free from all such services; but as it was for security of property to hold of some great man who could protect the proprietor from violence, the generality of estates became feudal. For the same reason men possessed of great estates paid feu and swore fealty to the sovereign [2].

It appears from this that it must have been a very difficult matter to secure property, especially if it was

[1] Dalrymple, *Feudal Property*, p. 199. See above, p. 37, n. 2.

[2] This paragraph is a summary of pp. 36-39 above.

small, in those early times, and therefore nothing could have a worse consequence than the division of estates. The consequences of dividing the kingdom of France were sufficiently experienced, and the case would have been still worse in private estates. However, on account of the opposition from the rest of the sons, it was long before the right of primogeniture or the indivisibility of estates could be introduced, and in Germany it did not fully take place before the last century; but as the circumstances necessarily required it, estates were at last made indivisible, and since a single person was to be preferred, the oldest son would naturally be the person. This legal preference must be given for some quality that is altogether indisputable. If it were to be given to wisdom or valour, there might be great disputes, but among brothers there can be [no] contest who is the oldest. In the beginnings of society age itself is very much respected; and to this day, among the Tartars, the king is not succeeded by his son, but by that one of the royal family who is oldest.

Primogeniture, when introduced, would naturally occasion succession by representation for the following reason: the younger brothers at first would think it hard that their older brother should be preferred to them, and if he died they would still think it harder that his son, an infant, should come in before them; accordingly in many places this has been disputed in single combat [1]. Bruce and Balliol disputed on this account. According to our notions, Balliol had the best right, for he was descended from the oldest daughter, though Bruce was a step nearer the common stock. The difficulty of introducing this at first gave rise to a new species of succession, by which, when a father died, his estate went to his eldest son, but if he died while his children

[1] 'Non minus agitatum etiam bellis et pugnis singularibus, an nepos ex filio priore filio posteriori sit praeferendus.' Grotius, *De iure belli et pacis*, lib. ii. cap. vii. § 30.

were minors, or if he died while his father was alive, his brother, not his sons, succeeded. This was attended with one inconvenience, that on the death of the youngest his sons were preferred to those of the other brothers. By the Roman law a grandson succeeded only to his father's part: he might succeed as a son, but not as an oldest son. The brothers naturally thought that they were nearer the father than any grandson he could have; but as this was a hardship to the brother's claim, so it was also a hardship to cut off the reasonable expectation which the grandson had if his father had lived. This last circumstance after[wards] gave occasion to lineal succession. When this difficulty is got over there is little dispute about collateral succession. In feudal lordships a woman could not succeed, as she was incapable of performing military services; but they could succeed to lands where there was required any other kind of service[1]. Of fiefs there are two kinds, masculine and feminine. France, to the crown of which no woman can succeed, is an instance of the former, and England of the latter.

There are some niceties whimsical enough in the Scotch law with regard to succession of collaterals. If the second brother has an estate and dies, it goes to the third and not to the oldest, who is supposed to have been sufficiently provided for. Conquest[2] on the contrary ascends, but it does not go to the oldest, but to the immediately older brother. By the English law the old brother excludes the whole blood from one half of the estate by conquest, in other countries the preference is not so great[3].

[1] Dalrymple, *Feudal Property*, pp. 229-231.

[2] 'Conquest that falls to the heir of conquest is all heritable rights whereupon infeftment did or might follow, acquired by the deceased upon singular titles, i.e. to which he did not succeed as heir praeceptione herĕditatis or otherwise.' MacDouall, *Institute of the Laws of Scotland*, vol. ii. p. 297.

[3] This sentence is evidently corrupt. See Craig, *Ius feudale*, ed. J. Baillie, 1732, pp. 334-336.

We must observe that the right of primogeniture hinders agriculture[1]. If the whole estate were divided among the sons, each one would improve his own part better than one can improve the whole; besides, tenants never cultivate a farm so well as if it were their own property. Primogeniture is also hurtful to the family, for, while it provides for one, it suffers all the rest in a few generations to be reduced to beggary[2]. In succession to a monarchy, however, it has one evident advantage, that it prevents all dangerous rivalships among the brothers.

There are some other kinds of succession that take place, or have taken place in several countries. Thus in some countries the youngest son succeeds to the father. There is something like this among our tenants to this day: the older sons as they grow up are provided for, and the youngest, remaining with the father, succeeds to him.

So much for legal succession. We come next to testamentary. It is to be observed that there is no extension of property so great as this, and therefore it was long before it could be introduced; it was very natural to give a man a right to dispose of his property while he lived, but a testament supposes him to dispose of a right when, properly speaking, he can have none himself. He cannot be said to transfer his right, for the heir has no right in consequence of the testament till after the testator himself have none. Puffendorf whimsically accounts for this from the immortality of the soul[3]. At Rome the right of making testaments was introduced gradually. At first it was only allowed, and that too after the con-

[1] *W. of N.* bk. iii. ch. ii. vol. i. pp. 386–389.

[2] *Ibid.* p. 388.

[3] It is not Pufendorf but Leibnitz, quoted by him (*De iure naturae et gentium*, lib. iv. cap. x. § 4), who gives this explanation. Pufendorf says 'quod autem comminiscitur auctor novae methodi iurisprudentiae p. m. 56 id nescio an cordati sint adprobaturi.'

sent of the fellow citizens was asked and obtained, to childless people. This was much the same with adopting children[1]. When a person died and wanted to leave his estate to a son in exile, he would naturally request his neighbours not to take it from him after his own death. This request would be regarded, not so much on account of its being his will, as from a kind of piety for the dead. We naturally find a pleasure in remembering the last words of a friend and in executing his last injunctions, the solemnity of the occasion deeply impresses the mind; besides, we enter as it were into his dead body, and conceive what our living souls would feel if they were joined with his body, and how much we would be distressed to see our last injunctions not performed[2]. Such sentiments naturally inclined men to extend property a little farther than a man's lifetime.

This seems to have been the foundation of testamentary succession. It was a sort of impiety not to comply with the father's desire, though it was no injury to deprive the heir of the estate, as there was no law established in his favour, and as his being in exile cut off all reasonable expectation of succeeding. The injury is conceived to be done to the dead person, as we enter into what would be his sentiments were he to live again. It is to be observed that this practice is a considerable refinement in humanity, and never was practised in a rude nation. Before the twelve tables no Roman had a right to make a will[3]. Our Saxon ancestors had no right to dispose of their lands by testament[4], and in the history of the Old Testament we hear of no such practice. Piety for the dead could take

[1] Lord Kames, *Law Tracts*, vol. i. pp. 186-7; Dalrymple, *Feudal Property*, p. 152; Heineccius, *Antiq. Rom.* lib. ii. tit. x. § 2.

[2] Dalrymple, *Feudal Property*, p. 154.

[3] Above, p. 113.

[4] This too absolute assertion is probably a rash inference from Dalrymple's history of the alienation of land-property by will in *Feudal Property*, ch. iii. sect. 3, pp. 149-162.

place only with regard to the immediate successor, and therefore at first the right of making testaments extended no further, unless in case the person in whose favour it was made should refuse to succeed, in which case another might be appointed. This was a further extent of the right. Again, if a man died and left his sister's[1] son heir to him, that the estate might not go to foreign relations, the testator was allowed to say that if the pupil die at a certain age, the estate shall go to such another person. This was called pupillar substitution[2]. Thus property was still further extended.

The greatest of all extensions of property is that by entails. To give a man power over his property after his death is very considerable, but it is nothing to an extension of this power to the end of the world. In the beginnings of society the state of families is very different from what it is at present. As the wife was subject to the husband, and at the best only on the footing of a daughter, she seldom made any addition to the husband's estate unless by her own industry; but when female succession took place, and women came to be possessed of fortunes, they would not marry without a previous capitulation by which they insured themselves of good usage, and stipulated that some part of their fortune should go to their relations after their death. By this arose a new species of marriage from agreement which rendered the parties equally independent[3]. This great alteration in domestic affairs would naturally at first be complained of, and, as the ultimate cause of it was the succession of females, they would endeavour to prevent their opulence. On this account a law was made at Rome bringing matters to their ancient footing, called the Voconian law. To elude this law a *fide[i] commissum* was invented, by which, when

[1] A mistake. The pupil must be a descendant in the power of the testator.

[2] MS. reads 'popular succession.'

[3] Above, p. 77.

a man had a mind to leave his estate to a person whom the law would not allow, [he left it to someone else] and took his solemn promise that he would transfer it to the person for whom he intended it. Augustus made a law obliging the trustee always to restore it, and appointed a [fidei-]commissary praetor for that purpose [1]. The person to [2] whom the estate was left was called *heres fiduciarius*, and the person to whom it was to be restored was called *fide[i] commissarius*: thus property was extended beyond the first successor, and when this step was gained they easily advanced further and introduced entails.

Entails were first introduced into the modern law by the ecclesiastics, whose education made them acquainted with the Roman customs [3]. As they were the preachers of this doctrine, they naturally became the explainers and executors of wills till Theodosius and Valentinian [4] took it from them. In England William the Conqueror restored it to the ecclesiastics [5].

By the customs of our country [6] a man, if he leave a wife and children, can dispose only of a third by testament; and if he leave a wife without children, only a half. Lands after the introduction of the feudal system could only be disposed [of] by testament in the same way with military services, by the consent of the superior. Originally in England there were no entails by will, but by

[1] Heineccius, *Antiq. Rom.* lib. ii. tit. xxiii. §§ 2-4.

[2] MS. reads 'for.'

[3] The Roman origin of entails is denied in *W. of N.* bk. iii. ch. ii. vol. i. p. 388.

[4] MS. reads 'Theodosius Valentinus.' It is difficult to account for the statement in the text, which exaggerates enormously the powers of the ecclesiastics. Justinian considered it manifestly absurd that they should attempt to meddle with wills; *Cod.* lib. i. tit. iii. § 40 (41).

[5] Perhaps a rash inference from statements to the effect that anciently the probate of wills was in the county court, where the bishop and sheriff sat together, and that William the Conqueror divided the ecclesiastical from the civil jurisdiction: see Bacon, *New Abridgement of the Law*, s. v. Courts ecclesiastical, vol. i. p. 618.

[6] I.e. Scotland.

tenure. A man held an estate for himself and his heirs, but if he had no heirs he could not alienate it, it returned to the superior. But if he had heirs he could alienate it, and thus the lord was deprived of his right of reversion. A law[1] was afterwards made to secure this.

Upon the whole nothing can be more absurd than perpetual entails. In them the principle of testamentary succession can by no means take place. Piety to the dead can only take place when their memory is fresh in the minds of men: a power to dispose of estates for ever is manifestly absurd. The earth and the fullness of it belongs to every generation, and the preceding one can have no right to bind it up from posterity[2]; such extension of property is quite unnatural. The insensible progress of entails was owing to their not knowing how far the right of the dead might extend, if they had any at all. The utmost extent of entails should be to those who are alive at the person's death, for he can have no affection to those who are unborn. Entails are disadvantageous to the improvement of the country, and those lands where they have never taken place are always best cultivated: heirs of entailed estates have it not in their view to cultivate lands, and often they are not able to do it. A man who buys land has this entirely in view, and in general the new purchasers are the best cultivators.

[1] Stat. Westm. II, 13 Ed. I. cap. i. De donis conditionalibus.

[2] 'In the present state of Europe ...nothing can be more completely absurd [than entails]. They are founded upon the most absurd of all suppositions, the supposition that every successive generation of men have not an equal right to the earth and to all that it possesses; but that the property of the present generation should be restrained and regulated according to the fancy of those who died perhaps 500 years ago.' *W. of N.* bk. iii. ch. ii. vol. i. p. 388. 'Absurd' occurs twice, as in the text above.

[§ 5. *Fifth way of acquiring Property: Voluntary Transference.*]

In voluntary transference two things are required: first, a declaration of the intention both of the person who transfers, and of him to whom it is transferred: second, the actual delivery of the thing. In most cases the first of these is not binding without the latter, because there is no right without possession. If a man indeed have borrowed a thing and afterwards purchase it, there is no need of delivery, for it is already in his possession. Before possession you can have no right to the thing, though you may have a right to make the man keep his promise or contract. If I buy a horse from a man, and before delivery he sell him to a third person, I cannot demand the horse from the possessor, but only from the person who sold him. But if he has been delivered I can claim him from any person. Property therefore cannot be transferred without tradition or delivery. Grotius indeed justly observes that in the transference of a pledge there is no need of delivery, because in this case the thing is already in the man's possession[1]. In France, if a man declare his purpose to make a donation, and die before the delivery, the donation goes to the heir. This was also a custom among the Wisigoths. In transferring the property of lands and other large objects, what gives possession is not so easy to determine. As there cannot be an actual delivery, in our country a symbolical delivery is used; an ear or sheaf of corn signifies the whole field, a stone and turf, the estate to the centre of the earth, and the keys of the door, the house. By the Scotch law, if there be a transference of several estates, the purchaser must be infeft in each. By the English law infeftment in one

[1] *De iure belli et pacis*, lib. ii. cap. viii. § 25.

serves for all[1] when done in presence of the county court[2]. In Scotland it must be done on the land: it is enough in England if it be done in view of it. Besides delivery a charter or writing, showing on what terms the transference was made, is also requisite for security. Till the custom was abolished by a late statute, no vassal or possessor had a right of alienating his estate without the consent of the superior[3]. As he held it for military service, it was requisite that the estate should be resigned to the superior, who resigned it to the purchaser, as it was proper that his vassal should be of his own choosing. Afterwards, however, it became necessary to accept of creditors, and this was often used as a handle to elude the law. The seller gave a bond for a sum of borrowed money without any mention that it was a sale, by which means the lands were adjudged to the creditor, and the lord was obliged to accept of him as his vassal. In like manner, as the tenant was liable to oppression from a new superior, the lord could not dispose of his estate without consent of his vassal. If therefore either of them alienated any part of their estates without the other's consent, his right was forfeited.

The duty of vassals to their lords continued longer in Scotland than in England, which may be accounted for from the difference of their government, for that [of] England all along favoured democracy, and that of Scotland aristocracy. After society was fully established, there was no occasion for mutual consent, because the tenant was protected by law, whatever the lord was.

In the time of the civil wars[4] a new sort of delivery took place. When a person transferred his estate to another

[1] Scil. 'in the same county.'

[2] This should probably read 'as the feoffment and giving livery was anciently done in presence of the county court.' See Bacon, *Abridgement*, s.v. Feoffment, vol. ii. p. 492; Coke, *Littleton*, p. 253 a.

[3] In Scotland. The 'late statute' is 20 Geo. II. cap. 50.

[4] Of the Lancastrians and Yorkists.

for his own use it was not affected by forfeiture ; the person to whom it was transferred was considered as the bailiff, and took possession in the other's name.

[§ 6. *Of Servitudes.*]

The second species of real rights is servitudes or burdens which one man has on the property of another. These rights were at first personal, as they were entered into by a contract between the persons. It is necessary that I should have a road to the market town ; if a man's estate lie between me and it, I must bargain with him for the privilege of a road through it. This contract produces only a personal right, though I should bind him not to sell this estate without the burden ; but here was an inconveniency, for, if the land were sold and the new proprietor refused the road, I could not sue him on a personal right upon the former proprietor. Before I can come at the new purchaser, I must pursue the person from whom I had the right, who must pursue him to whom he sold it. If the land has gone through several hands this is very tedious and inconvenient. The law, to remedy this, made servitudes real rights, demandable *a quocumque possessore*.

Servitudes were *rusticae*, such as the right of a road to the town, or to the river, and of feeding so many cows on another man's pasture grounds, or *urbanae*, such as the right of leaning the beams of my house on your gable, the right of obliging him who is proprietor of the under-story to make his wall strong enough to support mine, and the like. These are all naturally personal rights and are only made real by lawyers. Life rents on estates and many other things are also servitudes, and are properly personal. Feudal burdens were only persons' rights, and therefore every new vassal must renew his homage and the promise of fealty.

In the beginning of the feudal law, if the proprietor did not perform his duty in every article he forfeited his feu; in like manner, if the tenant encroached on his lord's grounds, what he had feued returned to the superior. The right of the vassal is founded on the charter of the superior, and every article of it must be fulfilled, and every new possessor must renew the obligation. When tenants became independent and had a real property, they were said to have the *dominium directum*, not the *dominium utile*[1].

[§ 7. *Of Pledges and Mortgages.*]

Pledges and mortgages are certain securities for the payment of debts. At first they could not be claimed as real rights, though afterwards the law considered them as such. Pledges properly regard moveable subjects, and mortgages immoveable; if a pledge be not redeemed at a certain time, it is forfeited. As people in bad circumstances are naturally slothful, the negligence of debtors among the Romans gave occasion to the *lex commissaria*, by which the creditor was empowered to seize the pledge, and return the overplus if there was any. By the English law, if no day be named, the pledge falls to the pawntaker on the death of the pawner[2]. In immoveables, lands are mortgaged but not delivered, and in case of failure they are forfeited. The Roman law and ours are much the same on this head. If payment be not made within some few months after demand, the creditor adjudges the land for the whole sum and the penalty incurred; but his property is not secure without long possession, for the proprietor has a power of redeeming it within a reasonable time; but, as upon redemption much trouble must be

[1] By a slip of the lecturer or the reporter, 'directum' and 'utile' have been transposed. The text should read 'the dominium utile, not the dominium directum.' Dalrymple, *Feudal Property*, pp. 200, 238.

[2] Bacon, *Abridgement*, s. v. Bailment, vol. i. p. 239.

occasioned in examining old accounts and the like, the law[1] has made twenty years the stated time in England for redeeming mortgages.

Hypothecs are another kind of pledges really arising from contract, but made real rights by the civil law. By them anciently the landlord was empowered to detain the furniture and whole stock of the tenant if he turned bankrupt, and could claim them *a quocumque possessore.* This arose from the practice of keeping tenants by steel-bow, by which the whole stock in the farm was the landlord's. At present the landlord has only a right of preference, and we have not so many hypothecs as the Romans had.

All pledges are naturally personal rights, and are only made real by the civil law.

[§ 8. *Of Exclusive Privileges.*]

Exclusive privileges are the last division of real rights. Among these is the right of inheritance, which is not a creature of the civil law, but arises from nature. The heir, previous to any other person, has a privilege of demanding what belonged to the deceased, and after he is admitted heir it is his real property. Again, if a person start a wild beast, he has an exclusive privilege of pursuing, and whatever person comes in upon the chase is liable to punishment[2] because he breaks in upon his exclusive privilege. In the year 1701 an English man-of-war engaged with a French merchant fleet under convoy, which was just about to fall into their hands, when a Scotch privateer came and carried off the prize. A lawsuit commenced and the Scotch privateer was declared guilty of breach of property, but upon strict inquiry we shall find that it was only breach of privilege[3]. Though these and some other exclusive

[1] I.e. the practice of the courts. Bacon, *Abridgement*, vol. iii. p. 654.

[2] MS. erroneously reads 'not' here.

[3] No such case appears to have occurred in 1701. In 1677, however, a case (*King's Advocate* v. *Rankin*) was tried which is

privileges arise from nature, they are generally the creatures of the civil law. Such are monopolies and all privileges of corporations, which, though they might once be conducive to the interest of the country, are now prejudicial to it. The riches of a country consist in the plenty and cheapness of provisions, but their effect is to make everything dear. When a number of butchers have the sole privilege of selling meat, they may agree to make the price what they please, and we must buy from them whether it be good or bad. Even this privilege is not of advantage to the butchers themselves, because the other trades are also formed into corporations, and if they sell beef dear they must buy bread dear. But the great loss is to the public, to whom all things are rendered less comeatable, and all sorts of work worse done; towns are not well inhabited, and the suburbs are increased. The privilege, however, of vending a new book or a new machine for fourteen years has not so bad a tendency, it is a proper and adequate reward for merit. A right to servitudes and exclusive privileges, it is to be observed, may be acquired by prescription.

So much for the different kinds of real rights: we proceed now to personal rights, which arise either from contract, quasi-contract, or delinquency.

[§ 9.] *Of Contract.*

That obligation to performance which arises from contract is founded on the reasonable expectation pro-

possibly the one referred to. The frigate *Nightingale* pursued a Dutch privateer which was taking home three French prizes (England and France being then in alliance against Holland). When she returned from the pursuit, she found that Rankin, in command of a Scotch privateer, had captured one of the prizes. The court held that Rankin's action was injurious 'otherways than to assist the first attacter, unless it had been proven that the prize would have escaped' if he had not stopped her. W. M. Morison, *Decisions of the Court of Session*, 1811, pp. 11930–11936.

duced by a promise, which considerably differs from a mere declaration of intention. Though I say I have a mind to do such a thing for you, yet on account of some occurrences do not do it, I am not guilty of breach of promise. A promise is a declaration of your desire that the person for whom you promise should depend on you for the performance of it. Of consequence the promise produces an obligation, and the breach of it is an injury.

Breach of contract is naturally the slightest of all injuries, because we naturally depend more on what we possess than what is in the hands of others. A man robbed of five pounds thinks himself much more injured than if he had lost five pounds by a contract. Accordingly in rude ages crimes of all kinds, except those that disturb the public peace, are slightly punished, and society is far advanced before a contract can sustain action or the breach of it be redressed. The causes of this were the little importance of contracts in those times, and the uncertainty of language.

The first contracts that sustained action would be those where the damage done was very great, and where there could be no doubt but the person once intended to perform. Accordingly among the ancients promises entered into with great solemnity first sustained action. Among them no stipulation could be made unless the contractors were personally present, and no promissory note in writing was binding. As no promises by the Roman law sustained action without a stipulation, so by the English a consideration or cause for the promise was at first necessary to make it obligatory. It was thought contrary to good manners to insist on a promise: if a man promised with his daughter a certain sum, there is a consideration, and therefore he was obliged to perform it; but if he promised it with any other man's daughter it was *sine causa*, and, unless she was a relation, could not sustain action. If I made you a promise it did not sustain action, but if I again promised not to forget my former promise, the latter promise was obligatory, and the former was the consideration that made it so[1].

By the civil law the first promises that sustained action were those entered into in presence of a court where there could be no doubt of the intention, and accordingly recognizance of every promise was taken before some court. A recognizance is when a debtor comes before a court with the creditor, and acknowledges that he owes him a certain sum; a copy of this acknowledgment was given to the creditor and another lodged in the hands of the clerk, and whenever the creditor produced this, if it was found to correspond to the other, he might pursue for his money. Afterwards a recognizance before the magistrate of a staple town served the purpose[2].

The next contracts that sustained action were the *contractus reales*, or those which were entered into by the delivery of a thing to be returned itself, or in species, or in value. These are of four kinds, the *mutuum*, *commodatum*, *depositum* and *pignus*[3].

The *mutuum* is when I lend anything to be returned in value, as money. This soon sustained action.

Commodatum is when the thing itself is to be restored, as a borrowed horse.

Depositum is when a thing is committed to another's care but not to his use.

Pignus is a security for debt.

All these sustained action before the consensual contracts, which are also four, to wit, buying and selling, letting

[1] This appears to be an exaggerated or misreported account of the old rule, 'that wherever a defendant is under a moral obligation, or is liable in conscience and equity to pay, that is a sufficient consideration.' Cowper, *Reports*, p. 294. So a man may make himself liable for otherwise irrecoverable debts contracted when he was a minor, and a liability barred by the statute of limitations may be similarly revived.

[2] Bacon, *Abridgement*, s. v. Execution, vol. ii. pp. 330-332.

[3] *Instit.* lib. iii. tit. xiv.

and hiring, partnership, and commission. In buying, if the contract be not fulfilled, you lose your earnest money. Letting and hiring once comprehended leases, day's wages, building, and almost everything with regard to society. If the contract of commission was performed gratuitously it could not at first sustain any action, but if a reward was given, it was nearly the same with the *commodatum*. If a small price be paid for the loan of a thing it becomes letting and hiring. The *mutuum* does not infer interest, and in a bond, unless the interest be specified, it will carry none.

Besides these there was in the Roman law what was called a *pactum nudum*, when there was a bare promise without any consideration, which produced an exception or defence against the action of the pursuer[1]. As contracts deprive men of that liberty which every man wishes to enjoy, a very small defence set them free. Originally no contracts were sued before any court but the ecclesiastic, but they came gradually to civil courts[2]. The canon[3] law, which judged from principles of honour and virtue, obliged men to perform even those promises that were made gratuitously. This was imitated by the civil law; and by our law if a promise be clearly proven, he who promises must perform it. In general the law gave only action for damages till the court of chancery was introduced. It is indeed the natural idea of [a] court to redress injuries, and accordingly if a person refused to perform his contract he was only obliged to pay the loss which the other had sustained; but the court of chancery forced the person to a performance of the agreement.

Nothing can be more different than the present and ancient state of contracts. Execrations and the most

[1] 'Nuda pactio obligationem non parit, sed parit exceptionem.' *Digest*, lib. ii. tit. xiv. § 7.

[2] 'No contracts were' should be 'some cases of breach of faith were not.'

[3] MS. reads 'common.'

solemn ceremonies were scarce thought sufficient to secure the performance of a contract; drinking blood and water mixed, bleeding one another, promising before the altar, breaking a straw, and a number of other ceremonies to impress the mind, were invented. At present almost anything will make a contract obligatory.

There are some questions concerning contracts much agitated by lawyers, especially one in the case when the coin happens to be debased[1]. [If] I borrow £100 when the coin is 4 oz. [to] the pound, and it be afterwards debased to 2 oz., whether should I pay £100 of the new coin or £200? When the government makes any alteration in the coin it is to answer some urgent necessity. In 1705 the crown of France had a demand for ten million, and could raise only five[2]. They cried up the coin and paid the ten with five. As the government allows private persons to pay with the new coin, the injury is not great. The debasement of the coin cheapens for some time all commodities and provisions, as all are paid in the new coin, and therefore the uses of money may be served by the new as well as the old coin[3].

[§ 10. *Of Quasi-Contract.*]

Quasi-contract is founded on the duty of restitution. If you find a watch on the way, you are obliged to restore it by the right of property, because a man loses not property with possession. But if you and I balance accounts, and you pay me a sum which both think due, but you afterwards find you did not owe that sum, how

[1] Pufendorf, *De iure naturae et gentium*, lib. v. cap. vii. § 6.

[2] The date in the MS. is not clearly written and might be 1703, 1705, or 1706. The probability is that the reference is to the recoinage of 1708-9 mentioned in Melon, *Essai politique sur le commerce*, 1734 (in Daire's *Économistes financiers*, p. 721), and Dutot, *Réflexions politiques sur les finances et le commerce*, 1738 (in the same collection, p. 797), though on that occasion the augmentation was only 25 per cent.

[3] See below, Part ii. Div. ii. § 8.

will you claim it? You cannot ask it as your property, for you alienated that sum, nor can you claim it by contract, for there never was one made between us[1], yet it is evident that I am a gainer by your loss, and therefore restitution is due.

In the same manner if a man was called away by a sudden order of the state without leaving an attorney to manage a law suit that he had going on, and a friend undertakes this office without commission, as the defence is necessary, and the undertaking it prudent, restitution of his expenses are due. On the same principle were founded the *actiones contrariae* of the Roman law. If you lent me a horse which had cost me extraordinary expenses, by the contract commodate you could redemand your horse in the same [state] in which you lent him, but I could claim my extraordinary expenses by an *actio contraria*. The same principle takes place in many other cases. If a person borrows money, and gets three of his acquaintances sureties for him, jointly and severally, and if he turn bankrupt, the creditor pursues the ablest surety, who has a claim by the duty of restitution on the other two for their thirds. The Scotch law carries this still farther. If a bankrupt had two estates, and two creditors *A* and *B*: *A* has a security on both estates, *B* has security only on the best: *A* has a liberty of drawing his money from either estate he pleases, and draws from that on which *B* has his security. As *B* in this case is cut out, the law obliges *A* to give up his security on the other estate to *B*. The same was the case in the Roman law with regard to tutory.

[§ 11. *Of Delinquency*]

We come now to the third kind of personal rights, those to wit, *ex delicto*.

Delicts are of two kinds, as they arise *ex dolo* when

[1] 'Nam qui solvendi animo pecuniam dat, in hoc dare videtur, ut distrahat potius negotium quam contrahat.' *Instit.* lib. iii. tit. xxvii. § 6.

there is a blameable intention, or *ex culpa* when they are done through a culpable negligence.

Injury naturally excites the resentment of the spectator, and the punishment of the offender is reasonable as far as the indifferent spectator can go along with it. This is the natural measure of punishment. It is to be observed that our first approbation of punishment is not founded upon the regard to public utility which is commonly taken to be the foundation of it. It is our sympathy with the resentment of the sufferer which is the real principle. That it cannot be utility is manifest from the following example. Wool in England was conceived to be the source of public opulence, and it was made a capital crime to export that commodity[1]. Yet though wool was exported as formerly and men were convinced that the practice was pernicious, no jury, no evidence, could be got against the offenders. The exportation of wool is naturally no crime, and men could not be brought to consider it as punishable with death[2]. In the same manner, if a sentinel be put to death for leaving his post, though the punishment be just and the injury that might have ensued be very great, yet mankind can never enter into this punishment as if he had been a thief or a robber.

Resentment not only prompts to punishment, but points out the manner of it. Our resentment is not gratified unless the offender be punished for the particular offence done ourselves, and unless he be made sensible that it is for that action. A crime is always the violation of some right, natural or acquired, real or personal. The non-performance of a contract indeed

[1] 13 and 14 Car. II. cap. 18.

[2] The preamble of 7 and 8 W. III. cap. 28, quoted in *W. of N.* bk. iv. ch. viii. vol. ii. p. 232, says that owing to the severity of the penalty under 13 and 14 Car. II. cap. 18, 'the prosecution of offenders hath not been so effectually put in execution.'

is not a crime, unless it be through some fraudulent intention.

The greatest crime that can be done against any person is murder, of which the natural punishment is death, not as a compensation, but as a reasonable retaliation. In every civilized nation death has been the punishment of the murderer, but in barbarous nations a pecuniary compensation was accepted of, because then government was weak, and durst not meddle in the quarrels of individuals unless in the way of mediation. In the age of hunters particularly there was little more than the name of authority, and a man of superior influence can do no more than persuade the parties to an agreement. When one man killed another, the whole society met and advised the one party to give, and the other to take, a compensation. In America when one member of a family kills another, the society does not intermeddle with them, as this cannot hurt the peace of the society; they only take notice of it when one family attacks another[1]. It was long before the government could call a man before them and tell him what he must do, because it was long before people would submit to such absolute authority.

In the laws of all nations we have the remains of this ancient state of weakness. When government became more powerful, the murderer was not only obliged to make a compensation to the relations of the slain, but likewise to the public, who were put to the trouble of lending him their protection, on that occasion, against the revenge of those who were concerned. This was the state of criminal law among the Germans at the declension of the Roman Empire. The Germans were much farther advanced than the Americans at this day. Though they seldom punished with death, yet they seemed to make the punishment in some measure proportioned to the crime. A price was set

[1] Lafitau, *Mœurs des sauvages Amériquains*, tom. i. pp. 486, 487, 490. See above, p. 15.

on every person according to his station. There was one price paid for killing the king, and another for killing a slave. The compensation was proportioned to the dignity of the person and of his relations. What was paid to the prince for interposition was increased and diminished in the same proportion. It was a higher fine to kill a man belonging to a lord than one belonging to a little baron. To disturb the king's peace subjected to a greater fine than to disturb the peace of a baron or lord. If the injurer refused to pay the compensation he was left to the resentment of the injured, and if he was not able to pay it, he was obliged to implore the assistance of his friends. As the compensation was not adequate to the offence, the government, after it acquired strength, took this additional compensation to itself as the price of the offender's freedom. From this the sovereign acquired the right of pardoning criminals, for naturally he has no more right to pardon a crime than to discharge an unpaid debt.

Anciently a crime was considered in two lights, as committed against the family injured and against the peace. The government had the exclusive right of punishing those who had disturbed the peace and killed any of the king's vassals. The compensation to the government was afterwards changed into a capital punishment. After the king's pardon, the offender was free, and the relation had no right to pursue him. In England the offender can be punished for the relation as well as for the king. When an appeal[1] is made to the king, he cannot pardon, but appeals are seldom or never used, as it is difficult to bring them about. If a man was murdered, nobody but the wife could pursue for an appeal, or, if she was accessory, the legal

[1] 'Appeal is a word used in our law for the removal of a cause from an inferior court or judge to a superior; but more commonly for the accusation of a murderer, by a party who had interest in the person killed, or of a felon by one of his accomplices.' G. Jacob, *New Law Dictionary*, 8th ed. 1762, s. v. Appeal.

heir[1]. Any mistake in the process, such as a word wrong spelled, stopped the procedure[2], for the statute of amendment, which permitted courts to overlook errors, did not extend to appeals. Appeals in former times were often made in cases of maiming, hurting, &c.[3]

There are several kinds of murder by the English law. The word originally signified stealth, as the crime was usually committed in private. Afterwards felonious[4] killing of every kind was called murder, and compensation made for it accordingly. Murder arises either from malice prepense, or from sudden provocation, or from chance *per infortunium*. Of these the first alone is properly called murder, the second is manslaughter, and the last chance medley, which is often excusable and often justifiable. Murder committed *se defendendo* is when two persons quarrel, and the one is obliged to kill the other for his own safety. This is excusable, not justifiable homicide. Justifiable homicide is of two kinds. First, in defence [of] one's person, goods, or house. It differs from homicide *se defendendo* in this, that there is no quarrel, but an attack on the highway, or in a man's house. Second, homicide is justifiable in support of a constable or officer of justice.

These are the different species of murder and homicide, we shall next show what is the nature of each. When a person lies in wait for another and kills him, it is plainly murder. It is the same when a man kills another without provocation. By the English law there is no provocation without a blow; no words or menaces are sufficient. However, if a man give you a blow, and you return it and kill him, it is not murder, but manslaughter. If a man be shooting at tame fowl, or doing any other criminal action,

[1] Hawkins, *Pleas of the Crown*, bk. ii. ch. xxiii. §§ 36-43.

[2] *Ibid.* §§ 103-125.

[3] Jacob, *New Law Dictionary* (s. v. Appeal of Robbery), says, 'Appeals of rape and robbery are now much out of use, but the appeal of murder still continues, and is often brought.'

[4] MS. reads 'felony and.'

and without intending it, kill a man, it is murder. Where-ever there is any appearance of malice or forethought it is murder. If a person kills another in the afternoon for some provocation received in the forenoon, it is murder, but if he has only retired a few steps, and returned to do it immediately, it is not murder, but manslaughter. Homicide *se defendendo* is not punishable if there was no possibility of escape, but if a man had time to retire and draw his sword, it is punishable, because he might have escaped[1].

The Scotch law makes no distinction between manslaughter and murder[2]. In England manslaughter was introduced by what is called benefit of clergy. When civil government increased in authority, the punishment[s] of crimes were made more severe that the peace might be less disturbed. The clergy pled that this was not agreeable to the word of God, and as they derived their authority from Jesus Christ and the Pope, they would answer before no civil judicatory. They pretended that the scripture did not consider any crime where there was no malice or forethought as murder, and this they proved from Deuteronomy xixth. When any [clerical] person therefore had committed a crime, the bishop had a power to claim him and take him out of the hands of the secular power. If a person could get twelve persons to swear for him, he was acquitted. If not, the bishop judged whether he was corrigible or not. If he was incorrigible, he was degraded. The bishop could claim in this manner all clergy and beadles, wardens, or other persons who had

[1] Hawkins, *Pleas of the Crown*, bk. i. chs. xxviii–xxxi.

[2] 'As by intended homicide we mean not only that which is premeditated and the consequence of malice preconceived, but also that which is instantly conceived in the very encounter, so as to comprehend all slaughter where the intention to kill is antecedent even to the very blow; it follows that the homicide which is committed in *Rixa* or *Tulzie* will be construed by us to be intended homicide,' Alex. Bayne, *Institutions of the Criminal Law of Scotland*, 1748, pp. 33, 34.

any connexion with the Church, but the civil courts after-[wards] allowed him only to claim those that could read, as this [was] more immediately connected with the office of the clergy. Queen Anne afterwards extended the privileges arising from benefit of clergy, with regard to manslaughter, to all equally[1]. For chance medley a man forfeits his goods, but he has the power of suing for them again and of obtaining pardon. In justifiable homicide a man must plead not guilty of anything the court can meddle [with], and if he can bring in his evidence he is not arraigned[2].

Our resentment naturally falls upon inanimate as well as animate objects, and in many places the sword or instrument that had killed any person was considered as execrable, and accordingly was destroyed, particularly among the Athenians. By the English law if a man fell from a house and was killed, the house was forfeited by the law of deodand[3]. Deodand signifies to be given to the devil, by the same sort of metaphor that the scripture uses where it is said he blessed God in his heart, that is, he cursed him. Afterwards the clergy applied deodands to charitable uses. If a man was killed by an object at rest, only the part by which he was killed was forfeited.

[1] 'And forasmuch as when any person is convicted for any felony within the benefit of clergy, upon his prayer to have the benefit thereof allowed to him it hath been used to administer a book to him to try whether he can read as a clerk, which by experience is found to be of no use, be it therefore enacted' that such person 'shall not be required to read, but without any reading shall be allowed, taken, and reputed to be and punished as a clerk convict.' 5 and 6 Ann. cap. 6 (6 Ann. cap. 9 in *Statutes of the Realm*). The indulgence had already been extended to women (who were of course incapable of obtaining benefit of clergy) by 3 W. and M. cap. 9. The account of the origin of benefit of clergy in the text is far from accurate.

[2] Not quite accurately put. See Hawkins, *Pleas of the Crown*, bk. i. ch. xxix. § 25.

[3] This is erroneous, as nothing annexed to the freehold could be deodand. Probably 'house' is a copyist's error for 'horse.'

If he was killed [by falling] from the wheel of a wagon standing, only that wheel was deodand, but if the wagon was in motion, the whole team was forfeited. It was long questioned if a ship was forfeited by a man being killed in it, but as mariners are so much exposed, it was thought hard that it should [1].

A person may also be injured in his body by demembration, mutilation, assault and battery, or restraint on his liberty. Maiming and mutilation originally by the Roman law were compensated for in the same way with murder, and if the person was incapable, with the assistance of his friends, to pay the compensation, he was given over to the person maimed, to be maimed in the same manner, as we are acquainted by the Salic law, which gives us the form of their procedure. In the same manner all hurts among many nations, particularly among the Lombards, were compounded for; they paid so much for a tooth, so much more if it was a foretooth, so much for two teeth, but, what is very remarkable, though twenty were knocked out, the injured person could claim no more than the price of three. They had a precise sum for every member of the body. Among the Romans, if a man could not pay his composition, he was obliged to make satisfaction by the law of retaliation; he received as many blows as he gave. An eye went for an eye, and a tooth for a tooth. This custom continued long, and is in general reasonable, but in some cases it is not proper. If a man got his arm broken in wrestling, it was hard that another's should be broken for it in cold blood. In some cases it was impracticable, as when a man causes an abortion in a woman, he could not be punished in the same manner. This custom by degrees went out, and pecuniary fines, according to the circumstances of him who was to pay them, were introduced, and the praetor at Rome caused them to be received, but in some countries it continued longer, and there are remains of it

[1] Hawkins, *Pleas of the Crown*, bk. i. ch. xxvi.

in Holland to this day. When a person was maimed in any member that rendered him incapable of military service [1], the punishment was more severe.

By the Coventry Act, maiming in the face from malice or forethought was punished with death [2]. The reason of this was that Sir John Coventry had spoken impertinently against the king in parliament. The Prince of Wales, with some others, probably not without the king's permission, laid wait for him, and cut his ears and his face [3]. The parliament immediately enacted that maiming in the face from forethought should be punishable with death. There was never one, however, executed upon this law but one Cook, who lay in wait to murder his brother, but did not get it executed, only he maimed him in the face. He was therefore by the Coventry Act found guilty of deliberate malice. He pled that his intention was to murder, not to maim, but the court from the instrument he used found that he intended to maim as well as murder [4].

A man may also be injured by assault and battery. When a person is put to bodily fear it is assault, and when he is actually beat it is battery. Originally no assault by words subjected to punishment, unless there was likewise

[1] The term 'mayhem' or 'maim' was properly applied only to such injuries. Hawkins, *Pleas of the Crown*, bk. i. ch. xliv. § 1.

[2] 22 and 23 Car. II. cap. 1.

[3] 'The Prince of Wales' is an extraordinary mistake for 'the king's son,' i.e. Monmouth. Rapin's account is that the attack on Sir John 'was, by the king's order, committed to the Duke of Monmouth, his natural son, and the Duke had employed some other persons, who after the deed retired to his house.' *History of England*, translated by Tindal, vol. ii. p. 658. Sir John's nose was slit.

[4] In 1721 Arundel Cooke or Coke, an attorney, was tried at the Suffolk assizes with John Woodburne, his hired accomplice, for lying in wait for and disfiguring his brother-in-law, who had just been supping with him. Attempt to murder was not at that time a capital offence, and there is no doubt that Cooke did intend to murder his brother-in-law, and not merely to maim him. Yet both criminals were condemned, as stated in the text, and executed. *State Trials*, 1730, vol. vi. pp. 212-228.

a shaking of the fist, drawing an instrument or something of this kind. A composition was the first punishment for these crimes, but now it is fine and imprisonment.

A man may further be injured in his body by restraining his liberty, therefore the laws of every country are particularly careful of securing it. No magistrate in this country has an arbitrary power of imprisonment. It is indeed reasonable that he should have it in his power to imprison when there is ground of suspicion, though an innocent man may sometimes suffer a little by it. Nothing is more difficult than perfectly to secure liberty. If the person can bring some circumstances to alleviate the suspicion, he may be set at liberty upon bail, unless it be a capital crime. If the bail be not sufficient, it is unjust in the magistrate to accept of it, but if it be, he is punishable if he do not. If a person be wrongously kept in prison beyond the time when he ought to have been tried, he has so much a day according to his station.

In England, if a person be confined the day after the assizes, forty[1] days after he may have the benefit of the Habeas Corpus Act, that is, he may be carried to London at his own expense, but if he cannot afford this, he must wait till the next assizes. In Scotland there is no occasion for the Habeas Corpus Act. A person may be tried by the sheriff if he pleases, and at any rate can be carried to Edinburgh to the king's court. All this is for the security of liberty in free governments, but in despotic governments the will of the magistrate is law.

It is to be observed with respect to what is done through fear, that a bond given from this principle is not binding; no obligation is valid unless the person acted voluntar[il]y. However if a person is threatened to be pursued[2], and gives a bond to avoid it, the bond is valid, and the fear is not considered as a *metus iniustus*.

[1] 'Forty' should be 'not in any case more than twenty;' see above, p. 46, note 2.

[2] I. e. of course, prosecuted.

A rape or forcible marriage is capital, because the woman is so dishonoured that no other punishment can be a sufficient retaliation. Though forcible marriage be forbidden by law, yet if the woman afterwards consent, the friends can have no appeal, yet the king may pursue it.

A man may be injured in his reputation, by affronts, by words, and by writings. An affront in company is a real injury; if the affront be offered in words it is a verbal injury; if in writing it is a written injury. In all these the law gives redress. Affronts by the old law were punished in the same manner with assault and battery. Affronts in company are most atrocious crimes; the trifling fine of five or ten pounds is by no means an adequate compensation for them. Where the law denies justice, we are naturally led to take it ourselves. This introduced duelling in Europe, which brings along with it an additional injury; I must not only receive a box on the ear, but I am obliged to expose my life, or become altogether odious. It is to be observed that in Socrates' time the affront of giving the lie was little thought of; he does it himself without any ceremony.

Verbal injuries are redressed both by ancient and modern laws. When a person is accused by words, it sustains a process before a court of justice. If he be accused of forgery, theft, or any crime, as he may be subjected to great damages, he is entitled to sufficient redress. In the same manner if a person's right or title be slandered he suffers an injury. If I say you have no more right to your own house than I have, it is an injury, as it may excite those who have pretended titles. Though it be true, this is only an alleviation, and will not secure me from a prosecution. There are some offences that are only prosecuted in spiritual courts, as if a person call a woman a whore.

Written injuries are subjected to severer punishments than verbal ones, as they are more deliberate malice.

Abusive words in a libel give a process, though the same words would not if spoken. Libels and satires are punished according to the nature of the government. In aristocratical governments they are punished severely. Little petty princes may be quite destroyed by abusive libels, whereas kings and ministers of state in a free country, being far out of their reach, cannot be hurt by them. In [1] governments, and in Rome for a long time, they were not punished. Augustus at last revived the law subjecting the authors to a capital punishment[2]. In general people of circumstances take no notice of such libels unless it be absolutely necessary to clear themselves of some crime.

A person may be injured in his estate, real or personal. With regard to his real estate he may be injured either in his moveables or immoveables. In his immoveables he may be injured by arson or forcible entry. Arson is wilful fire-raising [3] either in the house of another, or in our own, so as to affect that of another. By the Roman, English and Scotch law this is punished capitally. If the fire be occasioned by negligence no punishment is inflicted. Forcible entry is the violently putting a man out of his estate. The laws are so strict on this head that the person ousted may retake his own by violence[4]. This was occasioned by the feudal customs, by which it was very common for barons and their vassals to deprive one another of their possessions, and this was the only way [that] then could be fallen on to get it restored. Afterwards it was enacted that if any person could prove

[1] Some words, possibly 'the Greek,' have evidently dropped out.

[2] Tacitus, *Ann.* lib. i. cap. 72.

[3] The term 'wilful fire-raising' is used for arson in Scotch law books. Bayne, *Institutions of the Criminal Law of Scotland*, p. 26.

[4] 'It seems that at the common law a man disseised of any lands or tenements (if he could not prevail by fair means) might lawfully regain the possession thereof by force.' Hawkins, *Pleas of the Crown*, bk. i. ch. lxiv. § 1.

that he was violent[ly] dispossessed, his estate should be restored[1]. But if the violent possessor had kept it three years, the old possessor must prove not only that he was dispossessed by violence, but that he has a real right to it, before it be restored[2].

A man may be injured in his moveables three ways, by theft, robbery, and piracy. Theft is the clandestinely taking away the property of another. This crime does not naturally excite that degree of resentment which prompts to capital punishment; and for a long time it was not punished with death. By the old Roman law the thief was obliged to restore what he had taken, and to add to it as much more. If he stole a sheep he restored two. There was, however, a peculiar distinction between the *fur manifestus* and *fur nec manifestus*. The former, as he was taken with the goods about him, paid quadruple, and the latter only double the value of things stolen. This they borrowed, it is said, from the Lacedaemonians[3], who taught their youth to steal and hide well, as they thought it improved them in that cunning which is necessary in war. However, the Lacedaemonians never encouraged the stealing the property of another. In their feasts nothing was prepared for their young men, and it was expected that they should purloin from the tables of their fathers what was sufficient for themselves; to steal such trifles as a crust of bread was indulged, but nothing else. The real reason of their punishing the *fur manifestus* more severely than another was that barbarous nations punish crimes according to the degree of resentment they excite, and when the thief was catched in the act their resentment was very high, and consequently disposed them to punish him severely. Since

[1] 5 Ric. II, cap. 7; 15 Ric. II, cap. 2; 8 Hen. VI, cap. 9; Hawkins, *P.C.*, bk. i. ch. lxiv. §§ 6, 7.

[2] 31 Eliz. cap. 11; Hawkins, *P.C.*, bk. i. ch. lxiv. § 8.

[3] But Heineccius, *Antiq. Rom.* lib. iv. tit. i. § 12, says they borrowed it 'ex iure Attico.'

the thirteenth century this crime has been punished capitally. The vassals of great lords were continually making incursions into the neighbouring territories and carrying off booty. When government came to be established, it naturally punished most severely those crimes to which men had the greatest propensity, and consequently endeavoured to restrain this practice. The Emperor Barbarossa first made this crime capital, and he was followed by all civilized nations, though undoubtedly the punishment is too great, for a thief is but a petty mean creature and does not excite a very high degree of resentment; he seems to be in some degree below this passion. By the old Scotch law theft in a landed gentleman was considered as treason[1], because the gentry were considered as theabettors and assistants of thieves and vagrants; and, as they made war on one another, which looked like an usurpation of sovereignty, they were considered as guilty of treason. By the English law any theft below a shilling was punished with the pillory, and above that with death. In Scotland it requires a much greater sum[2]. Nothing is theft with us but what belongs to particular persons. The man who stole deer in a forest or pigeons at a distance from a pigeon-house could not be punished till by a late statute[3]. House-breaking indeed, though there was not the value of a shilling carried off, was punished capitally. Such punishments, however necessary once, are certainly now too severe. Government [was] at first weak, and could not punish crimes, but was obliged to interpose in those cases in which the interest of society was concerned; but

[1] 'One circumstance in the offender, namely, his being a landed man, formerly made the punishment of this crime [theft] to be that of high treason.' Bayne, *Institutions of the Criminal Law of Scotland*, p. 46.

[2] No sum was specified, many circumstances besides value being taken into account.

[3] 2 Geo. III, cap. 29, or more probably an error for 'late statutes.' MacDouall, *Institute*, vol. i. p. 594; Bacon, *Abridgement*, s.v. 'Game.'

when it acquired more strength it made punishments severe that it might restrict the licentiousness of manners which lax discipline had introduced. Accordingly we find that the laws of the twelve tables made almost every crime capital. In Europe after the custom of compensation went out, they punished everything as treason, theft in a landed man, a servant killing his master, a curate his bishop, or a husband his wife[1] were all petty treason. Afterwards only crimes respecting the state were considered as treason; and this crime came by degrees to its proper extent.

Robbery, as it puts a man to the greatest bodily fear, is subjected to the greatest punishment: no occasion can save the robber, even though he should cover the injury by pretending to buy a man's goods after he has forced him to sell them to him[2].

Piracy is punished still more severely[3].

A man may be injured in his personal estate by fraud or forgery. The natural punishment of the *dolus malus* is not death, but some sort of ignominy such as the pillory. Some frauds, however, on account of the facility and security with which they may be committed, and the loss which they occasion, are justly subjected to capital punishment. When an insured ship, for instance, is cast away, it is difficult to prove that it was done by fraud; but if she be insured to the full value there is a great temptation to cast her away, and therefore the law, in order to intimidate the merchant, made death the punishment[4]. It was a question whether a ship ought to be insured for her value at the port whence she sets out, or at the port to which she is

[1] 'A husband his wife' should be 'a wife her husband.'

[2] Hawkins, *Pleas of the Crown*, bk. i. ch. xxxv. § 10, says that some hold that 'if a man meeting another going with his goods to market in order to sell them, compel him to sell them to him against his will, he is guilty of robbery, though he give for them more than they are worth.'

[3] *Ibid.* ch. xxxvii.

[4] 1 Ann. st. 2, cap. 9.

bound, and it was determined that it should be at the port where she sets out. If a Glasgow merchant sends out a ship with £3000 worth of goods for Virginia, they are worth more than £4000 when they arrive there; and if the merchant were allowed to insure for this last sum he would have a great temptation to make shipwreck of her. He can expect no more when he is at the expense of taking his goods to Virginia; he may meet with bad debtors, and he can lose nothing by the insurers. In the same manner it was anciently capital to steal anything from the plough, as it was so much exposed[1].

In England a bankrupt may have a discharge on surrendering himself and all his effects, but as he has it in his power to defraud his creditors, if he does not give up all he has, he is punishable by death[2]. Forgery is also punished capitally, and nobody complains that this punishment is too severe, because when contracts sustain action property can never be secure unless the forging of false ones be restrained. However, the forgery of every deed is not capital[3], but only the forgery of deeds payable to the bearer on demand, because any forgery of a deed regarding the conveyance of land may easily be discovered before any damage be done.

Perjury is not punished capitally[4].

As there are several ways of acquiring personal rights so there are several ways in which they expire. First, by payment of what is due by contract or quasi-contract, because the fulfilment of the obligation satisfies the other party. Secondly, by discharge or acquittance, even though the debt be not paid. This also takes place with regard

[1] Among 'certain offences which will not fall under the definition of theft, which however have been so called because they were declared to be punishable as theft,' Bayne mentions 'cutting and destroying the gear belonging to the plough.' *Institutions of the Criminal Law of Scotland*, p. 47.

[2] Hawkins, *Pleas of the Crown*, bk. i. ch. lvii.

[3] *Ibid.* chs. lviii, lxx.

[4] *Ibid.* ch. lxix.

to crimes, for when the king or the injured person choose to drop prosecution or to give a pardon, the person is free. Thirdly, by prescription. If a debt be not claimed within a certain time the debtor is free. This is very reasonable, for if a debt be not claimed for a long time the negligence of the debtor is encouraged. By the Scotch law, if he call for neither principal nor interest of a bond for forty years, it very justly prescribes. Nobody of common prudence would neglect any part of his affairs for forty years, if ever he intended to meddle with them again. According to strict law, if the interest be demanded in the thirty-ninth year the capital does not prescribe. Crimes likewise prescribe, and it is reasonable that they should, whether they be punished from a sympathy with the resentment of the sufferer, or from public utility, or to satisfy the public. Resentment wears out in a few years, and a person who has behaved well for twenty years, the time fixed on by our law, cannot be very dangerous to the public. Appeals by the English law prescribe in one year[1]; but an indictment does not prescribe so soon[2], because the king prosecutes for public security and not to gratify private resentment, and therefore the law favours his claim. At any rate it would be unreasonable to prosecute a man for a crime committed forty years ago, because he may now be a quite different man from what he was then. Besides, the thing is quite forgotten, and the end of punishing and public example is entirely lost. Treason itself prescribes in a few years[3]. From a resentment in law, however, if sentence have actually passed upon a person, and he have made his escape, he may be executed on his former sentence: the escape is considered as a new crime. However, this is not very

[1] This applies only to appeals of death. See Hawkins, *Pleas of the Crown*, bk. ii. ch. xxiii. § 48.

[2] *Ibid.* ch. xxvi. § 41.

[3] Three years, under 7 & 8 W. III, cap. 3.

natural, and if a man live quietly after his return he is seldom troubled. We had an instance of an earl who had been sentenced in 1715 and had returned to his native country and lived peaceably in it till the year 1745, when he again joined the rebels and was executed on his former sentence[1]. Dr. Cameron suffered in Scotland in the same manner[2]. In every country, if a person return after twenty years he is not troubled; it would be thought invidious in the officers of justice to meddle with him.

Some general observations on the criminal law is all that remains on this subject.

Resentment seems best to account for the punishment of crimes. If a person fires a pistol down a street, though he do no harm, public utility requires that he should be punished; but such crimes are by the laws of every country more slightly punished than if some mischief had ensued. The reason is plain. Resentment never rises to any great pitch unless some injury be actually done; some things that are in themselves criminal are not punished unless some bad consequence follow. A man meets with little resentment for riding an unruly horse in the market-place, but if he kill anybody, resentment is very high. For the same reason, deodands, though inanimate objects, are accounted execrable. In many cases the resentment falls upon the very member of the body which perpetrated the

[1] This was Charles Ratcliffe, who claimed to be Earl of Derwentwater in succession to his brother James. Both were condemned to death in 1716, but Charles escaped from prison. In 1745 he was captured on board a vessel said to be going to the assistance of the rebels, and was arraigned and executed in London without another trial. He had resided abroad, not in Scotland as stated in the text. Howell's *State Trials*, 1813, vol. xviii. p. 430 sqq.

[2] Dr. Archibald Cameron, Lochiel's brother, was executed in London in 1753 on the strength of a bill of attainder passed against him in 1746. *Ibid.* vol. xix. p. 734 sqq. 'Suffered in Scotland' is probably a mistake of the reporter for 'suffered after being captured in Scotland,' or some equivalent phrase.

action. Resentment is on the whole a very indiscriminating principle, and pays little attention to the disposition of the mind.

Certain persons are not to be considered as subjects of punishment, such as idiots, madmen, and children. We are not so much shocked by an action done by a madman, as one done by another person. We think binding the only punishment adequate to their crimes.

This is all we intended on the injuries that may be done to a man as a man.

Having now considered man as a member of a state, as a member of a family, and as a man, we proceed to police, [the] second division of jurisprudence.

PART II: OF POLICE

[DIVISION I. CLEANLINESS AND SECURITY.]

POLICE is the second general division of jurisprudence. The name is French, and is originally derived from the Greek πολιτεία, which properly signified the policy of civil government, but now it only means the regulation of the inferior parts of government, viz:—cleanliness, security and cheapness or plenty[1]. The two former, to wit, the proper method of carrying dirt from the streets, and the execution of justice, so far as it regards regulations for preventing crimes or the method of keeping a city guard, though useful, are too mean to be considered in a general discourse of this kind. An observation or two before we proceed to the third particular is all that is necessary.

We observe then, that in cities where there is most police and the greatest number of regulations concerning it, there is not always the greatest security. In Paris the regulations concerning police are so numerous as not to be comprehended in several volumes; in London there are

[1] Johnson (*Dictionary*, 1755) describes 'police' as of French origin, and mentions πολιτεία as the original of 'policy.' He defines 'police' as 'the regulation and government of a city or country, so far as regards the inhabitants;' and 'policy' as 'the art of government, chiefly with respect to foreign powers.'

only two or three simple regulations. Yet in Paris scarce a night passes without somebody being killed, while in London, which is a larger city, there are scarce three or four in a year. On this account one would be apt to think, that the more police there is the less security; but this is not the cause. In England as well as in France, during the time of the feudal government, and as late as Queen Elizabeth's reign, great numbers of retainers were kept idle about the noblemen's houses[1], to keep the tenants in awe. These retainers, when turned out, had no other way of getting their subsistence but by committing robberies, and living on plunder, which occasioned the greatest disorder. A remain of the feudal manners, still preserved in France, gives occasion to the difference. The nobility at Paris keep far more menial servants than ours, who are often turned out on their own account or through the caprice of their masters, and, being in the most indigent circumstances, are forced to commit the most dreadful crimes. In Glasgow, where almost nobody has more than one servant, there are fewer capital crimes than in Edinburgh. In Glasgow there is not one in several years; but not a year passes in Edinburgh without some such disorders. Upon this principle, therefore, it is not so much the police that prevents the commission of crimes as the having as few persons as possible to live upon others. Nothing tends so much to corrupt mankind as dependency, while independency still increases the honesty of the people.

The establishment of commerce and manufactures, which brings about this independency, is the best police for preventing crimes[2]. The common people have better wages in

[1] Hume, *History of England under the House of Tudor*, vol. ii. p. 735. Cp. above, p. 35.

[2] In *W. of N.* bk. ii. ch. iii. vol. i. pp. 338-340, the want of industry in towns where courts and parliaments reside is attributed to the fact that the inhabitants are not employed by capital.

this way than in any other, and in consequence of this a general probity of manners takes place through the whole country. Nobody will be so mad as to expose himself upon the highway, when he can make better bread in an honest and industrious manner. The nobility of Paris and London are no doubt much upon a level; but the common people of the former, being much more dependent, are not to be compared with those of the latter: and for the same reason the commonalty in Scotland differ from those in England, though the nobility too[1] are much upon a level.

Thus far for the two first particulars which come under the general division of police.

[1] I.e. the nobility of England and Scotland as well as the nobility of Paris and London.

[DIVISION II. CHEAPNESS OR PLENTY.]

[§ 1. *Of the Natural Wants of Mankind.*]

In the following part of this discourse we are to confine ourselves to the consideration of cheapness or plenty, or, which is the same thing, the most proper way of procuring wealth and abundance. Cheapness is in fact the same thing with plenty. It is only on account of the plenty of water that it is so cheap as to be got for the lifting; and on account of the scarcity of diamonds (for their real use seems not yet to be discovered) that they are so dear [1]. To ascertain the most proper method of obtaining these conveniences it will be necessary to show first wherein opulence consists, and still previous to this we must consider what are the natural wants of mankind which are to be supplied; and if we differ from common opinions, we shall at least give the reasons for our non-conformity.

Nature produces for every animal everything that is sufficient to support it without having recourse to the improvement of the original production. Food, clothes and lodging are all the wants of any animal whatever [2], and most

[1] The cheapness of water on account of its abundance is an ancient commonplace. Barbeyrac on Pufendorf, *De iure naturae et gentium*, lib. v. cap. i. § 4, quotes Plato, *Euthydem.* 304 B, τὸ γὰρ σπάνιον, ὦ Εὐθύδημε, τίμιον· τὸ δὲ ὕδωρ εὐωνύτατον ἄριστον ὂν ὡς ἔφη Πίνδαρος. The low value of useful water arising from its plentifulness is contrasted with the high value of useless diamonds arising from their scarcity by Law, *Money and Trade considered*, 1705, ch. i, and by Joseph Harris, *Essay on Money and Coins*, 1757, pt. i. § 3.

[2] 'Les choses nécessaires à la

of the animal creation are sufficiently provided for by nature in all those wants to which their condition is liable. Such is the delicacy of man alone, that no object is produced to his liking. He finds that in everything there is need of improvement. Though the practice of savages shows that his food needs no preparation, yet being acquainted with fire, he finds that it can be rendered more wholesome and easily digested, and thereby may preserve him from many diseases which are very violent among them. But it is not only his food that requires this improvement; his puny constitution is hurt also by the intemperature of the air he breathes in, which, though not very capable of improvement, must be brought to a proper temperament for his body, and an artificial atmosphere prepared for this purpose. The human skin cannot endure the inclemencies of the weather, and even in those countries where the air is warmer than the natural warmth of the constitution, and where they have no need of clothes, it must be stained and painted to be able to endure the hardships of the sun and rain. In general, however, the necessities of man are not so great but that they can be supplied by the unassisted labour of the individual. All the above necessities everyone can provide for himself, such as animals and fruits for his food, and skins for his clothing.

As the delicacy of a man's body requires much greater provision than that of any other animal, the same or rather the much greater delicacy of his mind requires a still greater provision to which all the different arts [are] subservient. Man is the only animal who is possessed of such a nicety that the very colour of an object hurts him. Among different objects a different division or arrangement of them pleases. The taste of beauty, which consists

vie sont la nourriture, le vêtement et le logement,' Cantillon, *Essai sur la nature du commerce en général*, 1755, p. 163. Cf. *Moral Sentiments*, 1st ed., pt. i. sect. iv. ch. ii., 6th ed., pt. i. sect. iii. ch. ii.

chiefly in the three following particulars, proper variety, easy connexion, and simple order, is the cause of all this niceness. Nothing without variety pleases us; a long uniform wall is a disagreeable object. Too much variety, such as the crowded objects of a parterre, is also disagreeable. Uniformity tires the mind; too much variety, too far increased, occasions an over-great dissipation of it. Easy connexion also renders objects agreeable; when we see no reason for the contiguity of the parts, when they are without any natural connexion, when they have neither a proper resemblance nor contrast, they never fail of being disagreeable. If simplicity of order be not observed, so as that the whole may be easily comprehended, it hurts the delicacy of our taste. Again, imitation and painting render objects more agreeable. To see upon a plain, trees, forests, and other such representations, is an agreeable surprise to the mind[1]. Variety of objects also renders them agreeable. What we are every day accustomed to does but very indifferently affect us. Gems and diamonds are on this account much esteemed by us. In like manner our pinchbeck and many of our toys[2] were so much valued by the Indians, that in bartering their jewels and diamonds for them they thought they had made by much the better bargain.

[§ 2. *That all the Arts are subservient to the Natural Wants of Mankind.*]

Those qualities, which are the ground of preference, and which give occasion to pleasure and pain, are the cause of many insignificant demands, which we by no means stand

[1] 'Of the Imitative Arts,' *Essays*, p. 137.

[2] Johnson (*Dictionary*, 1755) gives as the first meaning of toy, 'a petty commodity; a trifle; a thing of no value,' and quotes from Abbot, 'They exchange for knives, glasses, and such toys, great abundance of gold and pearl.'

in need of. The whole industry of human life is employed not in procuring the supply of our three humble necessities, food, clothes and lodging, but in procuring the conveniences of it according to the nicety and delicacy of our taste. To improve and multiply the materials, which are the principal objects of our necessities, gives occasion to all the variety of the arts.

Agriculture, of which the principal object is the supply of food, introduces not only the tilling of the ground, but also the planting of trees, the producing of flax, hemp, and innumerable other things of a similar kind. By these again are introduced different manufactures, which are so very capable of improvement. The metals dug from the bowels of the earth furnish materials for tools, by which many of these arts are practised. Commerce and navigation are also subservient to the same purposes by collecting the produce of these several arts. By these again other subsidiary [arts] are occasioned. Writing, to record the multitude of transactions, and geometry, which serves many useful purposes. Law and government, too, seem to propose no other object but this; they secure the individual who has enlarged his property, that he may peaceably enjoy the fruits of it. By law and government all the different arts flourish, and that inequality of fortune to which they give occasion is sufficiently preserved. By law and government domestic peace is enjoyed and security from the foreign invader. Wisdom and virtue too derive their lustre from supplying these necessities. For as the establishment of law and government is the highest effort of human prudence and wisdom, the causes cannot have a different influence from what the effects have. Besides, it is by the wisdom and probity of those with whom we live that a propriety of conduct is pointed out to us, and the proper means of attaining it. Their valour defends us, their benevolence supplies us, the hungry is fed, the naked is clothed, by the exertion of these divine qualities. Thus, according to the above representation, all things are subservient to supplying our threefold necessities.

[§ 3. *That Opulence arises from the Division of Labour.*]

In an uncivilized nation, and where labour is undivided[1], everything is provided for that the natural wants of mankind require; yet, when the nation is cultivated and labour divided, a more liberal provision is allotted them; and it is on this account that a common day labourer in Britain has more luxury in his way of living than an Indian[2] sovereign. The woollen coat he wears requires very considerable preparations—the wool-gatherer, the dresser, the spinster, the dyer, the weaver, the tailor, and many more, must all be employed before the labourer is clothed. The tools by which all this is effectuated employ a still greater number of artists—the loom-maker, miln-wright, rope-maker, not to mention the bricklayer, the tree-feller, the miner, the smelter, the forger, the smith, &c. Besides his dress, consider all his household furniture, his coarse linens, his shoes, his coals dug out of the earth or brought by sea, his kitchen utensils and different plates, those that are employed in providing his bread and beer, the sower, the brewer, the reaper, the baker, his glass windows and the art required in preparing [them], without which our northern climate could hardly be inhabited. When we examine the conveniences of the day labourer, we find

[1] The term 'division of labour' does not appear to be an old one. Mandeville, in part ii. (published in 1729) of the *Fable of the Bees*, Dialogue vi. p. 335, makes Cleomenes say that people enjoying quiet will soon learn 'to divide and subdivide their labour,' but Horatius does not understand the phrase without explanation. See too the index to part ii. s. v. Labour.

[2] I. e. of course, American Indian. 'A king of a large and fruitful territory there [America], feeds, lodges, and is clad worse than a day labourer in England.' Locke, *Civil Government*, § 41.

that even in his easy simple manner he cannot be accommodated without the assistance of a great number, and yet this is nothing compared with the luxury of the nobility. An European prince, however, does not so far exceed a commoner, as the latter does the chief of a savage nation[1]. It is easy to conceive how the rich can be so well provided for, as they can direct so many hands to serve their purposes. They are supported by the industry of the peasant. In a savage nation every one enjoys the whole fruit of his own labour[2], yet their indigence is greater than anywhere.

It is the division of labour which increases the opulence of a country.

In a civilized society, though there is a division of labour,

[1] The whole of this passage from the beginning of the paragraph reappears without much alteration in *W. of N.* bk. i. ch. i. vol. i. pp. 12-14. Locke had said: ''Tis not barely the ploughman's pains, the reaper's and thresher's toil, and the baker's sweat [that] is to be counted into the bread we eat; the labour of those who broke the oxen, who digged and wrought the iron and stones, who felled and framed the timber employed about the plough, mill, oven, or any other utensils, which are a vast number, requisite to this corn, from its being seed to be sown to its being made bread, must all be charged on the account of labour.' *Civil Government*, § 43. Mandeville had wondered 'what a number of people, how many different trades, and what a variety of skill and tools must be employed' to produce the 'thick parish gown' of the pauper (*Fable of the Bees*, pt. i. Remark P. 2nd ed., 1723, p. 182), and 'what a bustle is there to be made in several parts of the world before a fine scarlet or crimson cloth can be produced, what multiplicity of trades and artificers must be employed! Not only such as are obvious, as woolcombers, spinners, the weaver, the cloth-worker, the scourer, the dyer, the setter, the drawer and the packer; but others that are more remote and might seem foreign to it, as the mill-wright, the pewterer, and the chemist, which yet are all necessary, as well as a great number of other handicrafts, to have the tools, utensils, and other implements belonging to the trades already named' (*ibid.* 'A Search into the Nature of Society,' pp. 325, 326). A shorter reference to the number of operations requisite to provide a coat occurs in Harris, *Essay of Money and Coins*, pt. i. § 12.

[2] *W. of N.* bk. i. chs. vi, viii. vol. i. pp. 50, 67, 68.

there is no equal division, for there are a good many who work none at all [1]. The division of opulence is not according to the work. The opulence of the merchant is greater than that of all his clerks, though he works less [2]; and they again have six times more than an equal number of artisans, who are more employed [3]. The artisan who works at his ease within doors has far more than the poor labourer who trudges up and down without intermission. Thus, he who as it were bears the burden of society, has the fewest advantages.

[§ 4. *How the Division of Labour multiplies the Product.*]

We shall next show how this division of labour occasions a multiplication of the product, or, which is the same thing, how opulence arises from it. In order to this let us observe the effect of the division of labour in some manufactures. If all the parts of a pin were made by one man, if the same person dug the ore, [s]melted it, and split the wire, it would take him a whole year to make one pin, and this pin must therefore be sold at the expense of his maintenance for that time, which, taking [it] at a moderate computation, would at least be six pounds for a pin. If the labour is so far divided that the wire is ready-made, he will not make above twenty per day, which, allowing ten pence for wages, makes the pin a half-penny [4]. The pin-maker therefore divides the labour among a great number of different persons; the cutting, pointing, heading, and gilding are all separate professions. Two or three are employed in making the head, one or two in putting it on, and so on, to the putting

[1] *W. of N.* Introduction, vol. i. p. 2.

[2] *Ibid.* bk. i. ch. vi. pp. 50, 51.

[3] I. e. who work harder.

[4] MS. reads 'two pence,' the copyist probably having misread '½d.'

them in the paper, being in all eighteen [1]. By this division every one can with great ease make 2000 a day [2]. The same is the case in the linen and woollen manufactures. Some arts, however, there are which will not admit of this division, and therefore they cannot keep pace with other manufactures and arts. Such are farming and grazing. This is entirely owing to the return of the seasons, by which one man can only be for a short time employed in any one operation. In countries where the season[s] do not make such alterations it is otherwise. In France the corn is better and cheaper than in England [3]. But our toys, which have no dependence on the climate, and in which labour can be divided, are far superior to those of France [4].

When labour is thus divided, and so much done by one man in proportion, the surplus above their maintenance is considerable, which each man can exchange for a fourth [5] of what he could have done if he had finished it alone.

[1] *W. of N.* bk. i. ch. i. vol. i. pp. 6, 7. The fifth volume of the *Encyclopédie*, 1755, s. v. 'Épingle,' contains an elaborate description of the eighteen operations, contributed by 'M. Delaire, qui décrivait la fabrication de l'épingle dans les ateliers même des ouvriers, ... tandis qu'il faisait imprimer à Paris son analyse . . . du chancelier Bacon,' (p. 807). If Adam Smith had relied on an English authority, he might have mentioned a larger number. 'Notwithstanding that there is scarce any commodity cheaper than pins, there is none that passes through more hands ere they come to be sold. They reckon twenty-five workmen successively employed in each pin between the drawing of the brass wire and the sticking of the pin in the paper.' Ephraim Chambers, *Cyclopaedia*, s.v. 'Pin,' vol. ii. 2nd ed. 1738, 4th ed. 1741.

[2] This figure is not from the *Encyclopédie*, and the number produced per man in the small factory spoken of in *W. of N.* was 4800.

[3] *Ibid.* bk. i. ch. i. vol. i. pp. 7, 8.

[4] In *W. of N.* bk. i. ch. i. vol. i. p. 9, it is not the toys, but 'the hardware and the coarse woollens of England' which 'are beyond all comparison superior.'

[5] 'A fourth of' is probably a mistake of the copyist for '4 times.' The calculation is perhaps from Cantillon, who says that the labour of 25 adults is sufficient to procure for 100 others all the necessaries of life. *Essai*, pp. 113, 114.

By this means the commodity becomes far cheaper, and the labour dearer. It is to be observed that the price of labour by no means determines the opulence of society; it is only when a little labour can procure abundance. On this account a rich nation, when its manufactures are greatly improven, may have an advantage over a poor one by underselling it. The cotton and other commodities from China would undersell any made with us, were it not for the long carriage, and other taxes that are laid upon them [1]. We must not judge of the dearness of labour by the money or coin that is paid for it [2]. One penny in some places will purchase as much as eighteenpence in others. In the country of the Mogul, where the day's wages are only twopence, labour is better rewarded than in some of our sugar islands, where men are almost starving with four or five shillings a day. Coin, therefore, can be no proper estimate. Further, though human labour be employed both in the multiplication of commodities and of money, yet the chance of success is not equal. A farmer, by the proper cultivation of an acre, is sure of increase; but the miner may work again and again without success. Commodities must therefore multiply in greater proportion than gold and silver [3].

But again [4], the quantity of work which is done by the division of labour is much increased by the three following

[1] According to the fashion of the time China is here regarded as a rich nation. See Cannan, *History of the Theories of Production and Distribution*, 1893, p. 12, note.

[2] According to Defoe, *Plan of the English Commerce*, 1728, the manufactures of China, India, and other Eastern countries 'push themselves upon the world by the mere stress of their cheapness' (p. 65). A page or two further on he says that in China men get 2*d*. a day for towing boats from the canal banks, while in the American colonies five shillings a day and in Jamaica six or seven shillings a day are regular wages (pp. 66, 67).

[3] And therefore will become cheaper, so that the same income in coin will indicate a larger amount of real opulence as time goes on.

[4] I.e. 'to return to our main subject again.'

articles: first, increase of dexterity; secondly, the saving of time lost in passing from one species of labour to another; and thirdly, the invention of machinery. Of these in order:

First, when any kind of labour is reduced to a simple operation, a frequency of action insensibly fits men to a dexterity in accomplishing it. A country smith not accustomed to make nails will work very hard for three or four hundred a day, and those too very bad; but a boy used to it will easily make two thousand, and those incomparably better; yet the improvement of dexterity in this very complex manufacture can never be equal to that in others. A nail-maker changes postures, blows the bellows, changes tools, &c., and therefore the quantity produced cannot be so great as in manufactures of pins and buttons, where the work is reduced to simple operations[1].

Secondly, there is always some time lost in passing from one species of labour to another, even when they are pretty much connected. When a person has been reading he must rest a little before he begin to write. This is still more the case with the country weaver, who is possessed of a little farm; he must saunter a little when he goes from one to the other. This in general is the case with the country labourers, they are always the greatest saunterers; the country employments of sowing, reaping, threshing being so different, they naturally acquire a habit of indolence, and are seldom very dexterous. By fixing every man to his own operation,

[1] *W. of N.* bk. i. ch. i. vol. i. p. 9. The *Encyclopédie*, tom. i. 1751, s. v. 'Art' says, 'Lorsqu'une manufacture est nombreuse, chaque opération occupe un homme différent. Tel ouvrier ne fait et ne fera de sa vie qu'une seule et unique chose; tel autre une autre chose: d'où il arrive que chacune s'exécute bien et promptement, et que l'ouvrage le mieux fait est encore celui qu'on a à meilleur marché.'

and preventing the shifting from one piece of labour to another, the quantity of work must be greatly increased [1].

Thirdly, the quantity of work is greatly increased by the invention of machines. Two men and three horses will do more in a day with the plough than twenty men without it. The miller and his servant will do more with the water miln than a dozen with the hand miln, though it, too, be a machine [2]. The division of labour no doubt first gave occasion to the invention of machines. If a man's business in life is the performance of two or three things, the bent of his mind will be to find out the cleverest way of doing it; but when the force of his mind is divided it cannot be expected that he should be so successful [3]. We have not, nor cannot have, any complete history of the invention of machines, because most of them are at first imperfect, and receive gradual improvements and increase of powers from those who use them. It was probably a farmer who made the original plough, though the improvements might be owing to some other. Some miserable slave who had perhaps been employed for a long time in grinding corn between two stones, probably first found out the method of supporting the upper stone by a spindle. A miln-wright perhaps found out the way of turning the spindle with the hand, but he who contrived that the outer wheel should go by water was a philosopher, whose business it is to do nothing, but observe every-

[1] *W. of N.* bk. i. ch. i. vol. i. p. 10, where, however, the example of the little rest between reading and writing is omitted.

[2] *Ibid.* loc. cit., it is considered 'unnecessary to give any example.'

[3] 'If one will wholly apply himself to the making of bows and arrows, whilst another provides food, a third builds huts, a fourth makes garments, and a fifth utensils, they not only become useful to one another, but the callings themselves will, in the same number of years, receive much greater improvements than if all had been promiscuously followed by every one of the five.' Mandeville, *Fable of the Bees*, pt. ii. Dialogue vi. pp. 335, 336.

thing. They must have extensive views of things, who, as in this case, bring in the assistance of new powers not formerly applied. Whether he was an artisan, or whatever he was who first executed this, he must have been a philosopher. Fire machines, wind and water-milns were the invention of philosophers, whose dexterity too is increased by a division of labour[1]. They all divide themselves, according to the different branches, into the mechanical, moral, political, chemical philosophers.

Thus we have shown how the quantity of labour is increased by machines.

[§ 5. *What gives Occasion to the Division of Labour.*]

We have already shown that the division of labour is the immediate cause of opulence; we shall next consider what gives occasion to the division of labour[2], or from what principles in our nature it can best be accounted for. We cannot imagine this to be an effect of human prudence. It was indeed made a law by Sesostris that every man should follow the employment of his father[3], but this is by no means suitable to the dispositions of human nature, and can never long take place; every one is fond of being a gentleman, be his father what he would. They who are strongest and, in the bustle of society[4], have got above the weak, must have as many under as to defend them in their station. From necessary causes, therefore, there must be as many in the lower stations as there is occasion for,

[1] *W. of N.* bk. i. ch. i. vol. i. pp. 11, 12. Mandeville, *Fable of the Bees*, pt. ii. Dialogue iii. pp. 152, 153, is much less favourable to the philosophers' claim to be regarded as useful inventors.

[2] *W. of N.* bk. i. ch. ii. heading.

[3] *Ibid.* bk. iv. ch. ix. vol. ii. p. 266, where, however, Sesostris is not named, the reference being merely to Egypt and Hindostan.

[4] 'To what purpose is all the toil and bustle of this world?' *Moral Sentiments*, 1759, p. 108.

there must be as many up as down, and no division can be overstretched [1]. But it is not this which gives occasion to the division of labour; it flows from a direct propensity in human nature for one man to barter with another, which is common to all men, and known to no other animal. Nobody ever saw a dog, the most sagacious animal, exchange a bone with his companion for another. Two greyhounds, indeed, in running down a hare, seem to have something like compact or agreement betwixt them, but this is nothing else but a concurrence of the same passions. If an animal intends to truck, as it were, or gain anything from man, it is by its fondness and kindness. Man, in the same manner, works on the self love of his fellows, by setting before them a sufficient temptation to get what he wants. The language of this disposition is, 'Give me what I want, and you shall have what you want.' It is not from benevolence, as the dogs, but from self love that man expects anything. The brewer and the baker serve us not from benevolence, but from self love. No man but a beggar depends on benevolence, and even they would die in a week were their entire dependence upon it [2].

By this disposition to barter and exchange the surplus of one's labour for that of other people, in a nation of hunters, if any one has a talent for making bows and arrows better than his neighbours, he will at first make presents of them, and in return get presents of their game. By continuing this practice he will live better than before,

[1] This passage is absent from *W. of N.* bk. i. ch. ii. vol. i. p. 14.

[2] *Ibid.* pp. 14-16. Mandeville says: 'The whole superstructure is made up of the reciprocal services which men do to each other. How to get these services performed by others when we have occasion for them is the grand and almost constant solicitude in life of every individual person. To expect that others should serve us for nothing is unreasonable; therefore all commerce that men can have together must be a continual bartering of one thing for another.' *Fable of the Bees*, pt. ii. Dialogue vi. p. 421.

and will have no occasion to provide for himself, as the surplus of his own labour does it more effectually [1].

This disposition to barter is by no means founded upon different genius and talents [2]. It is doubtful if there be any such difference at all, at least it is far less than we are aware of. Genius is more the effect of the division of labour than the latter is of it. The difference between a porter and a philosopher in the first four or five years of their life is, properly speaking, none at all. When they come to be employed in different occupations, their views widen and differ by degrees. As every one has this natural disposition to truck and barter, by which he provides for himself, there is no need for such different endowments; and accordingly, among savages there is always the greatest uniformity of character. In other animals of the same species we find a much greater difference than betwixt the philosopher and porter, antecedent to custom. The mastiff and spaniel have quite different powers, but though these animals are possessed of talents they cannot, as it were, bring them into the common stock and exchange their productions, and therefore their different talents are

[1] The example of the bow and arrow maker is in the passage in Mandeville, quoted above, p. 167 note. In the parallel passage in *W. of N.* bk. i. ch. ii. vol. i. p. 16, Mandeville's hut-maker also reappears.

[2] This contradicts a passage in Harris' *Essay on Money and Coins*, pt. i. § 11. 'Men are endued with various talents and propensities which naturally dispose and fit them for different occupations; and are ... under a necessity of betaking themselves to particular arts and employments from their inability of otherwise acquiring all the necessaries they want with ease and comfort. This creates a dependence of one man upon another, and naturally unites men into societies. In like manner, as all countries differ more or less, either in the kinds or goodness of their products, natural or artificial, particular men find their advantages, which extend to communities in general, by trading with the remotest nations.' Hume, 'Of the Original Contract,' requires his readers to 'consider how nearly equal all men are in their bodily force, and even in their mental powers and faculties, 'ere cultivated by educacation.' *Essays*, 1748, p. 291.

of no use to them[1]. It is quite otherwise among mankind; they can exchange their several productions according to their quantity or quality; the philosopher and the porter are both of advantage to each other. The porter is of use in carrying burdens for the philosopher, and in his turn he burns his coals cheaper by the philosopher's invention of the fire machine[2].

Thus we have shown that different genius is not the foundation of this disposition to barter which is the cause of the division of labour. The real foundation of it is that principle to persuade which so much prevails in human nature. When any arguments are offered to persuade, it is always expected that they should have their proper effect. If a person asserts anything about the moon, though it should not be true, he will feel a kind of uneasiness in being contradicted, and would be very glad that the person he is endeavouring to persuade should be of the same way of thinking with himself. We ought then mainly to cultivate the power of persuasion, and indeed we do so without intending it. Since a whole life is spent in the exercise of it, a ready method of bargaining with each other must undoubtedly be attained. As was before observed, no animal can do this but by gaining the favour of those whom they would persuade. Sometimes, indeed, animals seem to act in concert, but there never is anything like bargain among them. Monkeys, when they rob a garden, throw the fruit from one to another, till they deposit it in the hoard, but there is always a scramble about the division of the booty, and usually some of them are killed.

[1] *W. of N.* bk. i. ch. ii. vol. i. pp. 16-18.

[2] The steam engines of the time, used chiefly in draining mines, went by this name. Watt was working under the protection of the University of Glasgow, and on the eve of making his invention, when the lectures were delivered.

[§ 6. *That the Division of Labour must be proportioned to the Extent of Commerce.*]

From all that has been said we may observe that the division of labour must always be proportioned to the extent of commerce[1]. If ten people only want a certain commodity, the manufacture of it will never be so divided as if a thousand wanted it. Again, the division of labour, in order to opulence, becomes always more perfect by the easy method of conveyance in a country. If the road be infested with robbers, if it be deep and conveyance not easy, the progress of commerce must be stopped. Since the mending of roads in England forty or fifty years ago, its opulence has increased extremely. Water carriage is another convenience, as by it 300 ton can be conveyed at the expense of the tear and wear of the vessel, and the wages of five or six men, and that too in a shorter time than by a hundred wagons which will take six horses and a man each[2]. Thus the division of labour is the great cause of the increase of public opulence, which is always proportioned to the industry of the people[3], and not to the quantity of gold and silver, as is foolishly imagined, and the industry of the people is always proportioned to the division of labour.

Having thus shown what gives occasion to public opulence, in farther considering this subject we propose to consider:

First, what circumstances regulate the price of commodities:

[1] 'Limited by the extent of the market.' *W. of N.* bk. i. ch. iii. heading.

[2] In *W. of N.* bk. i. ch. iii. vol. i. p. 19, the ship only carries 200 tons and has six or eight men; the waggons have eight horses and two men, and carry four tons each.

[3] 'Plus il y a de travail dans un État, et plus l'État est censé riche naturellement.' Cantillon, *Essai*, p. 113.

Secondly, money in two different views, first as the measure of value, and then as the instrument of commerce:

Thirdly, the history of commerce, in which shall be taken notice of the causes of the slow progress of opulence, both in ancient and modern times, which causes shall be shown either to affect agriculture or arts and manufactures:

Lastly, the effects of a commercial spirit, on the government, temper, and manners of a people, whether good or bad, and the proper remedies. Of these in order.

[§ 7. *What Circumstances regulate the Price of Commodities.*]

Of every commodity there are two different prices, which though apparently independent, will be found to have a necessary connexion, viz. the natural price and the market price[1]. Both of these are regulated by certain circumstances. When men are induced to a certain species of industry, rather than any other[2], they must make as

[1] *W. of N.* bk. i. ch. vii. heading. Pufendorf distinguishes 'common or natural price' from 'legal price' ('pretium legitimum') fixed by the magistrate (*De iure naturae et gentium*, lib. v. cap. i. § 8), thus including both Adam Smith's kinds of price in 'natural price.' But he also says: 'In regulating this natural price, regard is to be had to the labour and expense of the merchant in importing and taking care of his goods; .... his time, his study, his care in getting, preserving, and sorting his commodities, as also his servant's wages, may fairly be rated by him.... But what sudden and frequent alterations the markets admit of, by reason of the plenty or scarcity of buyers, money, or commodities, is well known.' *Ibid.* § 10, Kennet's transl., 3rd ed. 1717.

[2] 'People that have children to educate that must get their livelihood, are always consulting and deliberating what trade or calling they are to bring them up to, till they are fixed; and thousands think on this that hardly think at all on anything else. First, they confine themselves to their circumstances, and he that can give but ten pounds with his son must not look out for a trade where they ask an hundred with an apprentice: but the next they

much by the employment as will maintain them while they are employed. An arrow-maker must be sure to exchange as much surplus product as will maintain him during as long time as he took to make them. But upon this principle in the different trades there must be a considerable difference, because some trades, such as those of the tailor and weaver, are not learned by casual observation and a little experience, like that of the day-labourer, but take a great deal of time and pains before they are acquired. When a person begins them, for a considerable time his work is of no use to his master or any other person, and therefore his master must be compensated, both for what maintains him and for what he spoils. When he comes to exercise his trade, he must be repaid what he has laid out, both of expenses and of apprentice fee, and as his life is not worth above ten or twelve years' purchase at most, his wages must be high on account of the risk he runs of not having the whole made up[1]. But again, there are many

think on is always which will be the most advantageous.' Mandeville, 'Essay on Charity and Charity Schools' in *Fable of the Bees*, pt. i. 2nd ed., p. 343; cp. Remark A, p. 45.

[1] 'Le fils d'un laboureur, à l'âge de sept ou douze ans, commence à aider son père, soit à garder les troupeaux, soit à remuer la terre, soit à d'autres ouvrages de la campagne, qui ne demandent point d'art ni d'habileté.

Si son père lui faisait apprendre un métier, il perdrait à son absence pendant tout le temps de son apprentissage, et serait encore obligé de payer son entretien et les frais de son apprentissage pendant plusieurs années : voilà donc un fils à charge à son père et dont le travail ne rapporte aucun avantage qu'au bout d'un certain nombre d'années. La vie d'un homme n'est calculée qu'à dix ou douze années ; et comme on en perd plusieurs à apprendre un métier, dont la plupart demandent en Angleterre sept années d'apprentissage, un laboureur ne voudrait jamais en faire apprendre aucun à son fils si les gens de métier ne gagnaient bien plus que les laboureurs. Ceux donc, qui emploient des artisans ou gens de métier, doivent nécessairement payer leur travail plus haut que celui d'un laboureur ou manœuvre ; et ce travail sera nécessairement cher à proportion du temps qu'on perd à l'apprendre et de la arts which require more extensive knowledge than is to be got during the time of an apprenticeship. A blacksmith and weaver may learn their business well enough without any previous knowledge of mathematics, but a watchmaker must be acquainted with several sciences in order to undertake his business well, such as arithmetic, geometry, and astronomy with regard to the equation of time, and their wages must be high in order to compensate the additional expense[1]. In general, this is the case in all the liberal arts, because after they have spent a long time in their education, it is ten to one if ever they make anything by it. Their wages therefore must be higher in proportion to the expense they have been at, the risk of not living long enough, and the risk of not having dexterity enough to manage their business. Among the lawyers there is not one among twenty that attains such knowledge and dexterity in his business as enables him to get back the expenses of his education, and many of them never make the price of their gown, as we say. The fees of lawyers are so far from being extravagant, as they are generally thought, that they are rather low in proportion. It is the eminence of the profession, and not the money made by it, that is the temptation for applying to it, and the dignity of that rank is to be considered as a part of what is made by it[2].

dépense et du risque qu'il faut pour s'y perfectionner.' Cantillon, *Essai*, pp. 23, 24.

[1] *W. of N.* bk. i. ch. x. pt. i. vol. i. pp. 106, 107. Cf. 'Scarcity enhances the price of things much oftener than the usefulness of them. Hence it is evident why those arts and sciences will always be the most lucrative that cannot be attained to but in great length of time, by tedious study and close application.' Mandeville, *Fable of the Bees*, pt. ii. Dialogue vi. p. 423.

[2] *W. of N.* bk. i. ch. x. pt. i. vol. i. pp. 110, 111. Cf. 'It is the hopes either of gain or reputation, of large revenues and great dignities, that promote learning; and when we say that any calling, art, or science is not encouraged, we mean no more by it than that the masters or professors of it are not sufficiently rewarded for their pains either with honour or

In the same manner we shall find that the price of gold and silver is not extravagant, if we consider it in this view, for in a gold or silver mine there is a great chance of missing it altogether. If we suppose an equal number of men employed in raising corn and digging silver, the former will make more than the latter, because perhaps of forty or fifty employed in a mine, only twenty make anything at all. Some of the rest may indeed make fortunes, but every corn man succeeds in his undertakings, so that upon the whole there is more made this way than the other. It is the ideal acquisition which is the principal temptation in a mine.

A man then has the natural price of his labour, when it is sufficient to maintain him during the time of labour, to defray the expense of education, and to compensate the risk of not living long enough, and of not succeeding in the business. When a man has this, there is sufficient encouragement to the labourer, and the commodity will be cultivated in proportion to the demand[1].

The market price of goods is regulated by quite other circumstances. When a buyer comes to the market, he never asks of the seller what expenses he has been at in producing them. The regulation of the market price of goods depends on the three following articles:—

First, the demand, or need for the commodity. There is no demand for a thing of little use; it is not a rational object of desire.

Secondly, the abundance or scarcity of the commodity in proportion to the need of it. If the commodity be scarce, the price is raised, but if the quantity be more than is sufficient to supply the demand, the price falls. Thus it is that diamonds and other precious stones

profit.' Mandeville, *Fable of the Bees*, pt. ii. Dialogue vi. p. 414.

[1] There is evidently a hiatus here, which may be supplied by the words 'and sold at its natural price.' Cf. *W. of N.* bk. i. ch. vii. 4th paragraph, vol. i. p. 57.

are dear, while iron, which is much more useful, is so many times cheaper, though this[1] depends principally on the last cause, viz.:—

Thirdly, the riches or poverty of those who demand. When there is not enough produced to serve everybody, the fortune of the bidders is the only regulation of the price. The story which is told of the merchant and the carrier in the deserts of Arabia is an evidence of this. The merchant gave 10,000 ducats for a certain quantity of water. His fortune here regulated the price, for if he had not had them, he could not have given them, and if his fortune had been less, the water would have been cheaper. When the commodity is scarce, the seller must be content with that degree of wealth which they have who buy it. The case is much the same as in an auction. If two persons have an equal fondness for a book, he whose fortune is largest will carry it. Hence things that are very rare go always to rich countries. The King of France only could purchase that large diamond of so many thousand pounds value[2]. Upon this principle, everything is dearer or cheaper according as it is the purchase of a higher or lower set of people. Utensils of gold are comeatable only by persons in certain circumstances. Those of silver fall to another set of people, and their prices are regulated by what the majority can give. The prices of corn and beer are regulated by what all the world can give, and on this account the wages of the day-labourer have a great influence upon the price of corn. When the price of corn rises, wages rise also, and *vice versa*[3]; when the quantity of corn falls short, as in

[1] I.e. the proportion between the value of precious stones and iron.

[2] The 'Regent' diamond, purchased for the King in 1717 for two million livres, according to Saint-Simon, who takes the credit of the purchase at a time of virtual bankruptcy to himself in conjunction with Law. *Mémoires*, ed. Chéruel et Regnier, tom. xiv. pp. 12–14.

[3] *W. of N.* bk. i. ch. viii. vol. i. p. 90.

a sea-voyage, it always occasions a famine, and then the price becomes enormous. Corn then becomes the purchase of a higher set of people, and the lower must live on turnips and potatoes.

Thus we have considered the two prices, the natural and the market price, which every commodity is supposed to have. We observed before that however seemingly independent they appear to be, they are necessarily connected. This will appear from the following considerations. If the market price of any commodity is very great, and the labour very highly rewarded, the market is prodigiously crowded with it, greater quantities of it are produced, and it can be sold to the inferior ranks of people. If for every ten diamonds there were ten thousand, they would become the purchase of everybody, because they would become very cheap, and would sink to their natural price. Again, when the market is overstocked, and there is not enough got for the labour of the manufacture, nobody will bind to it, they cannot have a subsistence by it, because the market price falls then below the natural price. It is alleged that as the price of corn sink[s], the wages of the labourer should sink, as he is then better rewarded. It is true that if provisions were long cheap, as more people would flock to this labour where the wages are high, through this concurrence of labour, the wages would come down, but we find that when the price of corn is doubled, the wages continue the same as before, because the labourers have no other way to turn themselves. The same is the case with menial servants[1].

From the above we may observe that whatever police tends to raise the market price above the natural, tends to diminish public opulence. Dearness and scarcity are in effect the same thing. When commodities are in abundance, they can be sold to the inferior ranks of people, who

[1] *W. of N.* bk. i. ch. viii. vol. i. pp. 90, 91. The reporter has evidently carried condensation to excess at this point.

can afford to give less for them, but not if they are scarce. So far, therefore, as goods are a conveniency to the society, the society lives less happy when only the few can possess them. Whatever therefore keeps goods above their natural price for a permanency, diminishes [a] nation's opulence. Such are

First, all taxes upon industry, upon leather, and upon shoes, which people grudge most, upon salt, beer, or whatever is the strong drink of the country, for no country wants[1] some kind of it. Man is an anxious animal, and must have his care swept off by something that can exhilarate the spirits. It is alleged that this tax upon beer is an artificial security against drunkenness, but if we attend to it, [we will find] that it by no means prevents it. In countries where strong liquors are cheap, as in France and Spain, the people are generally sober, but in northern countries, where they are dear, they do not get drunk with beer, but with spirituous liquors; nobody presses his friend to a glass of beer, unless he choose it[2].

Secondly, monopolies also destroy public opulence. The price of the monopolized goods is raised above what is sufficient for encouraging the labour. When only a certain person or persons have the liberty of importing a commodity, there is less of it imported than would otherwise be; the price of it is therefore higher, and fewer people supported by it. It is the concurrence of different labourers which always brings down the price. In monopolies, such as the Hudson's Bay and East India companies, the people engaged in them make the price what they please.

Thirdly, exclusive privileges of corporations have the same effect. The butchers and bakers raise the price of their goods as they please, because none but their

[1] I. e. of course, 'lacks' or 'is without.'

[2] *W. of N.* bk. iv. ch. iii. pt. ii. vol. ii. pp. 66–68.

own corporation is allowed to sell in the market, and therefore their meat must be taken, whether good or not. On this account there is always required a magistrate to fix the prices. For any free commodity, such as broad cloth, there is no occasion for this, but it is necessary with bakers, who may agree among themselves to make the quantity and price what they please. Even a magistrate is not a good enough expedient for this, as he must always settle the price at the outside, else the remedy must be worse than the disease, for nobody would apply to these businesses, and a famine would ensue. On this account bakers and brewers have always profitable trades [1].

As what raises the market price above the natural one diminishes public opulence, so what brings it down below it has the same effect.

It is only upon manufactures to be exported that this can usually be done by any law or regulation, such as the bounty allowed by the government upon coarse linen, by which it becomes exportable, when under twelve pence a yard [2]. The public paying a great part of the price, it can be sold cheaper to foreigners than what is sufficient for encouraging the labour. In the same manner, by the bounty of five shillings upon the quarter of corn when sold under forty [3] shillings, as the public pays an eighth part of the price, it can be sold just so much cheaper at a foreign market. By this bounty the commodity is rendered more comeatable, and a greater quantity of it produced, but then it breaks what may be called the natural balance of industry. The disposition to apply to

[1] See on the assize of bread, *W. of N.* bk. i. ch. x. ad fin.; vol. i. pp. 150, 151. See also bk. i. ch. vii. vol. i. pp. 64–66.

[2] This should read, 'upon coarse linen exported, when under eighteen pence a yard.' In *W. of N.* bk. iv. ch. viii. vol. ii. p. 227, the statute 29 Geo. II, cap. 15, is referred to and the value correctly given.

[3] A mistake for forty-eight. 1 W. & M. cap. 12. *W. of N.* bk. i. ch. xi. vol. i. p. 208.

the production of that commodity is not proportioned to the natural cause of the demand, but to both that and the annexed bounty. It[1] has not only this effect with regard to the particular commodity, but likewise people are called from other productions which are less encouraged, and thus the balance of industry is broken.

Again, after the ages of hunting and fishing, in which provisions were the immediate produce of their labour, when manufactures were introduced, nothing could be produced without a great deal of time. It was a long time before the weaver could carry to the market the cloth which he bought in flax. Every trade therefore requires a stock of food, clothes, and lodging to carry it on[2]. Suppose then, as is really the case in every country, that there is in store a stock of food, clothes, and lodging, the number of people that are employed must be in proportion to it[3]. If the price of one commodity is sunk below its natural price, while another is above it, there is a smaller quantity of the stored stock left to support the whole. On account of the natural connexion of all trades in the stock, by allowing bounties to one[4] you take away the stock from the rest. This has been the real consequence of the corn bounty.

The price of corn being sunk, the rent of the farms sinks also, yet the bounty upon corn, which was laid on at the time of the taxes[5], was intended to raise the rent, and had the effect for some time, because the tenants were assured of a price for their corn, both at home and abroad. But though the effects of the bounty encourag-

[1] I.e. the bounty. MS. reads 'but.'

[2] *W. of N.* bk. ii. Introduction, vol. i. p. 273.

[3] *W. of N.* Introduction, vol. i. pp. 2, 3.

[4] MS. reads 'me,' evidently a copyist's error.

[5] 'The Government of King William . . . was in no condition to refuse anything to the country gentlemen, from whom it was at that very time soliciting the first establishment of the annual land-tax.' *W. of N.* bk. i. ch. xi. vol. i. p. 208.

ing agriculture brought down the price of corn, yet it raised the grass farms, for the more corn the less grass. The price of grass being raised, butchers' meat, in consequence of its dependence upon it, must be raised also, so that if the price of corn is diminished, the price of other commodities is necessarily raised. The price of corn has indeed fallen from forty-two to thirty-five[1], but the price of hay has risen from twenty-five to near fifty shillings. As the price of hay has risen, horses are not so easily kept, and therefore the price of carriage has risen also. But whatever increases the price of carriage diminishes plenty in the market[2]. Upon the whole, therefore, it is by far the best police to leave things to their natural course, and allow no bounties, nor impose taxes on commodities.

Thus we have shown what circumstances regulate the price of commodities, which was the first thing proposed.

[§ 8. *Of Money as the Measure of Value and Medium of Exchange.*]

We come now to the second particular, to consider money, first as the measure of value and then as the medium of permutation or exchange. When people deal

[1] Red wheat is quoted at 33*s.*—35*s.* in the *London Chronicle* on Jan. 28, 1763, and at 33*s.*—36*s.* on Oct. 20 and 27, Nov. 3 and 10, 1763. The other weekly prices during the academical session of 1762-1763, and October to December, 1763, are somewhat lower.

[2] In *W. of N.* bk. i. ch. xi. vol. i. pp. 208-210, and bk. iv. ch. v. vol. ii. pp. 81-84, Adam Smith rejects the theory that the bounty had lowered the home price, and shows that by stimulating the foreign demand it must have rather tended to raise it. He even speaks of the 'very moderate supposition' that the bounty may have kept the price 4*s.* per quarter higher than it would otherwise have been. Having done this, he proceeds to argue that every alteration in the price of corn must be nominal and not real. He has therefore no need for the argument in the text above as to hay.

in many species of goods, one of them must be considered as the measure of value. Suppose there were only three commodities, sheep, corn, and oxen, we can easily remember them comparatively, but if we have a hundred different commodities, there are ninety-nine values of each arising from a comparison with each of the rest. As these cannot easily be remembered, men naturally fall upon one of them to be a common standard with which they compare all the rest. This will naturally at first be the commodity with which they are best acquainted. Accordingly we find that black cattle and sheep were the standard in Homer's time. The armour of one of his heroes was worth nine oxen, and that of another worth an hundred[1]. Black cattle was the common standard in ancient Greece. In Italy, and particularly in Tuscany, everything was compared with sheep, as this was their principal commodity. This is what may be called the natural measure of value. In like manner there were natural measures of quantity, such as fathoms, cubits, inches, taken from the proportion of the human body, once in use with every nation. But by a little observation they found that one man's arm was longer or shorter than another's, and that one was not to be compared with the other, and therefore wise men who attended to these things would endeavour to fix upon some more accurate measure, that equal quantities might be of equal values. This method became absolutely necessary when people came to deal in many commodities, and in great quantities of them. Though an inch was altogether inconsiderable when their dealings were confined to a few yards, more accuracy was required

[1] Glaucus and Diomedes, *Iliad*, vi. 236; *W. of N.* bk. i. ch. iv. vol. i. p. 24. The quotation is a stock one, occurring in Pliny, *H. N.* lib. xxxiii. cap. iii; Pufendorf, *De iure naturae et gentium*, lib. v. cap. v. § 1; Martin-Leake, *Historical Account of English Money*, 2nd ed. 1745, p. 4; and (with a mistake as to the numbers) E. Chambers, *Cyclopaedia*, 2nd ed. 1738, s. v. 'Money.'

when they came to deal in some thousands. We find, in countries where their dealings are small, the remains of this inaccuracy. The cast of the balance is nothing thought of in their coarse commodities.

Since, then, there must of necessity be a common standard of which equal quantities should be of equal values, metals in general seemed best to answer this purpose, and of these the value of gold and silver could best be ascertained. The temper of steel cannot be precisely known, but what degree of alloy is in gold and silver can be exactly found out. Gold and silver were therefore fixed upon as the most exact standard to compare goods with, and were therefore considered as the most proper measure of value.

In consequence of gold and silver becoming the measure of value, it came also to be the instrument of commerce. It soon became necessary that goods should be carried to market, and they could never be cleverly[1] exchanged unless the measure of value was also the instrument of commerce. In the age of shepherds it might be no great inconvenience that cattle should be the medium of exchange, as the expense of maintaining them was nothing, the whole country being considered as one great common; but when lands came to be divided, and the division of labour introduced, this custom would be productive of very considerable inconveniences. The butcher and shoemaker might at times have no use for one another's commodities. The farmer very often cannot maintain upon his ground a cow more than he has. It would be a very great hard-

[1] The second meaning for 'clever' given by Johnson (*Dictionary*, 1755) is 'just, fit, proper, commodious.' He says: 'This is a low word, scarcely ever used but in burlesque or conversation; and applied to anything a man likes, without a settled meaning.' See the quotations in Murray, *New English Dictionary*.

ship on a Glasgow merchant to give him a cow for one of his commodities. To remedy this, those materials which were before considered as the measure of value, came also to be the instrument of exchange. Gold and silver had all advantages. They can be kept without expense, they do not waste, and they are very portable. Gold and silver, however, do not derive their whole utility from being the medium of exchange; though they never had been used as money, they are more valuable than any other metals. They have a superior beauty, are capable of a finer polish, and are more proper for making any instrument, except those with an edge. For all these reasons, gold and silver came to be the proper measure of value, and the instrument of exchange; but in order to render them more proper for these purposes, it was necessary that both their weight and their fineness should be ascertained. At first their balances were not very accurate, and therefore frauds were easily committed. However, this was remedied by degrees; but common business would not allow of the experiments which are necessary to fix precisely the degree of fineness. Though with a great quantity of alloy, they are to appearance good. It was necessary therefore, to facilitate exchange, that they should fall upon some expedient to ascertain with accuracy both weight and fineness. Coinage most effectually secures both these. The public, finding how much it would tend to facilitate commerce, put a stamp upon certain pieces that whoever saw them might have the public faith that they were of a certain weight and fineness; and this would be what was at first marked upon the coin, as being of most importance[1].

[1] Aristotle, *Politics*, 1257 a 38–41, quoted in Pufendorf, *De iure naturae et gentium*, lib. v. cap. i. § 12. On the properties which have been observed in gold and silver coins, and have therefore been regarded as qualities necessary for a good measure of value and medium of exchange, see Grotius, *De iure belli et pacis*,

Accordingly, the coins of every country appear to have borne[1] the names of the weights corresponding to them[2], and they contained the denomination they expressed. The British pound sterling seems originally to have been a pound weight of pure silver[3].

As gold could be easily exchanged into silver, the latter came always to be the standard or measure of value. As there cannot be two standards, and in the greater part of purchases silver is necessary, we never say a man is worth so many guineas, but always pounds[4].

It is to be observed that the measure of quantity has always increased, while that of value has decreased. The British pound has now decreased to less than a third of its original value, which was sixty-three shillings, while the measure of quantity has considerably increased. The reason is that the interest of the government requires this. It is the interest of the baker and the brewer to make the measure of quantity as little as possible; and therefore there are inspectors appointed who, when it is brought down, always settle it a little farther up. All our measures, which were taken from the Roman foot, fathom, and inch,

lib. ii. cap. xii. § 17; Pufendorf, *De iure naturae et gentium*, lib. v. cap. i. § 13; Locke, *Some Considerations of the Consequences of the Lowering of Interest and Raising the Value of Money*, 2nd ed. 1696, p. 31; Law, *Money and Trade considered*, 1705, ch. i.; Hutcheson, *Introduction to Moral Philosophy*, p. 211; Montesquieu, *Esprit des lois*, liv. xxii. ch. ii; Cantillon, *Essai*, pp. 153, 355–357; Harris, *Money and Coins*, pt. i. §§ 22–27. Taken together, these passages include all the properties enumerated by Jevons (*Money and the Mechanism of Exchange*, 1875, ch. v.), viz. utility, portability, indestructibility, homogeneity, divisibility, stability of value, cognisability, and one in addition, the quality of not requiring to be fed like cattle. The five given in the text above are to be found in Harris. Divisibility, which he also mentions, reappears in *W. of N.* bk. i. ch. iv. vol. i. pp. 24, 25.

[1] MS. reads 'been.'

[2] Harris, *Money and Coins*, pt. i. § 28.

[3] *W. of N.* bk. i. ch. iv. vol. i. p. 27.

[4] *Ibid.* ch. v. vol. i. p. 41. Harris, *Money and Coins*, pt. i. §§ 34, 35.

are now a great deal more. In like manner what was called Troy weight, from Troy, a town in Champaigne[1], where then the greatest commerce was carried on, gave rise to a heavier weight, because there was usually given the cast of the balance along with it, and as this rendered dealings inaccurate, it was necessary that this cast of the balance should be determined. Accordingly, averdupois (*avoir du poise*[2]), or heavy weight, was settled at thirteen ounces; but as this was a number not easily divided, it was settled at sixteen, the ounces being made proportioned to it[3].

Thus the measure of quantity has been increasing; we shall next show how the coin decreased. When the government takes the coinage into its own hands, the expenses naturally fall upon it, and if any private man coins, he must lessen the value or have nothing but his labour for his pains; and besides, as no man's authority can be so great as to make his coin pass in common payments, he must forge the stamp of the government. As the government took the task upon themselves, they would endeavour, in order to prevent frauds, to prevent counterfeiting the king's coin, and encroaching on his prerogative; besides, as the public faith was engaged, it was necessary to prevent all kinds of fraud, because it was likewise necessary that people should be obliged to receive the coin according to its denomination, and that if any refused it after a legal tender of payment was made, the debtor should be free, and the creditor guilty of felony[4]. In rude and

[1] In *W. of N.* bk. i. ch. iv. vol. i. p. 27, Adam Smith writes, 'Troyes in Champaign' and 'Troyes weight.'

[2] The spelling of the MS. is retained.

[3] This account of the origin of avoirdupois weight may perhaps be the result of an inaccurate recollection of Martin-Leake. *Historical Account of English Money*, 2nd ed. 1745, pp. 30, 31. The original number of ounces in the pound avoirdupois is there given as fifteen.

[4] To refuse legal tender was never felony.

barbarous periods the government was laid under many temptations to debase the coin, or, according to the mint language, to raise it; when, for instance, on any important occasion, such as paying of debts, or of soldiers, it has occasion for two millions, but has no more than one, it calls in the coin of the country, and, mixing with it a greater quantity of alloy, makes it come out two millions, as like as possible to what it was before. Many operations of this kind have been performed in every country; but England, from the freedom which it has almost uninterruptedly enjoyed, has been less troubled with this than any other nation. There it has only fallen to one-third, but in many other countries it is not a fiftieth of its original value.

The inconveniences of such practices are very great. The debasement of the coin hinders commerce, or, at least, greatly embarrasses it. A new calculation must be made how much of the new coin must be given for so much of the old. People are disposed to keep their goods from the market, as they know not what they will get for them. Thus, a stagnation of commerce is occasioned; besides, the debasing of the coin takes away the public faith. Nobody will lend any sum to the government, or bargain with it, as he perhaps may be paid with one half of it. As there is a fraud committed by the government, every subject must be allowed to do the same, and pay his debts with the new money, which is less than he owed. This scheme, however, serves the purpose for some small time, on the following account. The use of money is twofold: for the payment of debts, and the purchasing of commodities. When the coin is debased, a debt of twenty shillings is then paid with ten; but if the new coin be carried to a foreign market, it will give nothing but the old value. All day-labourers are paid in the new coin. The necessities of life must be sold at what the greater part of people can give, and consequently their price will for some time be diminished. However, the king himself loses much, though he gains in the meantime. His doubling it is no doubt a present advantage, but it necessarily diminishes his revenue, because all his taxes are paid in the new coin. To prevent this loss the French, and indeed all other nations on a like occasion, when they double the money by edict without re-coinage, make the augmentation after the money is called in, and before it goes out, and a diminution is made before next term of payment [1]. A diminution has always a worse effect than an augmentation. An augmentation injures the creditor, a diminution the debtor, who should always be favoured [2]. If I bind for ten pounds and be obliged to pay fifteen, common industry must be excessively embarrassed [3].

The coins of most countries are either of copper, silver, or gold. We are obliged even to receive payment in sixpences, which sometimes is the occasion of confusion and loss of time. The different coins are regulated, not by the caprice of the government, but by the market price of gold and silver, and according to this the proportion of gold and silver [is] settled. This proportion sometimes varies a little. The guineas some time ago were valued at

[1] The French understood by an augmentation without recoinage an increase of the number of livres (a money of account, not actual coins) which go to a coin of given weight, and by a diminution a decrease of this number. Melon gives an example in which a debtor who has borrowed 2400 livres in 100 louis d'or is obliged to repay 120 louis d'or of the same weight when there is a diminution of one-sixth and the number of livres equal to a louis d'or consequently reduced from 24 to 20. *Essai politique* 1734, ch. xii. in Daire's *Économistes financiers*, p. 715.

[2] 'Les diminutions favorisent le créancier, et les augmentations le débiteur; et tout le reste égal en matière d'Etat, c'est le débiteur qui doit être favorisé.' *Ibid.* ch. xii. ad fin. Dutot criticizes the proposition and the historical examples adduced in support of it somewhat severely. *Réflexions politiques sur les finances et le commerce*, 1738, ch. i. (*ibid.* pp. 789, sqq.)

[3] *W. of N.* bk. i. ch. iv. vol. i. pp. 28, 29, strongly condemns augmentations or debasements, but says nothing of diminutions.

twenty-two shillings, and at other times they have been at twenty[1]. The gold rises more in proportion in Britain than anywhere else, and as it makes the silver of somewhat less value it is the cause of a real inconvenience. As silver buys more gold abroad than at home, by sending abroad silver they bring gold in return, which buys more silver here than it does abroad. By this means a kind of trade is made of it, the gold coin increasing and the silver[2] diminishing[3]. Some time ago a proposal was given in to remedy this, but it was thought so complex a case that they resolved for that time not to meddle with it.

[§ 9. *That National Opulence does not consist in Money.*]

We have shown what rendered money the measure of value, but it is to be observed that labour, not money, is the true measure of value[4]. National opulence consists therefore in the quantity of goods, and the facility of barter. This shall be next considered.

[1] Guineas were twenty-shilling pieces when first coined in 1663, but were soon taken at 21*s*., and later at 21*s*. 6*d*. Immediately before the great silver recoinage they passed at 30*s*. The act 7 and 8 Will. III, cap. 10, provided that they should not be taken at more than 26*s*., but prescribed no lower limit. Cap. 19 of the same year reduced this maximum to 22*s*. and the current value, which was recognized by the revenue officers, fell to 21*s*. 6*d*. in 1699, after the House of Commons had passed a resolution declaring that the act 7 and 8 Will. III, cap. 19, did not oblige any one to accept guineas at 22*s*. The maximum was reduced to 21*s*. by proclamation, Dec. 22, 1717, in pursuance of Newton's *Representation* (in *Select Tracts on Money*, 1856, pp. 274-279). See Ruding, *Annals of the Coinage*, 1817, vol. ii. pp. 405-410, 427, 446; Snelling, *View of the Gold Coin and Coinage of England*, 1763, pp. 30-32; *London Gazette*, Dec. 21-4, 1717.

[2] MS. reads 'value.'

[3] *W. of N.* bk. i. ch. v. vol. i. pp. 42-46; Harris, *Essay on Money and Coins*, pt. ii. §§ 25, 39; below, p. 203.

[4] *W. of N.* bk. i. ch. v. vol. i. pp. 30-38.

The more money that is necessary to circulate the goods of any country, the more is the quantity of goods diminished. Suppose that the whole stock of Scotland in corn, cattle, money, &c. amounts to twenty millions, and if one million in cash is necessary to carry on the circulation, there will be in the country only nineteen millions of food, clothes, and lodging, and the people have less by one million than they would have if there were no occasion for this expedient of money. It is therefore evident that the poverty of any country increases as the money increases, money being a dead stock [1] in itself, supplying no convenience of life. Money in this respect may be compared to the high roads of a country, which bear neither corn nor grass themselves, but circulate all the corn and grass in the country. If we could find any way to save the ground taken up by highways, we would increase considerably the quantity of commodities, and have more to carry to the market [2]. In the same manner as [the worth of] a piece of ground does not lie in the number of highways that run through it, so the riches of a country does not consist in the quantity of money employed to circulate commerce, but in the great abundance of the necessaries of life. If we could therefore fall on a method to send the half of our money abroad to be converted into goods, and at the same time supply the channel of circulation at home, we would greatly increase the wealth of the country.

Hence the beneficial effects of the erection of banks and paper credit. It is easy to show that the erection of banks is of advantage to the commerce of a country. Suppose as above that the whole stock of Scotland amounted to twenty millions, and that two millions are employed in the

[1] Harris speaks of laying up 'a kind of dead stock of the precious metals against any emergencies that might happen.' *Essay on Money and Coins*, pt. i. § 51.

[2] *W. of N.* bk. ii. ch. ii. vol. i. p. 322.

circulation of it, [and] the other eighteen are in commodities. If then the banks in Scotland issued out notes to the value of two millions, and reserved among them £300,000 to answer immediate demands, there would be one million seven hundred thousand pounds circulating in cash, and two millions of paper money besides. The natural circulation however is two million and the channel will receive no more. What is over will be sent abroad to bring home materials for food, clothes, and lodging. That this has a tendency to enrich a nation may be seen at first sight, for whatever commodities are imported, just so much is added to the opulence of the country. The only objection against paper money is that it drains the country of gold and silver, that bank notes will not circulate in a foreign market, and that foreign commodities must be paid in specie. This is no doubt the case; but if we consider attentively we will find that this is no real hurt to a country. The opulence of a nation does not consist in the quantity of coin, but in the abundance of commodities which are necessary for life, and whatever tends to increase these tends so far to increase the riches of a country.

Money is fit for none of the necessaries of life. It cannot of itself afford either food, clothes, or lodging, but must be exchanged for commodities fit for these purposes. If all the coin of the nation were exported, and our commodities proportionably increased, it might be recalled on any sudden emergency sooner than anyone could well imagine. Goods will always bring in money, and as long as the stock of commodities in any nation increases, they have it in their power to augment the quantity of coin, if thought necessary, by exporting their stock to foreign countries. This reasoning is confirmed by matter of fact. We find that the commerce of every nation in Europe has been prodigiously increased by the erection of banks. In this country everybody is sensible of their good effects, and our American colonies, where most of the commerce is carried on by paper circulation, are in a most flourishing condition [1].

What first gave occasion to the establishment of banks was to facilitate the transference of money. This at this day is the only design of the bank at Amsterdam. When commerce is carried to a high pitch, the delivery of gold and silver consumes a great deal of time. When a great merchant had ten or twenty thousand pounds to give away, he would take almost a week to count it out in guineas and shillings. A bank bill prevents all this trouble. Before the erection of the bank [2] at Amsterdam, the method the merchants fell upon to lessen the trouble of counting out great quantities of cash, was to keep certain sums put up in bags to answer immediate demands. In this case you must either trust the honesty of the merchant, or you must take the trouble of counting it over. If you trusted his fidelity, frequent frauds would be committed, if not, your trouble was not lessened. The inconveniences arising from this gave occasion to the erection of that bank, of which the whole transaction is this: you deposit a certain sum of money there, and the bank gives you a bill to that extent. This money is secure, and you never call for it, because the bill will generally sell above par, and it is therefore an advantage to yourself to let it lie; the bank has no office for payment, because there is seldom any payment demanded. In this manner the bank of Amsterdam has a good effect in facilitating commerce, and its notes circulate only there; the credit of that city is not in the least endangered by the bank. In 1701 [3], when the French army was at Utrecht, a sudden demand was made upon it, and all Holland was alarmed with the expected fatal

[1] *W. of N.* bk. v. ch. iii. vol. ii. p. 542.

[2] MS. reads 'banks.'

[3] A mistake for 1672, the date given in *W. of N.* bk. iv. ch. iii. vol. ii. pp. 59, 61.

consequences, but no danger ensued. Before this a suspicion prevailed that the bankers had fallen into a custom of trading with the money, but at that time it was found that a great quantity of the money had been scorched by a fire that happened in the neighbourhood about fifty years before that[1]. This plainly showed that there was no ground for the suspicion, and the credit of the bank remained unhurt. It has been affirmed by some that the bank of Amsterdam has always money in its stores to the amount of eighty or ninety millions; but this has lately been shown by an ingenious gentleman to be false, from a comparison of the trade of London and Amsterdam[2].

The constitution of the banks in Britain differs widely from that in Amsterdam. Here there is only about a sixth part of the stock kept in readiness for answering demands, and the rest is employed in trade. Originally they were

[1] 'Soon after the bank was established.' *W. of N.* bk. iv. ch. iii. vol. ii. p. 61.

[2] The 'ingenious gentleman' is Nicolas Magens (the 'Mr. Meggens' of *W. of N.* bk. i. ch. xi. vol. i. pp. 218, 222). He says: 'Now it is known that although Amsterdam has in proportion to its inhabitants more merchants than London; but as London contains four to one more people than Amsterdam, there are more merchants and men of business who keep accounts with the Bank. The utmost which appear in the London Directory are 2800, and most probably at Amsterdam not half so many; and although many have accounts with the Bank who are not resident in Amsterdam, it is the same in respect to London; and if it was even admitted that there were in Amsterdam 3000, and each of these to have on advance 10,000 guilders, the amount is 30,000,000 of guilders; and if 20,000, 60,000,000, which I am persuaded is much nearer the truth than what is asserted above' [i. e. by Melon, eighty millions sterling, and by Davenant, thirty-six millions sterling]. *Universal Merchant* (anon.), edited by William Horsley, 1753, p. 33. The story of the scorched money is not taken from Magens. The description of the bank in *W. of N.* bk. iv. ch. iii. vol. ii. pp. 54–62, was obtained from Mr. Henry Hope, no printed account having ever appeared 'satisfactory or even intelligible' to Adam Smith, as he says in the Preface or 'Advertisement' to the 4th edition of *W. of N.*

on the same footing with the Amsterdam bank, but the directors taking liberty to send out money, they gradually came to their present situation. The ruin of a bank would not be so dangerous as is commonly imagined. Suppose all the money in Scotland was issued by one bank, and that it became bankrupt, a very few individuals would be ruined by it, but not many; because the quantity of cash or paper that people have in their hands bears no proportion to their wealth. Neither would the wealth of the whole country be much hurt by it, because the hundredth part of the riches of a country does not consist in money. The only method to prevent the bad consequence arising from the ruin of banks, is to give monopolies to none, but to encourage the erection of as many as possible. When several are established in a country, a mutual jealousy prevails, they are continually making unexpected runs on one another. This puts them on their guard and obliges them to provide themselves against such demands. Was there but one bank in Scotland it would perhaps be a little more enterprising, as it would have no rival, and by mismanagement might become bankrupt; but a number puts this beyond all danger: even though one did break, every individual [would] have very few of its notes. From all these considerations it is manifest that banks are beneficial to the commerce of a country, and that it is a bad police to restrain them.

Several political writers have published treatises to show the pernicious nature of banks and paper money. Mun, a London merchant, published one with this intention, in answer to a book that had been written on the opposite before. He affirms that as England is drained of its money, it must go to ruin. The circulation of paper banishes gold and silver from the country; all other goods which we have in our possession being spent upon our subsistence, gradually diminish, and must at last come to an end. Money never decays, a stock of it will last for ever, and by keeping up great quantities of it in the country we shall insure our riches as long as the world stands. This reasoning was in those days thought very satisfactory, but from what has been said before concerning the nature of public opulence, it appears evidently absurd[1].

Some time after that, Mr. Gee, likewise a merchant, wrote with the same intention[2]. He endeavours to show that England would soon be ruined by trade with foreign countries; by the exchange he calculates that the balance is always against us, and consequently that in almost all our commercial dealings with other nations we are losers[3]; as they drain us of our money, we must soon come to ruin. The absurdity of this is likewise evident from former considerations, and we find that though no stop was put to the manner of carrying on foreign commerce by any regulations, the nation has prodigiously increased in riches, and is still increasing[4]. He proposed indeed some regulations to prevent our ruin from this quarter, which if the government had been [so] foolish [as] to have com-

[1] No work attributed to Mun was published with the intention of showing the pernicious nature of banks and paper money, and as his principal work, *England's Treasure by Foreign Trade*, 1664, was reprinted at Glasgow in 1755, it is not likely that Adam Smith was criticizing it before he had seen it. The most plausible explanation is that he was using the proved utility of banks and paper money as an argument against the theory that the wealth of a country is represented by its stock of the precious metals. He would say that if the contention of writers like Mun and Gee were correct, paper money must be most pernicious, and the reporter would misunderstand him to mean that Mun and Gee held that paper money was pernicious. *W. of N.* bk. iv. ch. i. vol. ii. pp. 4-7 contains a correct summary of Mun's argument and a nearly verbatim quotation from the fourth chapter of *England's Treasure*.

[2] I. e. according to the explanation suggested in the preceding note, 'with the intention of insisting on the accumulation of treasure.' Joshua Gee's *Trade and Navigation of Great Britain Considered*, 1730, was reprinted at Glasgow in 1750 and 1755.

[3] Chapters i-xii, xxxiv.

[4] Hume, 'Of the Balance of

plied with, they would more probably have impoverished the nation [1].

Mr. Hume published some essays [2] showing the absurdity of these and other such doctrines. He proves very ingeniously that money must always bear a certain proportion to the quantity of commodities in every country; that whenever [3] money is accumulated beyond the proportion of commodities in any country, the price of goods will necessarily rise; that this country will be undersold at the foreign market, and consequently the money must depart into other nations; but on the contrary whenever the quantity of money falls below the proportion of goods, the price of goods diminishes, the country undersells others in foreign markets, and consequently money returns in great plenty. Thus money and goods will keep near about a certain level in every country [4]. Mr. Hume's reasoning is exceedingly ingenious. He seems, however, to have gone a little into the notion that public opulence consists in money [5], which was considered above.

We may observe upon this that human industry always multiplies goods and money together, though not always in the same proportion. The labour of men will always be employed in producing whatever is the object of human desire, and things will increase in proportion as it is in the power of man to cultivate them. Corn and other commodities of that kind must always be produced in greater abundance than gold, precious stones, and the like,

Trade,' uses the same argument against Gee. *Political Discourses*, 1752, p. 81.

[1] Gee's 'regulations' (chs. xxiv-xxxiii.) are chiefly directed towards extracting wealth from the colonies by various encouragements and restrictions.

[2] 'Of Money,' 'Of the Balance of Trade,' in *Political Discourses*, 1752, and 'Of the Jealousy of Trade' in *Essays and Treatises*, 1758.

[3] MS. reads 'wherever.'

[4] 'Of the Balance of Trade.' *Political Discourses*, 1752, p. 82 sqq.

[5] Perhaps where he argues against paper money. 'Of Money' and 'Of the Balance of Trade.' *Ibid.* pp. 43-45, 89-91.

because they are more within the reach of human industry. Almost any part of the surface of the earth may, by proper culture, be made capable of producing corn, but gold is not to be found everywhere, and even where it is to be found, it lies concealed in the bowels of the earth, and to produce a small quantity of it, long time and much labour are requisite[1]. For these reasons money never increases in proportion to the increase of goods, and consequently money will be sold at a cheaper rate in proportion as a country becomes opulent. In savage nations money gives a vast price, because savages have no money but [what] they acquire by plunder, for they have not that knowledge which is necessary for producing money in their own country. But when a nation arrives at a certain degree of improvement in the arts, its value diminishes; then they begin to search the mines and manufacture it themselves. From the fall of the Roman Empire to the discovery of the West Indies, the value of money was very high, and continually increasing. Since that latter period its value has decreased considerably[2].

Mr. Locke, too, published a treatise to show the pernicious consequences of allowing the nation to be drained of money. His notions were likewise founded upon the idea that public opulence consists in money, though he treats the matter in a more philosophical light than the rest. He affirms, with Mr. Mun, that if there is no money in a nation it must soon come to ruin, that all commodities are soon spent, but money lasts for ever[3].

[1] Cp. § 7 above.

[2] The 'Digression concerning the variations in the value of silver during the course of the four last centuries' in *W. of N.* bk. i. ch. xi. vol. i. pp. 187-227 deals with three periods—1350 to 1570, when silver rose; 1570 to about 1640, when it fell; and 1570 to 1766, when it remained nearly stationary.

[3] It is difficult to discover any relation between this summary and Locke's *Some Considerations of the Consequences of the Lowering of Interest and Raising the Value of*

Upon the whole we may observe on this subject, that the reason why our riches do not consist in money but commodities is, that money cannot be used for any of the purposes of life, but that commodities are fitted for our subsistence. The consumptibility, if we may use the word, of goods, is the great cause of human industry [1], and an industrious people will always produce more than they consume. It is easy to show how small a proportion the cash in every country bears to the public opulence. It is generally supposed that there are thirty millions of money circulating in Britain [2], but the annual consumption amounts to much more than a hundred millions, for, computing the inhabitants of the island at ten millions, and allowing ten pounds per annum for the subsistence of each person, which is by much too little, the whole annual consumption amounts to that sum. So it appears that the circulating cash bears but a small proportion to the whole opulence of the country. It is probable, however, that there are not thirty millions in Britain, and in that case the proportion will be still less.

It is said by some who support the notion that the

Money, 1691, or the other two tracts reprinted along with it in 1696 under the title of *Several Papers relating to Money, Interest and Trade, &c.* But as the summary agrees with that in *W. of N.* bk. iv. ch. i. vol. ii. pp. 2, 3, it is impossible in this case to suppose error on the part of the reporter. Adam Smith probably had in his mind pp. 17, 18 and 77-79 of *Some Considerations* (1696 edition), and perhaps also §§ 46-50 of *Civil Government*, where the indestructibility of money is insisted on.

[1] 'Le commerce est l'échange des biens distribués par la nature en différents endroits, et que l'intérêt réciproque nous rend communs.

Tous ces biens se communiquent à nous en circulant d'un endroit à l'autre, jusqu'à ce que nos besoins satisfaits les aient consumés. La circulation est donc l'essence du commerce, la consommation en est la fin.' Dutot, *Réflexions politiques sur les finances et le commerce*, 1738, ch. iii. art. 7 ad init. (p. 898 in Daire's *Économistes financiers*); *W. of N.* bk. iv. ch. viii. vol. ii. p. 244.

[2] 'The most exaggerated computation which I remember to have either seen or heard of' *W. of N.* bk. iv. ch. i. vol. ii. p. 15.

riches of a country consists in money, that when a person retires from trade he turns his stock immediately into cash. It is plain, however, that the reason of this is that as money is the instrument of commerce, a man can change it for the necessaries and elegancies of life more easily than anything else. Even the miser who locks up his gold in his chest has this end in view. No man in his senses hoards up money for its own sake, but he considers that by keeping money always by him, he has it in his power to supply at once all the necessities of himself and his family.

This opinion that riches consist in money, as it is absurd in speculation, so it has given occasion to many prejudicial errors in practice, some of which are the following.

[§ 10. *Of Prohibiting the Exportation of Coin.*]

It was owing to these tenets that the government prohibited the exportation of coin [1], which prohibition has been extremely hurtful to the commerce of the country, because whatever quantity of money there is in any country above what is sufficient for the circulation is merely a dead stock.

In King William's time there were two species of coin, milled and unmilled. The unmilled was frequently clipped by different persons in its circulation. This occasioned frequent disorders among the people, and therefore the parliament ordered all the clipped money to be brought into the mint, and the government was at the expense of recoining it, which operation cost them about two millions. As they had been at this expense, they thought it just and proper to prohibit the exportation of money for the future [2]. The merchants, however,

[1] MS. reads 'corn.'

[2] There is evidently an omission at this point which may perhaps be supplied by the words, 'Till the Restoration, indeed, it had been unlawful to export any gold

complained of this hardship, and were then allowed to export money to a small extent[1]. The great complaint, however, was always scarcity of money. In order to remedy this, the government established a common office for coining money where every one might get their gold and silver turned into coin without any expense[2]. The consequence of this was that as coin was of no more value than bullion, a great deal of coin was melted down and exported. To prevent this it was rendered felony to melt coin[3]; but it is so simple an operation, and so easily gone about, that the law was easily eluded. The immediate effect of this regulation was that more coin was exported than ever. This might have been easily prevented by fixing a certain price upon the coinage of bullion, or by ordaining the master of the mint to be paid by the persons who brought their money to be coined; but such a regulation was never thought of.

Any regulation of the above kind is very absurd, for there is no fear if things be left to their free course that any nation will want money sufficient for the circulation of their commodities, and every prohibition of exportation is always ineffectual, and very often occasions the exportation of more than otherwise would be. Suppose, for instance, the Portuguese prohibited from exporting their money by a capital punishment. As they have few goods to give in exchange for ours, their foreign trade must cease; or if they attempt to smuggle, the British merchant

or silver.' See 9 Ed. III, st. 2, cap. 1, 2 Hen. VI, cap. 6, and the summary in Hale, *History of the Pleas of the Crown*, 1736, vol. i. pp. 655, 656.

[1] This probably refers to 15 Car. II, cap. 7, which allowed the exportation of foreign coin and bullion.

[2] Free and gratuitous coinage was established by 18 & 19 Car. II, cap. 5. Above, p. 59; *W. of N.* bk. iv. ch. vi. vol. ii. p. 131.

[3] To melt coin, though punishable, does not appear to have ever been felony. The act referred to is probably 6 & 7 Will. III, cap. 17, of which § 2 is directed against the practice of making ingots in imitation of the Spanish. For the explanation of the mistake see above, p. 59, note 5.

must lay such a price upon his goods as will be sufficient to reward him for the risk he runs of being detected, and the Portuguese merchant, being obliged to buy his goods too dear, must be a loser. In general, every prohibition of this kind hurts the commerce of a country. Every unnecessary accumulation of money is a dead stock which might be employed in enriching the nation by foreign commerce. It likewise raises the price of goods and makes the country undersold at foreign markets.

It is to be observed that prohibiting the exportation of money is really one great cause of the poverty of Spain and Portugal. When they got possession of the mines of Mexico and Peru, they thought they could command all Europe by the continual supplies which they received from thence, if they could keep the money among them, and therefore they prohibited the exportation of it. But this had a quite contrary effect, for when money is, as it were, dammed up to an unnatural height, and there is more than the circulation requires, the consequences are very unfavourable to the country. For it is impossible that the exportation of gold and silver can be wholly stopped, as the balance of trade must be against them, that is, they must buy more than they sell, and it is indispensably necessary that this balance be paid in money. Every commodity rises to an extravagant height. The Portuguese pay for English cloth, additional to the natural price of it, the expense and risk of carrying it there, for nobody ever saw a Spanish or Portuguese ship in a British harbour. All the goods sent to those countries are carried by ourselves and consigned to the British factors, to be disposed of by them. But besides the carriage and insurance, the British merchant must be paid for the risk of having his money seized in Portugal, in consequence of the prohibition. All risk of forfeiture or penalty must lie upon the goods[1]. This has a miserable

[1] Law, *Money and Trade Considered*, ch. ii. 2nd ed. pp. 21, 22.

effect upon the domestic industry of those countries, and has put a stop to their manufactures. Nobody ever saw a piece of Spanish cloth in any other country, yet they have the best materials in the world, and with the same art that we have, might monopolise the trade of Europe. It drew the attention of the nations who trade with them in these commodities, when a general, on a certain occasion, presented to his majesty the regiment of which he had the command clothed in the manufactures of Spain. In general they export no manufactured commodities, swords and armour excepted, as they have confessedly the best steel in the world, but only the spontaneous productions of the country, such as fruits and wines.

Regulations of a similar nature were made in Britain in King William's time[1]. Money was thought to constitute opulence, and therefore the accumulation of it commanded the whole of the public attention. They coined all money brought in for nothing, and the expenses of coinage, which amounted to about £140,000[2], were entirely thrown away; and, besides, great encouragement was given to exportation, because, as gold and silver were coined for nothing, coined money could never be dearer than bullion. As the exportation of bullion was free, they melted down the coin and sent it abroad. At present there is a great temptation to such practices, for an oz. of pure silver at mint price is exactly valued at 5*s.* 2*d.*, but bullion is often bought at 5*s.* 6*d.* As nothing is lost in melting, here is a profit of 4*d.* per oz. It is on this account that we seldom or never see a new shilling, and it is one of the causes that silver is so scarce in proportion to gold[3].

[1] The lecturer now returns from the digression contained in the last two paragraphs.

[2] MS. reads 'fourteen thousand pounds,' which is obviously much too little. In Lord Liverpool's *Treatise on the Coins of the Realm*, 1805, p. 75, the Mint charges are stated to have been £179,431 6*s.*

[3] See above, p. 190 and notes.

[§ 11. *Of the Balance of Trade.*]

The idea of public opulence consisting in money has been productive of other bad effects. Upon this principle most pernicious regulations have been established. Those species of commerce which drain us of our money are thought disadvantageous, and those which increase it beneficial, therefore the former are prohibited and the latter encouraged. As France is thought to produce more of the elegancies of life than this country, and as we take much from them, and they need little from us, the balance of trade is against us, and therefore almost all our trade with France is prohibited by great taxes and duties on importation. On the other hand, as Spain and Portugal take more of our commodities than we of theirs, the balance is in our favours, and this trade is not only allowed, but encouraged. The absurdity of these regulations will appear on the least reflection. All commerce that is carried on betwixt any two countries must necessarily be advantageous to both. The very intention of commerce is to exchange your own commodities for others which you think will be more convenient for you. When two men trade between themselves it is undoubtedly for the advantage of both. The one has perhaps more of one species of commodities than he has occasion for, he therefore exchanges a certain quantity of it with the other, for another commodity that will be more useful to him. The other agrees to the bargain on the same account, and in this manner the mutual commerce is advantageous to both. The case is exactly the same betwixt any two nations[1]. The goods which the English merchants want to import from France are certainly more valuable to them than what they give for them. Our very desire to purchase them shows that we have more use for them than either

[1] *W. of N.* bk. iv. ch. ii. vol. i. p. 29.

the money or the commodities which we give for them. It may be said indeed that money lasts for ever, but that claret and cambrics are soon consumed. This is true: but what is the intention of industry if it be not to produce those things which are capable of being used, and are conducive to the convenience and comfort of human life? Unless we use the produce of our industry, unless we can subsist more people in a better way, what avails it? Besides, if we have money to spend upon foreign commodities, what purpose serves it to keep it in the country? If the circulation of commodities require it, there will be none to spare; and if the channel of circulation be full, no more is necessary. And if only a certain sum be necessary for that purpose, why throw more into it?

Again, by prohibiting the exportation of goods to foreign markets, the industry of the country is greatly discouraged. It is a very great motive to industry, that people have it in their power to exchange the produce of their labour for what they please, and wherever there is any restraint on people in this respect, they will not be so vigorous in improving manufactures. If we be prohibited to send corn and cloth to France, that industry is stopped which raises corn and prepares cloth for the French market. It may be said indeed that if we were allowed to trade with France we would not exchange our commodities with theirs, but our money, and thus human industry is by no means discouraged; but if we attend to it, we shall find that it comes to the same thing at last. By hindering people to dispose of their money as they think proper, you discourage those manufactures by which this money is gained. All jealousies therefore between different nations, and prejudices of this kind, are extremely [hurtful] to commerce, and limit public opulence[1]. This is always the case betwixt France and us in the time of war.

[1] Hume, 'Of the Jealousy of Trade,' in *Essays and Treatises*, 1758, passim.

In general we may observe that these jealousies and prohibitions are most hurtful to the richest nations, and that in proportion as a free commerce would be advantageous. When a rich man and a poor man deal with one another, both of them will increase their riches, if they deal prudently, but the rich man's stock will increase in a greater proportion than the poor man's. In like manner when a rich and a poor nation engage in trade, the rich nation will have the greatest advantage, and therefore the prohibition of this commerce is most hurtful to it of the two. All our trade with France is prohibited by the high duties imposed on every French commodity imported. It would, however, have been better police to encourage our trade with France. If any foreign commerce is to be prohibited, it ought to be that with Spain and Portugal. This would have been most advantageous to England. France is much more populous, a more extensive country, farther advanced in arts and manufactures of every kind, and the industry which a commerce with that country would have excited[1] at home would have been much greater. Twenty millions of people perhaps in a great society, working as it were to one another's hands, from the nature of the division of labour before explained, would produce a thousand times more goods than another society consisting only of two or three millions. It were happy therefore, both for this country and for France, that all national prejudices were rooted out, and a free and uninterrupted commerce established.

It may be observed in general that we never heard of any nation ruined by this balance of trade. When Gee published his book, the balance with all nations was against us, except Spain and Portugal[2]. It was then

[1] MS. reads 'exerted.'

[2] And Holland, according to the Custom House accounts, which, however, Gee finds it convenient to reject as untrustworthy in this case. *Trade and Navigation*, chs. xii, xxxiv.

thought that in a few years we would be reduced to an absolute state of poverty. This indeed has been the cry of all political writers since the time of Charles II; notwithstanding all this, we find ourselves far richer than before, and, when there is occasion for it, we can raise much more money than ever has been done. A late minister of state levied in one year twenty-three millions[1] with greater ease than Lord Godolphin could levy six in Queen Anne's time. The French and Dutch writers, embracing the same principle, frequently alarmed their country with the same groundless terror, but they still continue to flourish. It is to be observed that the poverty of a nation can never proceed from foreign trade if carried on with wisdom and prudence. The poverty of a nation proceeds from much the same causes with those which render an individual poor. When a man consumes more than he gains by his industry, he must impoverish himself unless he has some other way of subsistence. In the same manner, if a nation consume more than it produces, poverty is inevitable; if its annual produce be ninety millions and its annual consumption an hundred, then it spends, eats, and drinks, tears, wears, ten millions more than it produces, and its stock of opulence must gradually [go] to nothing.

[§ 12. *Of the Opinion that no Expense at Home can be hurtful.*]

There is still another bad effect proceeding from that absurd notion, that national opulence consists in money. It is commonly imagined that whatever people

[1] For the service of the year 1760 £19,616,119, and for that of 1761 £18,299,153, were voted, and these amounts were far in excess of the votes for any other year before Adam Smith left Glasgow (Sinclair, *History of the Public Revenue*, pt. iii. 1790, p. 69). Pitt resigned Oct. 5, 1761, but Newcastle continued in office till May,

spend in their own country cannot diminish public opulence, if you take care of exports and imports. This is the foundation of Dr. Mandeville's system that private vices are public benefits: what is spent at home is all spent among ourselves, none of it goes out of the country[1]. But it is evident that when any man tears, and wears, and spends his stock, without employing himself in any species of industry, the nation is at the end of the year so much the poorer by it. If he spend only the interest of the money he does no harm, as the capital still remains, and is employed in promoting industry, but if he spend the capital, the whole is gone. To illustrate this let us make a supposition, that my father at his death, instead of a thousand pounds in cash, leaves me the necessaries and conveniences of life to the same value, which is precisely the same as if he left it in money, because I afterwards purchase them in money. I get a number of idle folks about me and eat, drink, tear, and wear, till the whole is consumed. By this, I not only reduce myself to want, but certainly rob the public stock of a thousand pounds, as it is spent and nothing produced for it. As a farther illustration of the hurt which the public receives from such practices, let us suppose that this island was invaded by a numerous band of Tartars, a people who are still in the state of shepherds, a people who lead a roving life, and have little or no idea of industry. Here they would find all commodities for the taking, they would put on fine clothes, eat, drink, tear, and wear everything they laid their hands upon. The consequence would be that from the highest degree of opulence the whole country would be reduced to the

1762, so that either 1760 or 1761 may be referred to. In *W. of N.* bk. iv. ch. i. vol. ii. p. 17, it is remarked that 'the expense of 1761, for example, amounted to more than nineteen millions.' 'Levied' should be 'raised,' as more than half the amounts were borrowed.

[1] In *Fable of the Bees*, pt. i. Remark (L), Mandeville rather argues against the doctrine.

lowest pitch of misery, and brought back to its ancient state. The thirty millions of money would probably remain for some time, but all the necessaries of life would be consumed. This shows the absurdity of that opinion that no home consumption can hurt the opulence of a country.

Upon this principle that no public expense employed at home can be hurtful, a war in Germany is thought a dreadful calamity, as it drains the country of money, and a land war is always thought more prejudicial than a sea one for the same reason; but upon reflection, we will find that it is the same thing to the nation, how or where its stock be spent. If I purchase a thousand pounds' worth of French wines, and drink them all when they come home, the country is two thousand pounds poorer, because both the goods and money are gone; if I spend a thousand pounds worth of goods at home upon myself the country is only deprived of one thousand pounds, as the money still remains; but in maintaining an army in a distant war it is the same thing whether we pay them in goods or money, because the consumption is the same at any rate. Perhaps it is the better police to pay them in money, as goods are better fitted for the purposes of life at home[1]. For the same reason there is no difference between land and sea wars, as is commonly imagined.

From the above considerations it appears that Britain should by all means be made a free port, that there should be no interruptions of any kind made to foreign trade, that if it were possible to defray the expenses of government by any other method, all duties, customs, and excise should be abolished, and that free commerce and liberty of exchange should be allowed with all nations, and for all things.

[1] In *W. of N.* bk. iv. ch. i. vol. ii. pp. 18, 19, 'the finer and more improved manufactures' are said to be the best medium for defraying the expense of distant wars.

But still further, and on the same principles as above, an apology is made for the public debt. Say they, though we [owe] at present above a hundred millions[1], we owe it to ourselves, or at least very little of it to foreigners. It is just the right hand owing the left, and on the whole can be little or no disadvantage. But [it] is to be considered that the interest of this hundred millions is paid by industrious people, and given to support idle people who are employed in gathering it. Thus industry is taxed to support idleness. If the debt had not been contracted, by prudence and economy the nation would have been much richer than at present. Their industry would not be hurt by the oppression of those idle people who live upon it. Instead of the brewer paying taxes which are often improper, the stock might have been lent out to such industrious people as would have made six or seven per cent. by it, and have given better interest than the government does: this stock would then have been employed for the country['s] welfare. When there are such heavy taxes to pay, every merchant must carry on less trade than he would otherwise do; he has his taxes to pay before he sell any of his commodities. This narrows, as it were, his stock, and hinders his trade from being so extensive as it otherwise would be[2]. To stop this clamour, Sir Robert Walpole endeavoured to show that the public debt was no inconvenience[3], though it is to

[1] According to *W. of N.* bk. v. ch. iii. vol. ii. p. 523, the debt in 1764 amounted to £139,516,807.

[2] *W. of N.* bk. v. ch. iii. vol. ii. pp. 526-529.

[3] Walpole took half a million from the Sinking Fund in 1733, but he does not appear to have contended that the debt was no inconvenience either in debate in the House of Commons on that occasion (see *Historical Register*, 1733, pp. 218, 219, 222, 223) or in his pamphlet, *Some Considerations concerning the Public Funds, the Public Revenues, and the Annual Supplies*, 1735. Hume, however, in the earlier editions of his *Political Discourses*, said that arguments in favour of 'the new paradox, that public encumbrances are of themselves advantageous, independent

be supposed that a man of his abilities saw the contrary himself.

[§ 13. *Of the Scheme of Mr. Law.*]

The last bad effect that shall be taken notice of is the notion of Mr. Law, a Scotch merchant. He thought that national opulence consists in money, and that the value of gold and silver is arbitrary, and depends on constitution and agreement. He imagined that the idea of value might be brought to paper, and it preferred to money. If this could be done, he thought it would be a great convenience, as the government then might do what it pleased, raise armies, pay soldiers, and be at any expense whatever. Mr. Law proposed his scheme to the Scotch parliament in 1701[1]. It was rejected, and he went over to France, where his project was relished by the Duke of Orleans. In this book[2] he agrees with the fore-mentioned writers that, the balance of trade being against a nation, it must soon be drained of its money. In order to turn the balance of trade in our favours, he proposed to the Scotch Parliament the following scheme:

of the necessity of contracting them,' might naturally have passed for trials of wit among rhetoricians, 'had we not seen such absurd maxims patronized by great ministers ... And these puzzling arguments (for they deserve not the name of specious), though they could not be the foundation of Lord Orford's conduct—for he had more sense—served at least to keep his partisans in countenance and perplex the understanding of the nation.' 'Of Public Credit,' *Political Discourses*, 1752, p. 126. After 1768 this reference to Lord Orford was omitted (see Hume's *Essays*, edited by T. H. Green and T. H. Grose, 1875, vol. i. pp. 362, 363).

[1] A mistake for '1705.' In the 2nd edition of *Money and Trade*, 1720, the bookseller requests the reader to receive favourably 'the following pages, which consist of some heads of a scheme which Mr. Law proposed to the Parliament of Scotland in the year 1705.' The year given in the text above was the date of Law's *Proposals and Reasons for Constituting a Council of Trade in Scotland.*

[2] I. e. *Money and Trade Considered: with a Proposal for supplying the Nation with Money*, 1705.

As there was little gold or silver in this country he thought they might fall upon some other method of creating money, independent of it, to wit, by paper. On this account he proposed the erecting of a land bank at Edinburgh, in which it is to be observed, he falls into many blunders concerning tenures and the nature of property. At this bank they were to keep by them only twenty or thirty thousand pounds to answer small demands, and to give out notes for land. For two acres of arable land they were to issue out a note of equal value, and if any extraordinary demand was made upon them, they would pay so much of it in money, and so much in land. By this means in a very short time the whole land of Scotland would go from hand to hand, as a twenty-shilling note does[1].

As this project never was executed, it is hard to say what the consequence might have been; it is, however, obviously liable to the following inconveniences. Taking the land rent of Scotland at five millions per annum, though it be much more, at twenty years' purchase it amounts to an hundred millions; there would then be just so much currency in the country, and if one million was then necessary for circulation there would just be ninety-nine millions for no purpose, as none of it could go abroad; they would not have been able to maintain one man more than formerly, as their food, clothes, and lodging would not have been increased, and every commodity would have risen to ninety-nine times its present value.

Mr. Law, not meeting with the encouragement he expected, went over to France in the year[2] 1714, and, as was before mentioned, found favour with the Duke of Orleans, then[3] Regent, and got liberty to erect a bank

[1] This paragraph appears to be intended as a summary of ch. vii. of *Money and Trade*.

[2] MS. reads 'years.'

[3] 'Then' refers not to 1714, but to the time when Law found suf-

there, which at first was only to the extent of six millions of livres[1] or £320,0[00] sterling. From this beginning he carried it on to a very great height, issued out many notes, and in a short time engrossed the whole circulation of France. As Mr. Law's notes were received in payment of the revenue[2], this contributed to the success of the scheme. This, too, had a greater effect in France than it could have had here, considering the number of taxes, and the manner in which they are levied. By this and other circumstances, his notes were always at par with gold and silver, especially as they were making continual changes in their coin. About that time twenty-eight livres, which were equal to eight ounces of pure silver, were raised to sixty[3], and as a diminution of coin is always the consequent of a sudden rise[4], this was daily expected. Mr. Law made his notes payable in what was called the money of the day[5]. Instead of promising to pay his notes, as we would say, in pounds sterling, he did it in crowns and half-crowns, which was a very proper method to make them par with gold and silver. Suppose that our coin were raised to double, a half-crown would become a crown, and so in this manner the bank notes and money would rise and fall together[6].

ficient favour to get liberty to erect a bank. Louis XIV died on Sept. 1, 1715. Orleans had seen Law, and spoken of him as 'un homme de qui il pourrait tirer des lumières' before that date (Saint-Simon, *Mémoires*, ed. Chéruel et Regnier, tom. xiii. p. 49).

[1] Paris Duverney, *Examen du livre intitulé Réflexions politiques sur les finances et le commerce*, 1740, tom. i. p. 207.

[2] *Ibid.* p. 210.

[3] 'About that time' apparently stands for 'between 1715 and May, 1718.' Dutot, *Réflexions politiques sur les finances et le commerce*, 1738, in Daire's *Économistes financiers*, pp. 810, 847; and Duverney, *Examen*, tom. i. pp. 216, 217.

[4] Above, p. 189.

[5] 'En écus du poids et titre du jour.' Duverney, *Examen*, tom. i. p. 209.

[6] It must be remembered that in Adam Smith's time the pound sterling was just as much a mere money of account as the French livre. Its practical identification with a particular coin is of

As Law wanted to make his notes above par, he fell upon the following scheme. He issued out his bank notes payable in livres tournois, by which, when the coin came to be diminished, he would not be obliged to pay above one-half[1]. The coin was not received in the market or elsewhere, as the diminution was still expected, and did not come for some time. This favoured his design, and kept the notes above par, by which the credit of his bank was established.

The next step Mr. Law fell upon was the relieving of the public debts, which amounted to 200[0] millions[2]. As he saw the diminution must needs come, he took another method to keep up his notes. He got a grant of the exclusive privilege of trading to Canada, and established the Mississippi Company. To this he joined the African, the Turkey, and the East India companies. He also farmed the tobacco and all the public revenues of France at 52 millions[3], for in France the whole

later date, and even now that coin is not called a pound, but a sovereign. Raising our coin to double would mean halving the quantity of silver coined into twenty shillings or '£1.' Law's notes for écus of a certain weight and fineness resembled Drummond's notes for guineas mentioned in *W. of N.* bk. i. ch. v. vol. i. p. 42.

[1] There appears to be some mistake or omission here. A diminution of the coin, i. e. a reduction of the number of livres in an écu of a certain weight and fineness would obviously increase the bullion value of notes for livres. So, if the coin were diminished 50 per cent. and no change made as regards the notes, Law would be obliged to pay double, not half. It may, however, have been supposed that the notes would be arbitrarily reduced when the coin was diminished, as an edict was soon issued declaring that this would not under any circumstances take place. The next two sentences in the text above describe the natural effect of this edict (see Duverney, *Examen*, tom. i. pp. 235, 236), and do not at all follow from the statement that Law would not be obliged to pay above a half.

[2] Dutot, in Daire's *Économistes financiers*, p. 806, gives the amount as 'deux milliards soixante-deux millions cent trente-huit mille une livres.'

[3] Duverney, *Examen*, tom. i. p. 249. MS. reads '12 millions.'

revenue is farmed by one man, who undertakes it and levies it without excisemen, and the farmers there are the richest in the country, and must be skilled in the finances and public revenues[1]. Mr. Law undertook this, and, having the whole trade of the country monopolized, it was difficult to say what profits he would make. He wanted to lend the government 80 or 90 millions [sterling], which he could easily do by issuing notes to that value, but then he saw that they would soon return upon him. To prevent this, his invention was set on work, and we shall see how far he succeeded. As the company he erected seemed to be in a very flourishing condition, shares were purchased in it at a very considerable rate. He opened a subscription to it at 500 livres, so that a navy ticket or *billet d'état* purchased a share into it, which raised them to a par, as they had for a long time been far below it. The government of France was never in such a miserable condition as then. The interest of the money which should have paid the *billets d'état* was seized upon for other purposes. Never was monarch more degraded than Lewis XIV. After the treaty of Utrecht he had occasion to borrow 8 millions of livres from Holland, and not only to give them his bond for 32 millions, but to get some merchants to be security for him[2]. Since that was the case, we need not be surprised that the *billets d'état* sold at great discount, as they bore no interest, and it was quite uncertain when they would be paid. Law published a declaration that one of these, which was granted for 500 livres, should purchase a share in the company, and thus they came again to par. The people still continuing in great expectations of profit, he in a few days opened a new subscription at 5000 livres,

[1] Duverney, *Examen*, tom. i. p. 252.

[2] Dutot, in Daire's *Économistes financiers*, p. 805, mentions these terms, and says that the loan was obtained from foreigners on the credit of a private person and his friends, but does not specify Holland.

and afterwards another at 10,000. At this time he was enabled to lend the government 1600 millions of livres at 3 per cent[1].

Had he stopped here, it is probable that he would have answered all engagements, but his future proceedings ruined all. It was impossible that the value of shares could long continue at such a high rate. He thought, however, that it was necessary to do all that he could to keep them up, as the whole fortunes of many people were in the bank. He had issued out notes to double the circulation of the country, which raised the price of everything to an enormous pitch, and consequently the exchange was against France in all foreign trade. This was principally occasioned by his opening an office to purchase 500 livres shares at 9000 livres[2], which obliged him to issue out many notes. People of prudence who were concerned opposed this scheme, and indeed it was the first thing that made his bank lose credit, and occasioned its dissolution. As he was not obliged to pay the capital sums, only the annual dividend of 200 livres arising from the profits[3], he might have let them fall to their original 500 without any great loss but that of reputation; but his buying up the shares occasioned his issuing out so many notes that they must of necessity return upon him. This was so much the case that he was obliged to open offices in different parts of Paris for the payment of them. When in this manner oppressed, he was making continual changes on the coin, in order to dissuade people from returning on the bank, and disgust them at gold and silver[4]. He cried up gold, but as coin

[1] Duverney, *Examen*, tom. i. pp. 250, 273, 289.

[2] *Ibid.* pp. 280, 281.

[3] The original fixed interest was only 4 per cent., or 20 livres on the shares of 500 livres; but a general meeting of the company, held on Dec. 30, 1719, resolved that the dividend should be 40 per cent., or 200 livres per share. *Ibid.* pp. 215, 267, 268, 317.

[4] 'Pour dégoûter les peuples des monnaies d'or et d'argent.' *Ibid.* p. 316.

cannot be kept much above the level of the metal, when it was so much depreciated, it was not taken. If a person had 20,000 guineas, as he was afraid that the coin would not continue at that value, he went to the bank and got it exchanged for notes. The same consideration prevented them from returning upon the bank, as they would there be paid in coin. By this means he not only prevented his notes from coming upon him, but filled his coffers with almost all the gold in the country. In order to accomplish this part of his scheme more perfectly, he most arbitrarily published an edict prohibiting any persons from keeping by them gold or silver, beyond a certain sum [1]. He also took away the severe penalties that were in force against the exportation of coin, and every person was allowed to export money free from duty [2]. By this means much of it went to Holland. He reasoned with himself, some instrument of change is necessary, paper, gold, and silver, at present are the medium; if gold and silver be utterly exported, paper only remains, and may be rendered the sole instrument of commerce. This he thought he had done effectually when by an edict he had swept a part into his coffers, and cleared the country of the remainder. They would therefore be obliged to take paper. At last, however, after a great number of expedients, he found it was impracticable. By paying out great sums, he kept off ruin for some months, but at last published an edict that all bank notes were to be paid only in one half: and indeed if he had stood to this, as some imagined he might have done, it would have been far better than to have suffered the after consequences. Upon this edict the credit of the bank was entirely broken, and the bank notes all on a sudden sunk to nothing [3]. This ruined an immense number of people. Britain can never be much hurt by

[1] Viz. 500 livres. Duverney, *Examen*, tom. i. p. 335.

[2] *Ibid.* pp. 320, 321.

[3] *Ibid.* tom. ii. pp. 6-8.

the breaking of a bank, because few people keep notes by them to any value[1]. A man worth £40,000 will scarce ever have £500 of notes by him. But the breaking of this bank in France occasioned the most dreadful confusion. The greatest part of people had their whole fortunes in notes, and were reduced to a state of beggary. The only people who were safe were the stock-jobbers who had sold out in time, or with their bank notes had purchased all the valuable goods and a great deal of land, though at the highest prices. These made immense fortunes by it.

The South Sea scheme in our own country was nothing to this. Nobody was under any obligations of going into it, the government had no share in it, and the loss was but a trifle in comparison. The clamour which Law's last edict made caused it soon to be rescinded[2], and the notes were again declared to be paid at value, but the bank never recovered its credit, and this had no effect. However, by raising the coin and other expedients, he kept it from May to October, and then[3] was obliged to leave France, which with difficulty he accomplished; his goods were confiscated and he died soon after[4]. This amazing scheme was founded on these two principles, that public opulence consists in money, and that the value of money is arbitrary, founded upon the common consent of mankind. Consistent with these principles he thought he might easily increase the public opulence if he could annex the idea of money to paper, and the government could never be at any loss to produce any effect that money could do. This scheme of Mr. Law's was by no means contemptible; he really believed in it, and was the dupe of it himself. It was thought he had provided well for himself, but it was found to be otherwise. If the Duke of Orleans had lived only

[1] Above, p. 195.

[2] Duverney, *Examen*, tom. ii. p. 11.

[3] In December, 1720. *Ibid.* p. 132.

[4] Not till 1729.

a few days longer it was agreed upon that he was to have been re-established. After his death it was not thought expedient to have it put in execution [1].

This scheme of Law's was imitated all over Europe. It gave occasion to the South Sea Company in England, which turned out at last a mere fraud, and, could it have been carried to as great an extent as Law's, would have been productive of the same consequences. It was erected in the latter end of Queen Anne's reign, and the intention of it was to carry on a trade to the South Seas. For this purpose they bought up the greater part of the debts of the nation. Their stock, however, was not great, and the profits which could be expected from it were very inconsiderable; the expectations of the people were never greatly raised, and its fall was not very prejudicial to the nation.

[§ 14. *Of Interest.*]

We have only two things further to mention relating to the price of commodities, to wit, interest and exchange.

It is commonly supposed that the premium of interest depends upon the value of gold and silver [2]. The value of these are regulated by their quantity, for as the quantity increases, the value diminishes, and as the quantity de-

[1] In *W. of N.* bk. ii. ch. ii. vol. i. p. 318, Adam Smith declines to give any account of the 'different operations' of Law's scheme because they have been so fully and clearly explained by Du-verney.

[2] In *W. of N.* bk. ii. ch. iv. vol. i. p. 357, the common opinion is attributed to Locke, Law, Montesquieu, and 'many other writers,' and it is remarked that 'this notion, which at first sight seems so plausible, has been so fully exposed by Mr. Hume, that it is perhaps unnecessary to say anything more about it.' See Locke, *Some Considerations of the Consequences of the Lowering of Interest and Raising the Value of Money*, 2nd ed., 1696, pp. 6, 10, 11; Law, *Money and Trade Considered*, 2nd ed., p. 17, and *Mémoires sur les banques* in Daire's *Économistes financiers*, p. 518; Montesquieu, *Esprit des lois*, liv. xxii. ch. vi; Hume, 'Of Interest,' *Political Discourses*, 1752, pp. 61-78.

creases, the value rises. If we attend to it, however, we shall find that the premium of interest is regulated by the quantity of stock. About the time of the discovery of the West Indies it is to be observed that common interest was at 10 or 12 per cent, and since that time it has gradually diminished. The plain reason is this. Under the feudal constitution there could be very little accumulation of stock, which will appear from considering the situation of those three orders of men, which made up the whole body of the people: the peasants, the landlords, and the merchants. The peasants had leases which depended upon the caprice of their masters; they could never increase in wealth, because the landlord was ready to squeeze it all from them, and therefore they had no motive to acquire it. As little could the landlords increase their wealth, as they lived so indolent a life, and were involved in perpetual wars[1]. The merchants again were oppressed by all ranks, and were not able to secure the produce of their industry from rapine and violence. Thus there could be little accumulation of wealth at all; but after the fall of the feudal government these obstacles to industry were removed, and the stock of commodities began gradually to increase.

We may further observe that what one trade lends to another is not so much to be considered as money, as commodities[2]. No doubt it is generally money which one man delivers another in loan, but then it is immediately turned into stock, and thus the quantity of stock enables you to make a greater number of loans. The price of interest is entirely regulated by this circumstance. If there be few who have it in their power to lend money, and a great number of people who want to borrow it, the price of interest must be high; but if the quantity of stock on hand be so great as to enable a great number to lend, it must fall proportionably.

[1] Above, pp. 36, 37; *W. of N.* bk. iii. ch. ii. vol. i. pp. 389, 390.
[2] *Ibid.* bk. ii. ch. iv. vol. i. p. 354.

[§ 15. *Of Exchange.*]

Exchange is a method invented by merchants to facilitate the payment of money at a distance. Suppose I owe £100 to a merchant at London, I apply to a banker in Glasgow for a bill upon another merchant in London, payable to my creditor. For this I must not only give the banker £100, but I must also reward him for his trouble. This reward is called the price, or premium, of exchange. Between Glasgow and London it is sometimes at 2 per cent., sometimes more, sometimes less. Between London and Glasgow again it is sometimes 4 or 5 per cent. below par; and between Glasgow and the West India colonies it is often at 50 per cent. below par. The value of exchange is always regulated by the risk of sending money between two places. It is often, however, greater than the risk can be supposed to be, and this is owing to paper circulation. Between Glasgow and London one can easily get £100 carried for fifteen or sixteen shillings; but as paper in Scotland makes a great part of the currency, and as there is an inconveniency in getting bank notes exchanged for gold and silver, a merchant chooses rather to pay 2 per cent. than take the trouble of changing the notes for cash, and sending the money [1]. This too is the cause of the high price of exchange between Virginia and Glasgow. In the American colonies the currency is paper, and their notes are 40 or 50 per cent. below par, because the funds are not sufficient. In every exchange you must pay the price, the risk, some profit to the banker, and so much for the degradation of money in notes. This is the cause of the rise of exchange. Whenever it rises beyond the price of insurance it is owing to the money of one country being lower than that of another. This was the cause of the high price of

[1] *W. of N.* bk. ii. ch. ii. vol. i. pp. 327, 328.

exchange between France and Holland about the time of the Mississippi Company. It was then at 80 or 90 per cent. All the money had been expelled from France by the scheme of Mr. Law, and the whole circulation was paper, and the credit of the bank had fallen. All these reasons conspired to raise the exchange to such an enormous pitch.

[§ 16. *Of the Causes of the slow Progress of Opulence.*]

We come now to the next thing proposed, to examine the causes of the slow progress of opulence. When one considers the effects of the division of labour, what an immediate tendency it has to improve the arts, it appears somewhat surprising that every nation should continue so long in a poor and indigent state as we find it does. The causes of this may be considered under these two heads: first, natural impediments; and secondly, the oppression of civil government.

A rude and barbarous people are ignorant of the effects of the division of labour, and it is long before one person, by continually working at different things, can produce any more than is necessary for his daily subsistence. Before labour can be divided some accumulation of stock is necessary; a poor man with no stock can never begin a manufacture. Before a man can commence farmer, he must at least have laid in a year's provision, because he does not receive the fruits of his labour till the end of the season. Agreeably to this, in a nation of hunters or shepherds no person can quit the common trade in which he is employed, and which affords him daily subsistence, till he have some stock to maintain him, and begin the new trade. Every one knows how difficult it is, even in a refined society, to raise one's self to moderate circumstances. It is still more difficult to raise one's self by those trades which require no art nor ingenuity. A porter or day-labourer must continue poor for ever. In the beginnings of society this is still more difficult. Bare subsistence is almost all that a savage can procure, and having no stock to begin upon, nothing to maintain him but what is produced by the exertion of his own strength, it is no wonder he continues long in an indigent state. The meanest labourer in a polished society has in many respects an advantage over a savage: he has more assistance in his labour; he has only one particular thing to do, which, by assiduity, he attains a facility in performing; he has also machines and instruments which greatly assist him. An Indian has not so much as a pick-axe, a spade, or a shovel, nor anything else but his own labour. This is one great cause of the slow progress of opulence in every country; till some stock be produced there can be no division of labour, and before a division of labour take place there can be very little accumulation of stock[1].

The other cause that was assigned was the nature of civil government. In the infancy of society, as has been often observed, government must be weak and feeble, and it is long before its authority can protect the industry of individuals from the rapacity of their neighbours. When people find themselves every moment in danger of being robbed of all they possess, they have no motive to be industrious. There could be little accumulation of stock, because the indolent, which would be the greatest number, would live upon the industrious, and spend whatever they produced. When the power of government becomes so great as to defend the produce of industry, another obstacle arises from a different quarter. Among neighbouring nations in a barbarous state there are perpetual wars, one continually invading and plundering the other, and though private property be secured from the violence of neighbours, it is in danger from hostile invasions. In this

[1] *W. of N.* bk. ii. Introduction, vol. i. pp. 273-275.

manner it is next to impossible that any accumulation of stock can be made. It is observable that among savage nations there are always more violent convulsions than among those farther advanced in refinement. Among the Tartars and Arabs, great bands of barbarians are always roaming from one place to another in quest of plunder, and they pillage every country as they go along. Thus large tracts of country are often laid waste, and all the effects carried away. Germany too was in the same condition about the fall of the Roman Empire; nothing can be more an obstacle to the progress of opulence.

We shall next consider the effect of oppressive measures, first, with regard to agriculture, and then with regard to commerce.

Agriculture is of all other arts the most beneficent to society, and whatever tends to retard its improvement is extremely prejudicial to the public interest. The produce of agriculture is much greater than that of any other manufacture. The rents of the whole lands in England amount to about 24 millions[1], and as the rent is generally about a third of the produce, the whole annual produce of the lands must be about 72 millions. This is much more than the produce of either the linen or woollen manufactures, for, as the annual consumption is computed to be about 100 millions, if you deduce from this the 72 millions, the produce of agriculture, there will remain only 28 millions for all the other manufactures of the nation. Whatever measures therefore discourage the improvement of this art are extremely prejudicial to the progress of opulence.

One great hindrance to the progress of agriculture is the throwing great tracts of land into the hands of single persons. If any man's estate be more than he is able to cultivate, a part of it is in a manner lost. When a nation

[1] Twenty millions is the estimate mentioned in *W. of N.* bk. v. ch. ii. pt. i. vol. ii. p. 411.

of savages takes possession of a country, the great and powerful divide the whole lands among them, and leave none for the lower ranks of people. In this manner the Celtae, and afterwards the Saxons, took possession of our own island [1]. When land is divided in great portions among the powerful, it is cultivated by slaves, which is a very unprofitable method of cultivation. The labour of a slave proceeds from no other motive but the dread of punishment, and if he could escape this, he would work none at all. Should he exert himself in the most extraordinary manner, he cannot have the least expectations of any reward; and as all the produce of his labour goes to his master, he has no encouragement to industry. A young slave may perhaps exert himself a little at first, in order to attain his master's favour; but he soon finds that it is all in vain, and that, be his behaviour what it will, he will always meet with the same severe treatment. When lands, therefore, are cultivated by slaves, they cannot be greatly improven, as they have no motive to industry. A cultivation of the same kind is that by villains. The landlord gave a man a piece of ground to cultivate, allowing him to maintain himself by it, and obliging him to restore whatever was over his own maintenance. This was equally unfavourable to the progress of agriculture, because the villains, who were a kind of slaves, had no motive to industry but their own maintenance. This objection lies equally against all cultivation by slaves. Some of the West India islands have indeed been cultivated by slaves, and have been greatly improven, but they might have been cultivated by freemen at less expense; and had not the profits of sugar been very great, the planters could not have supported the expense of slaves, but their profits have been so enormous, that all the extraordinary expense of slave cultivation has vanished before it [2]. In the northern

[1] *W. of N.* bk. ii. ch. ii. vol. i. pp. 386-390.

[2] *Ibid.* pp. 390-392.

colonies they employ few slaves, and, though they are in a very flourishing condition in those colonies, the lands are generally cultivated by the proprietors, which is the most favourable method to the progress of agriculture. A tenant of the best kind has always a rent to pay, and therefore has much less to lay out on improvements[1]. When a country sends out a colony, it may hinder a large tract of land to be occupied by a single person[2]; but when savages take possession of a country, they are subject to no laws, the strongest man takes possession of most ground, and therefore among them agriculture cannot be quickly promoted.

After villains went out, as was explained before[3], tenants by steel bow succeeded. The landlord gave a farm with a stock to a villain, which were restored with half of the produce, at the end of the year, to the landlord; but as the tenant had no stock, nor though he had[4], any encouragement to lay it out on improvements, this method always was unfavourable to agriculture. For the same reason that tithes, by depriving the farmer of a tenth of his produce, hinder improvement, this, though in a higher degree, was a hindrance, because the tenant was deprived of one-half of the produce. A great part of France is still cultivated by tenants of steel bow, and it is said that it still remains in some parts of the Highlands of Scotland[5].

The next species of cultivation was that by tenants, such as we have at present. Some of the tenants by steel bow, by extreme pinching and cunning, got a small stock laid up and offered their masters a fixed rent for the ground. Thus in progress of time the present method of cultivation was introduced, though it was long

[1] *W. of N.* bk. iii. ch. ii. vol. i. p. 397.

[2] As in the English North American colonies. *Ibid.* bk. iv. ch. vii. pt. ii. vol. ii. p. 152.

[3] Above, pp. 100, 101.

[4] I. e. 'nor, if he had possessed any stock.'

[5] *W. of N.* bk. iii. ch. ii. vol. i. p. 393.

liable to inconveniences. If the landlord sold his land, the new proprietor was not bound to the terms of agreement, and the tenant was often turned out of his farm; the landlord too invented a method to get rid of the tenant when he pleased by selling the estate to another, on whom he had a back bond to make him return the estate whenever the tenants were turned out. As the tenants were continually in danger of being turned out, they had no motive to improve the ground. This takes place to this day in every country of Europe, except Britain. In Scotland, contracts of this kind were rendered real rights in the reign of James III[1], and in England in that of Henry VII[2].

Besides these there were several other impediments to the progress of agriculture. At first all rents were paid in kind, by which, in a dear year, the tenants were in danger of being ruined. A diminution of produce seldom hurts the tenant who pays his rent in money, because the price of corn rises in proportion to its scarcity[3]. Society, however, is considerably advanced before money comes to be the whole instrument of commerce.

Another embarrassment was that the feudal lords sometimes allowed the king to levy subsidies from their tenants, which greatly discouraged their industry[4]. Besides all, under the tyranny of the feudal aristocracy, the landlords had nothing to stop them from squeezing their tenants and raising the rents of their lands as high as they pleased. England is better secured in this respect than

[1] Apparently a mistake for 'James II,' who, with the act of 1449, is mentioned in *W. of N.* bk. iii. ch. ii. vol. i. p. 395.

[2] *Ibid.* p. 394 gives the more exact date 'about the 14th of Henry VII,' for which see Bacon, *Abridgement*, s.v. Ejectment, vol. ii. p. 160, and cp. Blackstone, *Commentaries*, vol. iii. p. 201.

[3] This objection is not made in *W. of N.* bk. v. ch. ii. pt. ii. art. 1, vol. ii. p. 422, where rents in kind are condemned along with rents in service.

[4] *Ibid.* bk. iii. ch. ii. vol. i. pp. 396, 397.

any country, because everyone who hold[s] but 40*s.* a year for life has a vote for a member of parliament, by which, if he rent a farm, he is secure from oppression [1].

Several circumstances concurred to continue the engrossment of lands. The right of primogeniture was pretty early established, and hindered estates from being divided. The institution of entails is to this day attended with the same bad consequences [2]. The embarrassment, too, of the feudal law in transferring property, detarded the progress of agriculture. Any quantity of any other commodity may be bought or sold in an instant, but in purchasing four or five acres of land a great deal [of] time must be spent in examining the progress of writs [3], and getting your right legally constituted. This tends greatly to the engrossment of lands, and consequently stops their improvement. If all the forms in buying lands were abolished, every person almost who had got a little money would be ready to lay it out on land, and the land by passing through the different hands would be much better improved. There is no natural reason why a thousand acres should not be as easily purchased as a thousand yards of cloth. The keeping land out of the market always hinders its improvement. A merchant who buys a little piece of land has it in his eye to improve it, and make the most of it he can. Great and ancient families have seldom either stock or inclination to improve their estates, except a small piece of pleasure-ground about their house.

There are many errors in the police of almost every country, which have contributed greatly to stop the progress of agriculture. Our fathers, finding themselves once in every two or three years subject to the most grievous

[1] I. e. 'because every one who holds land to the value of 40*s.* a year for life has a vote for a member of parliament, in consequence of which fact he is secure from oppression if, instead of being content with his own property, he rents a farm.' Cf. *W. of N.* bk. iii. ch. ii. vol. i. p. 394.

[2] Above, p. 124.

[3] Scotch for 'investigating title.'

dearths, to escape that calamity prohibited the exportation of corn. This is still the police of the greater part of Europe, and it is the cause of all that dearth it is intended to prevent. In a plentiful year the corn of Spain, though the most fertile country in the world, is not worth the cutting down; they suffer it to lie rotting on the ground, because they would get nothing for it. The cause of this is not the indolence of the people, as is commonly imagined. The fact is, the farmer, finding he cannot dispose of his corn this year, will not risk a crop next year, but turns his grounds to grass. Next year a famine ensues, and he sows more than can be disposed of for the following season. It is to be observed that this was one great cause of the depopulation of ancient Italy. Exportation of corn was prohibited by severe penalties, and the importation of it encouraged by high premiums, so that the Italian farmers had no encouragement to industry, not being sure of a market. In the latter times of the Republic the Emperors tried several methods of promoting the cultivation of the country, but being ignorant that the real cause of their want was the immense quantity of corn daily imported from Egypt, and other parts of Africa, all their endeavours were ineffectual. Caligula and Claudius gave their soldiers land for nothing, upon condition that they would cultivate it, but as the soldiers had no other motive, very inconsiderable improvements were made. Virgil, too, published his Georgics to bring the cultivation of land into fashion, but all was in vain. Foreign corn was always sold cheaper than their own could be raised[1]. Agreeably to this we find Cato in the Third Book of Cicero's Offices, preferring pasturage of any kind to farming[2]. The Kings of Spain have also done all in their

[1] *W. of N.* bk. i. ch. xi. pt. i. vol. i. p. 159, and bk. iii. ch. ii. vol. i. p. 398.

[2] 'Third book' is a mistake. The passage referred to, which is given in full in *W. of N.* bk. i. ch. xi. pt. i. vol. i. p. 159, occurs in the last chapter of lib. ii.

power to promote the improvement of land. Philip IV went to the plough himself in order to set the fashion. He did everything for the farmers except bringing them a good market; he conferred the titles of nobility upon several farmers; he very absurdly endeavoured to oppress manufacturers with heavy taxes in order to force them to the country; he thought that in proportion as the inhabitants of towns became more numerous, those in the country decreased. This notion was highly ridiculous; for the populousness of a town is the very cause of the populousness of the country, because it gives greater encouragement to industry. Every man in a town must be fed by another in the country, and it is always a sign that the country is improving when men go to town. There are no parts of the country so well inhabited nor so well cultivated as those which lie in the neighbourhood of populous cities.

All these causes have hindered, and still hinder, the improvement of agriculture, the most important branch of industry. We may observe that the greater number of manufacturers there are in any country, agriculture is the more improved, and the causes which prevent the progress of these react, as it were, upon agriculture. It is easy to show that the free export and import of corn is favourable to agriculture. In England, the country has been better stored with corn, and the price of it has gradually sunk, since the exportation of it was permitted. The bounty on exportation does harm in other respects, but it increases the quantity of corn [1]. In Holland corn is cheaper and plentyer than anywhere else, and a dearth is there unknown. That country is as it were the magazine of corn for a great part of Europe: this is entirely owing to the free export and import they enjoy. If no improper regulations took

[1] Above, pp. 181, 182.

place, any country of Europe might do more than maintain itself with all sorts of grain.

The slow progress of arts and commerce is owing to causes of a like kind. In all places where slavery took place, the manufactures were carried on by slaves. It is impossible that they can be so well carried on by slaves as by freemen, because they can have no motive to labour but the dread of punishment, and can never invent any machine for facilitating their business. Freemen who have a stock of their own, can get anything accomplished which they think may be expedient for carrying on labour. If a carpenter think that a plane will serve his purpose better than a knife, he may go to a smith and get it made; but if a slave make any such proposal he is called a lazy rascal, and no experiments are made to give him ease. At present the Turks and Hungarians work mines of the same kind, situated upon opposite sides of the same range of mountains, but the Hungarians make a great deal more of them than the Turks, because they employ free men, while the Turks employ slaves. When the Hungarians meet with any obstacle every invention is on work to find out some easy way of surmounting it; but the Turks think of no other expedient but to set a greater number of slaves to work[1]. In the ancient world, as the arts were all carried on by slaves, no machinery could be invented, because they had no stock; after the fall of the Roman Empire, too, this was the case all over Europe.

In a rude society nothing is honourable but war. In

[1] 'On peut, par la commodité des machines que l'art invente ou applique, suppléer au travail forcé qu'ailleurs on fait faire aux esclaves. Les mines des Turcs, dans le bannat de Témeswar, étaient plus riches que celles de Hongrie; et elles ne produisaient pas tant, parce qu'ils n'imaginaient jamais que les bras de leurs esclaves.' Montesquieu, *Esprit des lois*, liv. xv. ch. viii. In *W. of N.* bk. iv. ch. ix. vol. ii. p. 269, Montesquieu is named as the authority for the statement, and 'neighbourhood' replaces the 'opposite sides of the same range of mountains,' which must have been obtained from some other source.

the Odyssey, Ulysses is sometimes asked, by way of affront, whether he be a pirate or a merchant[1]. At that time a merchant was reckoned odious and despicable; but a pirate or robber, as he was a man of military bravery, was treated with honour. We may observe that those principles of the human mind which are most beneficial to society, are by no means marked by nature as the most honourable. Hunger, thirst, and the passion for sex are the great supports of the human species, yet almost every expression of these excites contempt. In the same manner, that principle in the mind which prompts to truck, barter, and exchange, though it is the great foundation of arts, commerce, and the division of labour, yet it is not marked with anything amiable. To perform anything, or to give anything without a reward, is always generous and noble, but to barter one thing for another is mean. The plain reason for this is that these principles are so strongly implanted by nature that they have no occasion for that additional force which the weaker principles need. In rude ages this contempt rises to the highest pitch, and even in a refined society it is not utterly extinguished. In this country a small retailer is even in some degree odious at this day. When the trade of a merchant or mechanic was thus depreciated in the beginnings of society, no wonder that it was confined to the lowest ranks of people. Even when emancipated slaves began to practice these trades, it was impossible that much stock could accumulate in their hands, for the government oppressed them severely, and they were obliged to pay licences for their liberty of trading. In Doomsday-book we have an account of all the different traders in every

[1] *Odyssey*, ix. 252–255. Thucydides (i. 5), who is quoted by Grotius, *De iure belli et pacis*, lib. ii. cap. xv. § 5, refers to this and similar passages as evidence of the honourable character of piracy, but not as evidence of the despicable character of commerce.

county, how many of them were under the king, and how many under such a bishop, and what acknowledgments they were obliged to pay for their liberty of trading[1].

This mean and despicable idea which they had of merchants greatly obstructed the progress of commerce. The merchant is, as it were, the mean between the manufacturer and the consumer; the weaver must not go to the market himself, there must be somebody to do this for him. This person must be possessed of a considerable stock, to buy up the commodity and maintain the manufacturer; but when merchants were so despicable and laid under so great taxations for liberty of trade, they could never amass that degree of stock which is necessary for making the division of labour, and improving manufactures. The only persons in those days who made any money by trade were the Jews, who, as they were considered as vagabonds, had no liberty of purchasing lands, and had no other way to dispose of themselves but by becoming mechanics or merchants; their character could not be spoiled by merchandise, because they could not be more odious than their religion made them. Even they were grievously oppressed, and consequently the progress of opulence [was] greatly retarded.

Another thing which greatly retarded commerce was the imperfection of the law with regard to contracts, which were the last species of rights that sustained action, for originally the law gave no redress for any but those concluded on the spot[2]. At present all considerable commerce is carried on by commissions, and unless these sustained action, little could be done. The first action on contracts extended only to the moveable goods of the contractor, neither his lands nor his person could be touched; his goods were often very incon-

[1] *W. of N.* bk. iii. ch. iii. vol. i. pp. 399, 400.

[2] See above, pp. 132, 133, for the order in which the different kinds of contracts became enforceable.

siderable, and probity is none of the most prevalent virtues among a rude people. It is commerce that introduces probity and punctuality.

Another obstacle to the improvement of commerce was the difficulty of conveyance from one place to another. The country was then filled with retainers, a species of idle people who depended on the lords, whose violence and disorders rendered the going from one place to another very difficult. Besides, there were then no good highways. The want of navigable rivers in many places was[1] also an inconvenience. This is still the case in Asia and other Eastern countries: all inland commerce is carried on by great caravans, consisting of several thousands, for mutual defence, with waggons, &c. In our own country a man made his testament before he set out from Edinburgh to Aberdeen, and it was still more dangerous to go to foreign countries. The laws of every country to aliens and strangers are far from being favourable. It is difficult, or rather impossible, for them to obtain satisfaction. After this was a little remedied still conveyance by sea remained difficult. Piracy was an honourable occupation. Men were ignorant of navigation, and exposed to dangers on this account. The price of all these risks was laid upon the goods, and by this means they were so much raised above the natural price that the improvement of commerce was greatly retarded.

Another piece of police which was thought a wise institution by our forefathers had the same effect. This was the fairs and markets all over Europe. Till the sixteenth century all commerce was carried on by fairs. The fairs of Bartholomew[2], of Leipzig, of Troy in Champaigne, and even of Glasgow, are much talked of in antiquity. These

[1] MS. reads 'were.'

[2] 'Bartholomew fair at London for lean and Welsh black cattle.' Postlethwayt, *Dictionary of Trade and Commerce*, 1751, s. v. Fair.

were the most centrical places, and best fitted for carrying on business. All linen and black cattle were brought in from the country to these assignations or trysts, and, lest the purchaser should be disappointed, they were all brought on a certain day, and were not allowed to be sold on any other day. Forestallers, who went up and down the country buying up commodities, were severely punished, as this was a temptation not to bring them to the market. This might be necessary when it was not safe to go anywhere alone, but though you make no fairs, buyers and sellers will find a way to each other. Easy conveyance and other conveniences of trafficking will be of more advantage than the bringing them to a fixed market and thereby confining buying and selling to a certain season. All fairs, however necessary they then were, are now real nuisances. It is absurd to preserve in people a regard for their old customs, when the causes of them are removed.

Another obstacle to commerce was staple towns, which had the exclusive privilege of selling a certain commodity within that district. Calais, when it belonged to the English, was long the staple for wool[1]. As men were obliged to carry their wool to such a distance, its price was very high. It was however a very great advantage to any town to have the staple, and therefore the king gave it to that town with which he was best pleased, and took it away whenever it disobliged him[2]. Staple towns had all the disadvantages of fairs and markets with this additional one, that the staple commodity could be sold at no fair nor market except one. By this the liberty of

[1] Scil. 'exported.' The next sentence possibly refers not to Calais in particular, but to staple towns in general, since if 'such a distance' applies to Calais it would seem to indicate a belief that all wool, whether for foreign or domestic consumption, had to be carried there.

[2] See John Smith, *Memoirs of Wool*, 1747, ch. vii. esp. §§ 15, 16.

exchange, and consequently the division of labour, was diminished.

All taxes upon exportation and importation of goods also hinder commerce. Merchants at first were in so contemptible a state that the law, as it were, abandoned them, and it was no matter what they obliged them to pay. They, however, must lay the tax upon their goods, their price is raised, fewer of them are bought, manufactures are discouraged, and the division of labour hindered.

All monopolies and exclusive privileges of corporations, for whatever good ends they were at first instituted, have the same bad effect. In like manner the statute of apprenticeship, which was originally an imposition on government, has a bad tendency. It was imagined that the cause of so much bad cloth was that the weaver had not been properly educated, and therefore they made a statute that he should serve a seven years apprenticeship before he pretended to make any. But this is by no means a sufficient security against bad cloth. You yourself cannot inspect a large piece of cloth, this must be left to the stampmaster, whose credit must be depended upon[1]. Above all other causes the giving bounties for one commodity, and the discouraging another, diminishes the concurrence of opulence, and hurts the natural state of commerce.

Before we treat of the effects of police upon the manners of a people, we propose to consider taxes or revenue, which is in reality one of the causes that the progress of opulence has been so slow.

[1] *W. of N.* bk. i. ch. x. pt. ii. vol. i. pp. 125–130.

[PART III: OF REVENUE]

[*Introduction.*]

In the beginnings of society all public offices were performed by the magistrate without any reward, and he was fully satisfied with the eminence of his station. This is the case among the Tartars, Arabs, and Hottentots even to this day. Voluntary presents only are accepted, which have always a bad effect, but cannot be prevented while one is willing to give, and another to receive. It was in this manner, too, that the governors of the Roman provinces got their revenues. When government becomes so complex as to take up the whole attention of the public magistrate, he must undoubtedly have some reward, and if this be not given him by the public, he will fall upon some more dangerous method of obtaining it; few will be so generous as to exact nothing[1]. When applications are made, every one must bring his present, and the man who pays best will be best heard.

When government is a little farther advanced, magazines must be provided, ships built, palaces and other public buildings erected and kept up, and consequently a public revenue levied. At first indeed among the Romans there

[1] Above, p. 16.

was no revenue levied for carrying on war, because the soldiers required no pay. In savage nations this is always the case; every one of the Athenians went out to war at his own expense. The same was the case with our feudal lords; the burden of going to war was connected with the duty of the tenant or vassal. Such a practice cannot be of long duration, and accordingly we find that it ceased at Rome, and was the great cause of the dissolution of that republic. The governors of provinces made such grievous exactions from the people, that they alienated their affections, so that they gave no assistance in defending the state when it stood in need of assistance.

[§ 1. *Of Taxes on Possessions.*]

After the appropriation of land property, a portion of lands was commonly assigned for the maintenance of government. The free states of Greece had land set apart for this purpose, and we find Aristotle giving his opinion that private property should surround the royal lands, because those who were near a city were always for war, because they were sure of defence, and as the enemy would first come upon those lands which were near the boundaries[1]. In all [barbarous] countries we find lands appropriated to the purposes of sovereignty, and therefore little occasion for taxes and customs. We shall show that this is a bad police, and one cause of the slow progress of opulence.

Let us conceive what an immense tract of land would be required to support the British government. The annual expense of it in times of peace amounts to 3 millions, the whole land rents amount[2] to 24 millions[3]. Therefore

[1] He recommends that half the private property should be near the city, and the other half on the border, and that each citizen should have one lot in each portion. *Politics*, 1330 a 14–23.

[2] MS. reads 'amounts.'

[3] Above, p. 224.

the government must have an eighth part in its own hands. If we conceive, further, how such a tract of land would be cultivated, the quantity requisite would be prodigious. Allow it but to be half as well cultivated as the rest, which for many reasons would not be the case, the government would have in its hands a fourth of the whole country. By this therefore the stock of the country would be greatly diminished, and fewer people maintained. After government becomes expensive, it is the worst possible method to support it by a land rent. We may observe that the government in a civilized country is much more expensive than in a barbarous one; and when we say that one government is more expensive than another, it is the same as if we said that the one country is farther advanced in improvement than another. To say that the government is expensive and the people not oppressed is to say that the people are rich. There are many expenses necessary in a civilized country for which there is no occasion in one that is barbarous. Armies, fleets, fortified places, and public buildings, judges, and officers of the revenue must be supported, and if they be neglected, disorder will ensue. A land rent, to serve all these purposes, would be the most improper thing in the world.

All taxes may be considered under two divisions, to wit, taxes upon possessions and taxes upon consumptions. These are the two ways of making the subjects contribute to the support of government. The land tax is of the former kind, and all taxes upon commodities of the latter.

Possessions are of three kinds, to wit, land, stock, and money. It is easy to levy a tax upon land, because it is evident what quantity every one possesses, but it is very difficult to lay a tax upon stock or money without very arbitrary proceedings[1]. It is a hardship upon a man in trade to oblige him to show his books, which is the

[1] *W. of N.* bk. v. ch. ii. pt. ii. art. 2, vol. ii. p. 442.

only way in which we can know how much he is worth. It is a breach of liberty, and may be productive of very bad consequences by ruining his credit; the circumstances of people in trade are at some times far worse than at others. But if on account of this difficulty you were to tax land, and neither tax money nor stock, ye would do a piece of very great injustice. But though it be a difficult thing to tax money or stock without being oppressive, yet this method is used in several countries. In France, for example, in order to ascertain the circumstances of the subject, every bill is assigned, and all business transacted in presence of a public notary, and entered into his books, so that land, stock, and money are there all taxed in the same manner. Of these three only land is taxed in England[1], because to tax the other two has some appearance of despotism, and would greatly enrage a free people. Excepting the land tax, our taxes are generally upon commodities, and in these there is a much greater inequality than in the taxes on land possession. The consumptions of people are not always according to what they possess, but in proportion to their liberality. When taxes are laid upon commodities, their prices must rise, the concurrence of tradesmen must be prevented, an artificial dearth occasioned, less industry excited, and a smaller quantity of goods produced.

Taxes upon land possessions have this great advantage, that they are levied without any great expense; the whole land tax of England does not cost the government above eight or ten thousand pounds. Collectors are chosen by the gentlemen of the county, and are obliged to

[1] 'By what is called the land tax in England it was intended that stock should be taxed in the same proportion as land . . . the greater part of the stock of England is, perhaps, scarce rated at the fiftieth part of its annual value.' *W. of N.* bk. v. ch. ii. pt. 2, art. 2, vol. ii. pp. 443, 444.

[2] *Ibid.* art. 1, vol. ii. p. 418.

produce proper security for their carrying safely to the exchequer the money which they collect. The taxes of customs and excise, which produce such immense sums, are almost eaten up by the legions of officers that are employed in collecting them. These officers must have supervisors over them to examine their proceedings. The supervisors have over them collectors, who are under the commissioners, who have to account to the exchequer; to support these officers there must be levied a great deal more than the government requires, which is a manifest disadvantage.

Another advantage of a land tax is, that it does not tend to raise the price of commodities, as it is not paid in proportion to the corn and cattle, but in proportion to the rent. If the tenant pay the tax, he pays just so much less rent. Excise raises the price of commodities, and makes fewer people able to carry on business. If a man purchase £1000 worth of tobacco, he has an hundred pounds of tax to pay, and therefore cannot deal to such an extent as he would otherwise do; thus, as it requires greater stock to carry on trade, the dealers must be fewer, and the rich have, as it were, a monopoly against the poor. It was observed before that in England, from a kind of delicacy with regard to examining into the circumstances of particular persons, which is apparently an infringement upon liberty, no tax is laid upon stock or money, but all upon consumptions. Whatever advantages this method may have, there is evidently in it an inequality. The landlord who pays his annual land tax pays also a great part of the taxes on consumptions. On this account the landed interest complains first of a war, thinking the burden of it falls upon them, while on the other hand the monied men are gainers, and therefore oppose them. This perhaps occasions the continuance of what is called the Tory interest.

[§ 2. *Of Taxes on Consumptions.*]

Taxes upon possessions are naturally equal, but those upon consumptions naturally unequal, as they are sometimes paid by the merchant, sometimes by the consumer, and sometimes by the importer, who must be repaid it by the consumer. In Holland all goods are deposited in a public warehouse, one key of which is kept by the commissioner of the customs, and another by the owner of the goods. If the goods are exported, no tax is advanced, but if they go into the country the consumer pays down the price to the merchant and the custom to the commissioner. This method is much the same with the famous excise scheme of Sir Robert Walpole, which was at last his ruin. It was to this effect, that a general excise should be established, and all goods imported deposited in a public warehouse, and the tax should only be paid upon the inland sale of them [1]. Though this scheme be liable to inconveniences, such as subjecting the owner to anxiety from not having his goods entirely in his own power, yet it is plainly this which gives the Dutch so great an advantage over all the other nations of Europe. The Dutch are in a manner the carriers of the other Europeans; they bring corn from the Baltic and those places where it is cheap, and wines from those places where there has been a good vintage, and keep them by them till they hear of a dearth, and then export them to the places where it is. But in England the moment you bring the commodities to the country, you must pay the tax and sell them where you please. Thus the merchant may lie out of his interest for a long time, and therefore must sell his commodities dearer. The Dutch, having no tax to pay but upon inland sale, are enabled to sell cheaper than the English or any other nation.

Taxes on consumptions have however some advantage over those on possessions. They are not felt, being paid

[1] *W. of N.* bk. v. ch. ii. pt. ii. art. 4, vol. ii. pp. 481–484.

imperceptibly; but a person possessed of a thousand pounds of land-rent feels very sensibly an hundred pounds going from him. The taxes on consumptions are not so much murmured against, because they are laid upon the merchant, who lays them on the price of goods, and thus they are insensibly paid by the people. When we buy a pound of tea we do not reflect that the most part of the price is a duty paid to the government, and therefore pay it contentedly, as though it were only the natural price of the commodity. In the same manner when an additional tax is laid upon beer, the price of it must be raised, but the mob do not directly vent their malice against the government, who are the proper objects of it, but upon the brewers, as they confound the tax price with the natural one. Taxes upon consumptions therefore, which are paid by the merchant, seem most to favour liberty, and will always be favoured by this government. In Holland they buy a hogshead of wine and first pay the price to the merchant, and then so much to the officers of excise, as it were to get leave to drink it. We in reality do the very same thing, but as we do not feel it immediately, we imagine it all one price, and never reflect that we might drink port wine below sixpence a bottle, were it not for the duty.

Taxes on consumptions have still another advantage over those on possessions. If a person be possessed of a land-rent of an hundred pounds per annum, and this estate be valued at a high rate, he perhaps pays £20 to the government. The collector must be paid at a certain time of the year, and few people have so much self-command as to lay up money to be ready. He has therefore £20 to borrow to answer his present demands. When next payment comes, he has not only the tax to pay, but also the interest of the money borrowed the former year. He begins to encumber his estate; and thus upon examination it will be found that many landholders have been ruined. The best method of preventing this is to make the tenant pay the land tax in part payment of his rent[1]. The taxes on consumptions are not liable to this inconvenience. When a person finds that he is spending too much on the elegancies of life, he can immediately diminish his consumption. Taxes upon consumptions are therefore more eligible than taxes upon possessions, as they have not so great a tendency to ruin the circumstances of individuals.

It is to be observed that taxes both on consumptions and possessions are more or less advantageous to industry according to the manner in which they are levied. The land tax in England is permanent and uniform, and does not rise with the rent, which is regulated by the improvement of the land[2]; notwithstanding modern improvements it is the same that it was formerly. In France the tax rises proportionably to the rent, which is a great discouragement to the landholder. It has much the same effect with the tithes in England. When we know that the produce is to be divided with those who lay out nothing, it hinders us from laying out what we would otherwise do upon the improvement of our lands. We are better financiers than the French[3], as we have also the advantage of them in the following particulars.

In the method of levying our customs we have an advantage over the French. Our customs are all paid at once by the merchants, and goods, after their entry in the custom house books, may be carried by a permit through any part of the country without molestation and expense, except some trifles upon tolls, &c. In France a duty is paid at the end of almost every town they go into, equal, if not greater, to what is paid by us at first; inland

[1] *W. of N.* bk. v. ch. ii. pt. ii. art. 1, vol. ii. p. 418.

[2] *Ibid.*, with, however, the qualification that the owner of a portion only of a parish may find his land tax very slightly increased in consequence of his improvements.

[3] 'The French system of taxation seems in every respect inferior to the British.' *Ibid.* art. 4 ad fin., vol. ii. p. 504.

industry is embarrassed by theirs, and only foreign trade by ours.

We have another advantage in levying our taxes by commission, while theirs are levied by farm, by which means not one half of what they raise goes into the hands of the government. In England the whole expense of levying above seven millions does not come to £300,000. In France twenty-four millions are levied every year, and not above twelve goes to the expense of the government, the rest goes for defraying the expense of levying it, and for the profit of the farmer [1]. In England no excise officers are requisite but at the seaports, except a few up and down the country. The profits of the farmers in France would pay the expense of them all. In the collecting of our excise there is a regular subordination of officers who have their fixed salaries and nothing more, but in France the highest bidder has the place, and, as the man who undertakes it must advance the sum at a certain time, and runs a risk of not getting it up, he deserves a very high profit: besides, in an auction of this kind there are few bidders, as none are capable of undertaking the office but those who are brought up to business, and are possessed both of a great stock and credit, and can produce good security. When there are few bidders they can easily enter into an association among themselves, and have the whole at a very easy rate [2]. Upon the whole we may observe that the English are the best financiers in Europe, and their taxes are levied with more propriety than those of any country whatever [3].

Upon this subject it is in general to be observed that taxes upon exportation are much more hurtful than

[1] The amount paid into the treasury 'did not amount to fifteen millions sterling' in 1765, and the amount levied must have been about double. *W. of N.* bk. v. ch. ii. ad fin., vol. ii. p. 504.

[2] *Ibid.* pp. 499-504.

[3] 'Our state is not perfect, and might be mended, but it is as good or better than that of most of our neighbours.' *Ibid.* p. 497.

those upon importation. When the inhabitants of a country are in a manner prohibited by high taxes from exporting the produce of their industry, they are confined to home consumption, and their motives to industry are diminished. Taxes upon importation, on the contrary, encourage the manufacturing of these particular commodities. The tax upon Hamburgh linen, for example, hinders the importation of great quantities of it, and causes more linen to be manufactured at home. In general, however, all taxes upon importation are hurtful in this respect, that they divert the industry of the country to an unnatural channel. The more stock there is employed in one way, there is the less to be employed in another; but the effects of taxes upon exportation are still more pernicious. This is one great cause of the poverty of Spain; they have imposed a high tax on the exportation of every commodity, and think that by this means the taxes are paid by foreigners, whereas, if they were to impose a tax on importation, it would be paid by their own subjects[1], not reflecting that by bringing a burden on the exportation of commodities, they so far confine the consumption of them, and diminish industry[2].

To conclude all that is to be said of taxes, we may observe that the common prejudice that wealth consists in money has not been in this respect so hurtful as might have been imagined, and has even given occasion[3] to regulations not very inconvenient. Those nations to whom we give more goods than we receive, generally send us

[1] 'I have found ministers and others, both in their conversation and writings, maintain the erroneous maxim that high duties are to be laid upon commodities exported, because foreigners pay them; and, on the contrary, very moderate ones on such as are imported, because his majesty's subjects are at the charge of them.' Uztariz, *Theory and Practice of Commerce and Maritime Affairs*, transl. by John Kippax, 1751, vol. ii. p. 52; cp. vol. i. p. xiii.

[2] *W. of N.* bk. v. ch. ii. pt. ii. art. 4, vol. ii. pp. 495, 496.

[3] MS. reads 'occasions.'

manufactured goods; those on the contrary, from whom we receive more goods than we give, or with respect to whom the balance is in our favour, generally send us unmanufactured goods. To Russia, for example, we send fine linen and other manufactured goods, and for a small quantity of these receive, in return, great quantities of unmanufactured goods. This kind of trade is very advantageous, because goods in an unmanufactured and rude state afford employment and maintenance to a great number of persons. It is merely from the absurd notion that wealth consists in money, that the British encourage most of those branches of foreign trade, where the balance is paid in money.

There are still some other species of taxes, but as their nature is much the same, it is unnecessary to mention them.

Having thus given a general view of taxes, it will not be improper here, on account of their connexion, to consider the nature of stocks, and the causes of their rising and falling.

[§ 3. *Of Stocks.*]

Soon after the Revolution, on account of the necessities of government, it was necessary to borrow money from subjects, generally at a higher rate than common interest, to be repaid in a few years. The funds allotted for payment of this interest were taxes on certain commodities. These taxes were at first laid on for a certain number of years, according to the term for which the money was borrowed; but when, by various arts of government, these loans came to be perpetual, the taxes came, of course, to be perpetual, and thus the funds were mortgaged. Though they[1] were made perpetual when money could no longer be borrowed upon them, yet they were still redeemable

[1] I.e. the mortgaged taxes or funds. 'The funds' originally meant nothing but the aggregate produce of certain taxes.

upon paying up the money borrowed on them[1]. When these taxes were laid on, nothing would have shocked people more, than to have thought that they were to be perpetual, but their progress was so insensible, that it was never murmured at. What shocks at first will soon become easy from custom, which sanctifies everything. Thus [the] taxes were first laid on, and thus they came to the situation in which they are at present. When a sum of money is lent to a private person, the creditor can come upon the debtor when he pleases for both capital and interest; but it is not on this footing that the government borrows money; they give you a right to a perpetual annuity of three or four per cent., but not to redemand your capital. It seems very odd at first sight that the creditor should consent to such an inconvenience as that his money should never be paid up[2], but this is really his advantage. If you lend to the government a thousand pounds in time of war, as they have immediate use for it, they will perhaps be obliged to give you five per cent. of interest, and when peace comes they continue your annuity. You have it in your power to dispose of your annuity, and as your money is perfectly secure, and interest is paid by no private person with so much punctuality as by the government, you may very often sell the annuity of your £1000 at £1100 or more. The government, finding that these annuities sold above par, and for the same reason that people were much disposed to subscribe to the government funds, they resolved, as the funds were still redeemable, to take the advantage by paying up the sums borrowed at five per cent., and

[1] I.e. the stockholder's claim to his perpetual annuity from the mortgaged funds could be extinguished by repaying the capital borrowed from him. A detailed account of the early funds is given in *W. of N.* bk. v. ch. iii. vol. ii. pp. 513-517.

[2] Mortimer talks of 'the inconveniencies that might arise to contributors from being obliged to keep their money constantly in the hands of the government.' *Every Man his own Broker*, 5th ed., 1762, p. 12.

borrowing money at a lower rate[1]. This made the contractors with the government to be on their guard, and, as they saw their design, they would not lend them any more money, without at least some part of the interest should be irredeemable, perhaps two per cent. of the four they were to receive. In every fund therefore there was a part irredeemable[2], which made them continue to sell above par.

In the reigns of King William, Queen Anne, and in the beginning of that of King George I, the funds rose and fell, according to the credit of the government, as there was still some risk of a revolution. Of late, though there be no danger of a revolution, even in the times of peace stocks are sometimes at ten, twenty, or even fifty per cent. below par, and sometimes as much above it[3]. Nobody can suspect any risk of losing that money by change of government. How then comes it that stocks are thus everyday fluctuating without any visible cause? How comes it that good or bad news have such an influence on the rising and falling of stocks? The real cause is as follows:

Every misfortune in war makes peace to be at a greater distance, and every fortunate occurrence seems to favour its approach. When war continues, the necessities of government must be supplied, more money levied and new subscriptions opened for these purposes. As in war the interest must necessarily rise, every one is eager to be in the new subscription, and they who have annuities find that it will be for their advantage to sell out of the old stocks in prospect of a higher interest. The number of sellers, therefore, increases with the prospect of a war, and

[1] Details are given in *W. of N.* bk. v. ch. iii. vol. ii. pp. 515, 516.

[2] The 'irredeemables' of this period were terminable annuities. They were never so largely used as the arithmetical example in the text suggests. *Ibid.* vol. ii. pp. 516, 517.

[3] On March 3, 1763, 3 per cent. consols were quoted at $95\frac{1}{8}$. They had steadily risen in thirteen months from $62\frac{1}{4}$. See the *London Chronicle* for Feb. 3, 1762, and March 3, 1763.

consequently stocks fall. On the other hand, whenever there is a prospect of peace, as there are no expectations that new subscriptions will be opened, they who have annuities are not fond of selling them ; and therefore, the number of sellers decreasing, stocks must rise. In time of war, every one who has any stock runs to have it in the hands of the government, as it cannot be so advantageously employed anywhere else, as they get interest perhaps at seven or eight per cent., of which two or three perhaps is [ir]redeemable, and frequently a lottery ticket into the bargain. A person who has an annuity only at three per cent. will do all he can to sell it, that he may employ his stock to greater advantage, and for this reason will often sell it below par, and consequently stocks must necessarily fall. But in time of war, for the following reasons, even the new subscriptions come to sell below par.

As there are a great many stock-holders who are merchants, and who keep their stocks in the hands of the government that they may be ready to sell out on any sudden demand, and take the advantage of a good bargain when it casts up [1], and as these chances occur most frequently in time of war, they have often occasion to sell out, and thus more stock runs to the market, and the new subscriptions sink [2] below par. But further, in time of war, as was observed before, stock cannot be so advantageously employed, and everybody is tempted to subscribe. Even those whose circumstances are but very inconsiderable, subscribe for great sums in hopes that stocks will rise, and that they may sell out before the time of delivery, to great advantage ; but when things do not answer their expectations, and they are forced to sell out one way or another to support their credit, they are often obliged to sell below par. In this manner the new subscriptions may fall. Stock-jobbers that are well acquainted with their business, observe particularly when a number of indigent persons

[1] *W. of N.* bk. v. ch. iii. vol. ii. pp. 518, 519.

[2] MS. reads 'sinks.'

are in the subscriptions, and as they are soon obliged to sell out, and consequently stocks fall, it is their proper time to purchase them.

[§ 4. *Of Stock-jobbing.*]

The practice of stock-jobbing, or the buying stocks by time has, too, on all occasions, a very considerable influence on the rise and fall of stocks. The method in which this practice is carried on is as follows. A man who has not perhaps £1000 in the world, subscribes for £100,000, which is to be delivered at several fixed times, and in certain portions. He therefore hopes to get these several portions sold out to great advantage by the rising of the stocks before they fall due, but as anything he is worth would go if the stocks should fall, he uses all means to make them rise, he spreads reports at Change Alley that victories are gained, that peace is to be concluded, &c.[1] On the other hand, they who want to purchase a stock, and want that it should fall, propagate such reports as will sink the stocks as low as possible, such as that war will continue, that new subscriptions are thought on, &c. It is owing to this that, in time of war, our newspapers are so filled with invasions and schemes that never were thought of. In the language of Change Alley the buyer is called the bull[2], and the seller the bear[3], and as the bulls or bears predominate,

[1] Mortimer, *Every Man his own Broker*, 5th ed., pp. 31, 37–40.

[2] *Ibid.* p. 45, note. 'A Bull is the name by which the gentlemen of 'Change Alley choose to call all persons who contract to buy any quantity of government securities without an intention or ability to pay for it, and who consequently are obliged to sell it again either at a profit or a loss before the time comes when they have contracted to take it. . . . If he is asked a civil question, he answers with a surly look, and by his dejected, gloomy aspect and moroseness he not badly represents the animal he is named after.'

[3] *Ibid.* p. 47, note. 'A Bear in the language of 'Change Alley is a person who has agreed to sell any quantity of the public funds more than he is possessed of, and often without being possessed of any at all, but which nevertheless he is obliged to deliver against

stocks rise or fall. This practice of buying stocks by time is prohibited by the government, and accordingly, though they should not deliver up the stocks they have engaged for, the law gives no redress [1]. There is no natural reason why £1000 in the stocks should not be delivered, or the delivery of it enforced, as well as £1000 worth of goods; but after the South Sea Scheme this was thought upon as an expedient to prevent such practices, though it proved ineffectual. In the same manner, all laws against gaming never hinder it, and though there is no redress for a sum above £5 [2], yet all the great sums that are lost are punctually paid. Persons who game must keep their credit, else nobody will deal with them. It is quite the same in stock-jobbing, they who do not keep their credit will soon be turned out, and in the language of Change Alley be called lame duck [3]. It is unnecessary here to give any account of particular funds, as they are all of the same nature, and the security equal. If the interest of any sum of money be not paid by the funds allotted for that purpose, it is paid out of the sinking fund, which is the surplus of all the rest. There is perhaps some little difference in the facility of payment, but this is by no means considerable, and merits not our attention.

a certain time; before this time arrives he is continually going up and down seeking . . . whose property he can devour.' But see Murray, *New English Dictionary*, s. v. Bear.

[1] 7 Geo. II, cap. 8. 'An act to prevent the infamous practice of stock-jobbing.'

[2] Under 9 Ann. cap. 14, securities for sums over £10 lost at play were void, and if paid, such sums could be recovered from the winner.

[3] 'A name given in 'Change Alley to those who refuse to fulfil their contracts . . . The punishment for non-payment is banishment from Jonathan's, but they can still act as brokers at the offices.' Mortimer, *Every Man his own Broker*, 5th ed., p. 57, note.

[PART II: OF POLICE]

[*RESUMED*]

[§ 17. *Of the Influence of Commerce on Manners.*]

It[1] remains now that we consider the last division of police, and show the influence of commerce on the manners of a people. Whenever commerce is introduced into any country probity and punctuality always accompany it. These virtues in a rude and barbarous country are almost unknown. Of all the nations in Europe, the Dutch, the most commercial, are the most faithful to their word. The English are more so than the Scotch, but much inferior to the Dutch, and in the remote parts of this country they [are] far less so than in the commercial parts of it. This is not at all to be imputed to national character, as some pretend; there is no natural reason why an Englishman or a Scotchman should not be as punctual in performing agreements as a Dutchman. It is far more reducible to self-interest, that general principle which regulates the actions of every man, and which leads men to act in a certain manner from views of advantage, and is as deeply implanted in an Englishman as a Dutchman[2]. A dealer is afraid of losing his character,

[1] MS. reads 'In.'

[2] 'They make use of their skill and their wit to take advantage of other men's ignorance and folly they deal with; are great exacters where the law is in their

and is scrupulous in observing every engagement. When a person makes perhaps twenty contracts in a day, he cannot gain so much by endeavouring to impose on his neighbours, as the very appearance of a cheat would make him lose. When people seldom deal with one another, we find that they are somewhat disposed to cheat, because they can gain more by a smart trick than they can lose by the injury which it does their character.

They whom we call politicians are not the most remarkable men in the world for probity and punctuality[1]. Ambassadors from different nations are still less so; they are praised for any little advantage they can take, and pique themselves a good deal on this degree of refinement. The reason of this is that nations treat with one another not above twice or thrice in a century, and they may gain more by one piece of fraud, than [lose] by having a bad character. France has had this character with us ever since the reign of Lewis XIV, yet it has never in the least hurt either its interest or splendour. But if states were obliged to treat once or twice a day, as merchants do, it would be necessary to be more precise, in order to preserve their character. Wherever dealings are frequent, a man does not expect to gain so much by any one contract, as by probity and punctuality in the whole, and

own hands: in other points, where they deal with men that understand like themselves, and are under the reach of justice and laws, they are the plainest and best dealers in the world; which seems not to grow so much from a principle of conscience or morality, as from a custom or habit introduced by the necessity of trade among them, which depends as much upon common honesty as war does upon discipline, and without which all would break up, merchants would turn pedlars, and soldiers thieves.' Temple, *Observations upon the United Provinces*, in *Works*, 1757, vol. i. p. 154.

[1] *W. of N.* bk. iv. ch. ii. vol. ii. p. 41 contrasts a legislator governed by general principles with 'that insidious and crafty animal, vulgarly called a statesman or politician, whose councils are directed by the momentary fluctuation of affairs.'

a prudent dealer, who is sensible of his real interest, would rather choose to lose what he has a right to, than give any ground for suspicion. Everything of this kind is odious as it is rare. When the greater part of people are merchants, they always bring probity and punctuality into fashion, and these, therefore, are the principal virtues of a commercial nation.

There are some inconveniences, however, arising from a commercial spirit. The first we shall mention is that it confines the views of men. Where the division of labour is brought to perfection, every man has only a simple operation to perform; to this his whole attention is confined, and few ideas pass in his mind but what have an immediate connexion with it. When the mind is employed about a variety of objects, it is somehow expanded and enlarged, and on this account a country artist is generally acknowledged to have a range of thoughts much above a city one [1]. The former is perhaps a joiner, a house carpenter, and a cabinet-maker, all in one, and his attention must of course be employed about a number of objects of very different kinds. The latter is perhaps only a cabinet-maker; that particular kind of work employs all his thoughts, and as he had not an opportunity of comparing a number of objects, his views of things beyond his own trade are by no means so extensive as those of the former. This must be much more the case when a person's whole attention is bestowed on the seventeenth part of a pin [2] or the eightieth part of a button, so far divided are

[1] In *W. of N.* bk. i. ch. x. pt. ii. vol. i. p. 134, the superiority of the countryman over the townsman is not said to be 'generally acknowledged,' but only 'well known to every man whom either business or curiosity has led to converse much with both.'

[2] The eighteen operations mentioned on p. 164 above include putting the pins in paper. He who does this does not make part of a pin, so that the 'seventeenth part' here is consistent with the eighteen operations.

these manufactures. It is remarkable that in every commercial nation the low people are exceedingly stupid. The Dutch vulgar are eminently so, and the English are more so than the Scotch. The rule is general; in towns they are not so intelligent as in the country, nor in a rich country as in a poor one [1].

Another inconvenience attending commerce is that education is greatly neglected. In rich and commercial nations the division of labour, having reduced all trades to very simple operations, affords an opportunity of employing children very young. In this country [2], indeed, where the division of labour is not far advanced, even the meanest porter can read and write, because the price of education is cheap [3], and a parent can employ his child no other way at six or seven years of age. This, however, is not the case in the commercial parts of England. A boy of six or seven years of age at Birmingham can gain his threepence or sixpence a day, and parents find it to be their interest to set them soon to work; thus their education is neglected. The education which low people's children receive is not, indeed, at any rate considerable; however, it does them an immense deal of service, and the want of it is certainly one of their greatest misfortunes. By it they learn to read, and this gives them the benefit of religion, which is a great advantage, not only considered in a pious sense, but as it affords them subject for thought and speculation. From this we may observe the benefit of country schools, and, however much neglected, must acknowledge them to be an excellent institution. But, besides this want of education, there is another great loss which attends the putting boys too soon to work. The boy begins to find that his father is obliged to him, and therefore throws

[1] *W. of N.* bk. v. ch. i. pt. iii. art. 2, vol. ii. pp. 365-367

[2] Scotland.

[3] *W. of N.* bk. v. ch. i. pt. iii. art. 2, vol. ii. p. 369.

off his authority. When he is grown up he has no ideas with which he can amuse himself. When he is away from his work he must therefore betake himself to drunkenness and riot. Accordingly we find that in the commercial parts of England, the tradesmen are for the most part in this despicable condition; their work through half the week is sufficient to maintain them, and through want of education they have no amusement for the other, but riot and debauchery [1]. So it may very justly be said that the people who clothe the whole world are in rags themselves.

Another bad effect of commerce is that it sinks the courage of mankind, and tends to extinguish martial spirit. In all commercial countries the division of labour is infinite, and every one's thoughts are employed about one particular thing. In great trading towns, for example, the linen merchants are of several kinds, for the dealing in Hamburg and Irish linens are quite distinct professions. Some of the lawyers attend at King's Bench, some at the court of Common Pleas, and others at the Chancery. Each of them is, in a great measure, unacquainted with the business of his neighbour. In the same manner war comes to be a trade also. A man has then time to study only one branch of business, and it would be a great disadvantage to oblige every one to learn the military art and to keep himself in the practice of it. The defence of the country is therefore committed to a certain set of men who have nothing else ado, and among the bulk of the

[1] 'Those who are concerned in the manufactories of this kingdom know by experience that the poor do not labour upon an average above four days in a week, unless provisions happen to be very dear. ... When wheat and other provisions are at a low price ... idleness and debauchery generally take place.' *Considerations on Taxes as they are supposed to affect the Price of Labour in our Manufactories: also some reflections on the general behaviour and disposition of the Manufacturing Populace of this kingdom; showing by arguments drawn from experience that nothing but necessity will enforce labour, &c.*, 2nd ed. 1765, pp. 12, 13.

people military courage diminishes. By having their minds constantly employed on the arts of luxury, they grow effeminate and dastardly.

This is confirmed by universal experience.

In the year 1745 four or five thousand naked unarmed Highlanders took possession of the improved parts of this country without any opposition from the unwarlike inhabitants. They penetrated into England, and alarmed the whole nation, and had they not been opposed by a standing army, they would have seized the throne with little difficulty. Two hundred years ago such an attempt would have roused the spirit of the nation. Our ancestors were brave and warlike, their minds were not enervated by cultivating arts and commerce, and they were all ready with spirit and vigour to resist the most formidable foe. It is for the same reason, too, that an army of four or five hundred Europeans have often penetrated into the Mogul's country, and that the most numerous armies of the Chinese have always been overthrown by the Tartars. In those countries the division of labour and luxury have arrived at a very high pitch, they have no standing army, and the people are all intent on the arts of peace. Holland, were its barriers[1] removed, would be an easy prey. In the beginning of this century the standing army of the Dutch was beat in the field, and the rest of the inhabitants, instead of rising in arms to defend themselves, formed a design of deserting their country, and settling in the East Indies[2]. A commercial country may be formidable abroad, and may defend itself by fleets and standing armies, but when they

[1] Probably the Barrier fortresses. The removal of the dykes would not make Holland an easy prey.

[2] In 1672, not at the beginning of the eighteenth century. Hume, *History of Great Britain*, vol. ii. 1757, p. 226. It is perhaps not a mere coincidence that six pages earlier Hume uses the words 'would prove an easy prey' in speaking of the northern provinces of the Netherlands.

are overcome, and the enemy penetrates into the country, the conquest is easy. The same observation may be made with respect to Rome and Carthage. The Carthaginians were often victorious abroad, but when the war was carried into their own country, they had no share with the Romans. These are the disadvantages of a commercial spirit. The minds of men are contracted, and rendered incapable of elevation. Education is despised, or at least neglected, and heroic spirit is almost utterly extinguished. To remedy these defects would be an object worthy of serious attention.

Thus we have finished the three first great objects of law, to wit, justice, police, and revenue. We proceed now to treat of arms, the fourth part of the general division of jurisprudence.

[PART IV:] OF ARMS

[§ 1. *Of Militias.*]

In the beginning of society the defence of the state required no police, nor particular provision for it. The whole body of the people rose up to oppose any attempt that was made against them, and he who was chief in time of peace, naturally preserved his influence in time of war. But after the division of labour took place, it became necessary that some should stay at home, to be employed in agriculture and other arts, while the rest went out to war. After the appropriation of lands and the distinction of ranks were in some measure introduced, the cultivation of the ground would naturally fall to the meanest rank. The less laborious, but more honourable employment of military service, would be claimed by the highest order. Accordingly we find that this was the practice of all nations in their primitive state. The Roman *equites* or knights were originally horsemen in the army, and no slaves or those who did not pay taxes ever went out to war. In like manner among our ancestors only they who held by what was called knight's service were employed in the defence of the state, and the ancient villains were never considered as a part of the national force.

When the state was thus defended by men of honour

who would do their duty from this principle, there was no occasion for discipline. But when arts and manufactures increased, and were thought worthy of attention, and men found that they could rise in dignity by applying to them, and it became inconvenient for the rich to go out to war, from a principle of avarice, these arts, which were at first despised by the active and ambitious, soon came to claim their whole attention. The merchant who can make two or three thousand pounds at home will not incline to go out to war, but it was an amusement to an ancient knight who had nothing else ado. When the improvement of arts and manufactures was thought an object deserving the attention of the higher ranks, the defence of the state naturally became the province of the lower, because the rich can never be forced to do anything but what they please. In Rome, after the knights gave over serving in the army, the lowest of the people went in their stead, and in our own country, after the feudal militia went out, another of the lowest ranks succeeded. This therefore is the progress of military service in every country. Among a nation of hunters and shepherds, and even when a nation is advanced to agriculture, the whole body goes out together to make war. When arts and manufactures begin to advance, the whole cannot go out, and as these arts are laborious, and not very lucrative, for the reasons formerly adduced, the highest go out. After that, when arts and commerce are still farther advanced, and begin to be very lucrative, it falls to the meanest to defend the state[1]. This is our present condition in Great Britain.

[1] 'According to modern custom, armies are made up of the very dregs of a people, fellows too dissolute and worthless for any other occupation.' Hutcheson, *Introduction to Moral Philosophy*, p. 324. 'Our common soldiers are such a low, rascally set of people.' Hume, 'Of the Populousness of Ancient Nations,' *Political Discourses*, 1752, p. 188. Cp. with the whole section, *W. of N.* bk. v. ch. i. pt. i. vol. ii. pp. 274–281; and see above, pp. 26–29.

[§ 2. *Of Discipline.*]

When the whole body went out together there could be no occasion for military discipline, they being all, as it were, upon the same level, and as their common cause was so well discerned, it was quite unnecessary. When the highest orders went out, a principle of honour would supply the place of discipline, but when this office fell upon the lowest order, the most severe and rigid discipline became necessary, and accordingly we find that it has been introduced into all standing armies. In general, it is necessary that they should be kept under such authority as to be more afraid of their general and officers than of the enemy. It is the fear of their officers and of the rigid penalties of the martial law, which is the chief cause of their good behaviour, and it is to this principle that we owe their valiant actions. In the late war eight hundred Prussians defended a pass a whole day against several thousands of Austrians, and at night in their retreat deserted almost to a man. What could be the foundation of this courage? It was not a principle of honour, nor love to their country, nor a regard to their officers, for these would still have detained them; it was nothing but the dread of their officers, who were hanging, as it were, over their heads, and whom they durst not disobey. This, by the by, shows the governableness of our nature, and may also show how much that manly courage we so much boast of depends upon external circumstances. We may further observe how far this principle of fear may be carried. If a bold, fierce, and tyrannic adjutant be succeeded by one of a mild and gentle disposition, the ideas of terror are conveyed with the coat, and it is some time before it be perceived that he is not so terrible as the other.

[§ 3. *Of Standing Armies.*]

In this manner standing armies came to be introduced, and where there are none, the country is an easy prey to its enemies. The only thing to be observed concerning them is that they should be raised in the most convenient way, and with as little hurt as possible to the country. However much standing armies may be exclaimed against, in a certain period of society they must be introduced. A militia commanded by landed gentlemen in possession of the public offices of the nation can never have any prospect of sacrificing the liberties of the country for any person whatever. Such a militia would no doubt be the best security against the standing army of another nation.

Standing armies are of two kinds: the first is when the government gives offices to particular persons, and so much for every man they levy. From such a standing army as this, which is the model of our own, there is less danger than from the second kind, when the government makes a slump bargain with a general to lead out a certain number of troops for their assistance, which is the model of the standing armies in some little states of Italy. They make a bargain with some chieftain in those parts where the arts have not yet reached, and as the officers are all dependent on him, and he independent of the state, his employers lie at his mercy. But a standing army like ours is not so apt to turn their arms against the government, because the officers are men of honour, and have great connexions in the country. Yet on some occasions a standing army has proved dangerous to the liberties of the people, when that question concerning the power of the sovereign came to be disputed, as has been the case in our own country, because the standing army generally takes the side of the king[1]. The principle

[1] *W. of N.* bk. v. ch. i. pt. i. vol. ii. p. 290; and above, pp. 29, 30.

of the soldier is to obey his leader, and as the king appointed him and pays him, it is to him that he thinks he owes his service. This would never be the case if a proper militia were established. In Sweden, where it takes place, they are in no danger. Thus far concerning standing armies. It is needless to enter into any account of their pay, and other circumstances.

Having considered the laws of nature as we proposed, as they regard justice, police, revenue, and arms, we shall proceed to the last part of our plan, which is to consider the law of nations, or the claims which one nation may have upon another.

[PART V:]

OF THE LAWS OF NATIONS

[*Introduction.*]

It is to be observed that the rules which nations ought to observe, or do observe with one another, cannot be treated so accurately as private or public law. We find the rules of property pretty exactly established in every nation. The extent of the sovereign's power, as well as the duty of the subject, so far as justice is concerned, are pretty uniform everywhere. But with respect to the laws of nations, we can scarce mention any one regulation which is established with the common consent of all nations, and observed as such at all times [1]. This must necessarily be the case, for where there is no supreme legislative power nor judge to settle differences, we may always expect uncertainty and irregularity.

The laws of nations are such as take place either in peace or war. Those that take place in times of peace have been formerly explained, where it was shown with respect to aliens that they are entitled to security as to their persons and effects, but that they have no power to

[1] 'Vix ullum ius reperitur extra ius naturale . . . omnibus gentibus commune.' Grotius, *De iure belli et pacis*, lib. i. cap. i. § 14.

make a will, but all goes to the sovereign at their death[1]. The laws or rules observed in time of war shall be considered in the following order:

First, what is a just cause of war, or according to the Latin phrase, *quando liceat bellare*?

Secondly, what it is lawful for one nation to do to another in time of war, or *quantum liceat in bello*, and upon this head we shall consider the differences between the ancient and modern governments, and the great modifications of the latter.

Thirdly, what is due to neutral nations from the belligerent powers.

Fourthly, the rights of ambassadors between different nations.

[§ 1. *When is War Lawful?*]

First, *quando liceat bellare?* In general whatever is the foundation of a proper law suit before a court of justice may be a just occasion of war[2]. The foundation of a law suit is the violation of some perfect right whose performance may be extorted by force, and is so extorted in a rude society, but in modern times is decided by the magistrate, lest the society should be disturbed by every one taking justice at his own hands. When one nation encroaches on the property of another, or puts to death the subjects of another, imprisons them, or refuses them justice when injured, the sovereign is bound to demand satisfaction for the offence, as it is the intention of the government to protect its several members from foreign enemies, and if redress be refused, there is a foundation for war. In the same manner breach of contract, as when a debt is due by one nation to another, and payment refused, is a very just occasion of war. If, for example, the king of Prussia should

[1] Above, p. 65, where see note 2.

[2] 'Ac plane quot actionum forensium sunt fontes, totidem sunt belli; nam ubi iudicia deficiunt incipit bellum.' Grotius, *De iure belli et pacis*, lib. ii. cap. i. § 2.

refuse to pay the money advanced for him by the British nation in the time of the last war, a declaration of war against him would be just and reasonable. Every offence of the sovereign of one country against the sovereign of another, or of the sovereign against the subject, or of the subject of one country against the subject of another, without giving reasonable satisfaction, may be the cause of a war.

There seems to be only one exception to the general rule, that everything that is the subject of a law suit may be a cause of war, and that is with respect to quasi-contracts. In this case, indeed, it is difficult to determine whether a war would be reasonable or not, and we find no instance of a war declared upon the violation of this right. It must be allowed that the introduction of quasi-contract was the highest stretch of equity, and except in the Roman law it was never perfected nor introduced. In England, if you repair a man's house in his absence, you must trust to him for the payment of it, for you have no action by law. In the same manner, if a Russian do a piece of service to an English merchant, which, if he had not done, the merchant would have suffered extremely, and afterwards demand satisfaction for his trouble, if he be refused it and apply to the courts of justice, they will tell him that he must depend on the honour of the merchant for payment. Excepting this, everything which is the foundation of a proper law suit, will also make war just and reasonable.

[§ 2. *What is Lawful in War?*]

[Second,] *quantum liceat* [*in*] *bello?* How far a nation may push the resentment of an injury against the nation which has injured them, is not easy to determine. The practice of ancient and modern nations differs extremely. In general, when an injury is clearly and distinctly done, or when it is plainly intended and satisfaction refused, resentment is necessary and just. There are a few cases in which it is lawful even without satisfaction being demanded. If a robber was plainly intending to kill you, it would be quite lawful in you to do all you could to prevent him. The injury is plain. In the same manner, when one nation seems to be conspiring against another, though it may have done no real injury, it is necessary that it should be obliged to declare its intentions, and to give security when this demand would not subject it to inconveniences. Though this satisfaction be not demanded, when the King of Prussia saw his dominions about to be overwhelmed by the Elector of Saxony and the Queen of Hungary [1], it was quite right in him to be beforehand with them, and to take possession of their territories, and nothing would have been more absurd than for him to have told them that he was going to attack them. On the other hand, if it be only a debt that is due, it would be as unreasonable to go to war without demanding satisfaction, and it is only upon the dilatory and evasive manner of giving satisfaction that a war in this case becomes lawful.

But to consider a little more particularly what is lawful in war, suppose a subject of any government is injured, they who have injured him become natural objects of resentment, and also the government which protects him if it refuse satisfaction, but the greater part of the nation is perfectly innocent, and knows nothing about the affair. In the late war with France, not one out of twenty, either of the French or us, knew anything of the offences done. Upon what principle or foundation of justice therefore do we take their goods from them, and distress them in all possible ways? This can by no means be founded upon justice and equity, properly so called, it must be upon necessity, which, indeed, in this case, is a part of justice.

[1] In 1756.

Mr. Hutcheson[1] indeed very ingeniously accounts for this, but if we examine his opinion thoroughly, we shall find that he has not built his reasoning on a proper foundation. Every nation, says he, maintains and supports the government for its own good. If the government commit any offence against a neighbouring sovereign or subject, and its own people continue to support and protect it, as it were, in it, they thereby become accessory and liable to punishment along with [it]. As by the Roman law, if any of those slaves which every private person kept for his own advantage, had done any damage to another, one of these two things was to be done, he must either keep the slave no longer, or pay the damage, in like manner a nation must either allow itself to be liable for the damages, or give up the government altogether[2]. It is to be observed that in this reasoning, though excessively ingenious, the cases are not in the smallest degree parallel. A man can do with his slave as he pleases, he can either put him away, or pay what damages he has occasioned, but a nation in most cases can neither do the one nor the other. A government is often maintained, not for the nation's preservation, but its own. It was never the doctrine of any public law that the subjects had a right to dispose of the sovereign, not even in England, where his right has been so much contested. How then comes it that a nation should be guilty of an injury which was not in its power?

The real cause why the whole nation is thought a reasonable object of resentment is that we do not feel for those at a distance as we do for those near us. We have been injured by France, our resentment rises against the whole nation instead of the government, and they, through a blind indiscriminating faculty natural to man-

[1] MS. reads 'Hutchinson.'

[2] Hutcheson, *Introduction to Moral Philosophy*, pp. 276-277, 336. Cf. Grotius, *De iure belli et pacis*, lib. ii. cap. xxi. §§ 2, 7.

kind, become the objects of an unreasonable resentment. In a war between France and us, a Dane would naturally enter into the same sentiments that we do, and would involve together without distinction both the guilty and the innocent[1]. This is however quite contrary to the rules of justice, observed with regard to our own subjects. We would rather choose that ten guilty persons should escape than that one innocent person should suffer. Another cause is that it is often very difficult to get satisfaction from a subject or from a sovereign that may have offended. They are generally in the heart of the country, and perfectly well secured. If we could get at them no doubt they would be the first objects of our resentment, but as this is impossible, we must make reprisals some other way. We have suffered unjustly on account of our connexions, let them also suffer unjustly on account of theirs. In war there must always be the greatest injustice, but it is inevitable.

The practice of ancient and modern nations differs widely with regard to the length to which the outrages of war may be carried. Barbarians, if they do not kill those taken in war, may dispose of them as they please. As all who made war were considered as robbers and violators of the peace of society, such punishments were by no means thought inadequate. Even among the Romans, if the battering ram had once struck the walls, no agreement nor capitulation was allowed, but everything fell into the hands of the conquerors, and they were at liberty to use it as they pleased. So much was this the case in Cicero's time that he represents it as the greatest stretch of humanity that a capitulation was allowed after the ram had once struck the walls[2]. But though force and fraud were in

[1] I.e. an impartial foreigner would consider it quite natural that 'we' (the whole English and the whole French nation) should be enraged at each other.

[2] 'At Cicero (*Off.* i. 11) non tam quid fiat, quam quid natura aequum sit respiciens, sic ea de

former periods the great virtues of war, modern manners have come to a greater degree of refinement, both with respect to persons and effects. Captives in war are now by no means made slaves or liable to oppression: an officer is set free upon his parole or word of honour; and in the war between France and us, they generally treated our wounded prisoners better than their own wounded soldiers[1]. Indeed, there is no nation that pushes this point of gallantry farther than we do. When the sixpence a day which was allowed the French prisoners at Edinburgh and elsewhere, was thought insufficient to maintain them on account of the diminution it sustained before it came to their hands by sub-contracts, &c., a collection of £10,000 was generously made for them. In general prisoners of war are now as well treated as other people.

In the same manner cartel treaties, by which soldiers and sailors are valued at so much, and exchanged at the end of every campaign, the nation which has lost most prisoners paying the balance, is an evidence of our refinement in humanity[2]. In the late war indeed, we refused to enter into any such treaty with France for sailors, and by this wise regulation soon unmanned their navy, as we took a great many more than they[3]. It was the want of humanity

re pronuntiat: et cum iis, quos vi deviceris consulendum est, tum ii qui armis positis ad imperatorum fidem confugiunt quamvis murum aries percusserit, recipiendi.' Grotius, *De iure belli et pacis,* lib. iii. cap. xi. § 14.

[1] See e.g. *Gentleman's Magazine,* Jan., 1759, p. 42.

[2] 'The only cartel I remember in ancient history is that betwixt Demetrius Poliorcetes and the Rhodians; when it was agreed that a free citizen should be restored for 1000 drachmas, a slave bearing arms for 500.' Hume, 'Of the Populousness of Ancient Nations,' *Political Discourses,* 1752, p. 191. The *London Chronicle* for March 5, 1763, mentions £1,200,000 as the balance due for the maintenance, &c., of French prisoners. *W. of N.* bk. v. ch. iii. vol. ii. p. 524 gives £670,000 as the 'composition for French prisoners.' The practice of ransoming prisoners did not die out before 1780. See W. E. Hall, *International Law,* 4th ed., 1895, p. 428, note 1.

[3] See *Considerations on the Exchange of Seamen Prisoners of*

no doubt which rendered ancient towns so obstinate, for it was better to sustain the most terrible hardships than to surrender, but now the besieged know very well how they will be treated before they capitulate, and will run no great risk before they do so[1].

This superior degree of humanity was introduced during the time of Popery. We never find it among the Greeks and Romans, notwithstanding all their attainments. The Pope was considered as the common father of Christendom, the clergy were under his subjection, and he had intercourse by his legates with all the courts of Europe. By this they were more nearly connected, and he obliged them to treat one another with more humanity. The Holy War too, which at that time was undertaken by most of the princes in Europe, made them turn their arms against all those of a different religion, who they thought deserved to be treated in the most cruel manner, but when they came to be engaged in a war among themselves, as they had all been on one side in that common cause, and as they thought that Christians should not be treated in the same manner with infidels, a greater degree of humanity was introduced. From these causes, moderns behave differently from the ancients with regard to the persons of prisoners.

It is more from motives of policy than humanity that the effects of enemies are secured. When a French army invades Germany, the general makes a law that all the people who will live quietly, and do not rise against him, shall be secure in their persons and possessions, and he will punish a soldier as severely for injuring the peasants of his enemy's country as those of his own. But this is not the case in a sea war. An admiral seizes and plunders

War, 1758, a pamphlet on the other side.

[1] Grotius, *De iure belli et pacis*, lib. iii. cap. xii. § 8; Hume, 'Of the Populousness of Ancient Nations,' *Political Discourses*, 1752, p. 190.

all the merchant ships he can get. Many of the merchants have done as little harm as the peasants; why then this distinction? It is the interest of the general not to rob the peasants, because it would be difficult to march an army carrying all its provisions through the country of an enemy. But by engaging them to stay he is supplied without any other expedient. By this means war is so far from being a disadvantage in a well cultivated country, that many get rich by it. When the Netherlands is the seat of war all the peasants grow rich, for they pay no rent when the enemy are in the country, and provisions sell at a high rate. This is indeed at the expense of the landlords and better sort of people, who are generally ruined on such occasions. This is so much the case that all the poor people who are abroad, whenever they hear of a war, will not stay from their native country. It is quite otherways in a sea war. Every ship carries its own provisions, and has no dependence for them upon the ships which it meets.

Another cause of modern refinement is that courtesy, or rather gallantry, which takes place between hostile nations, by which even ambassadors are kept at their several courts. Anciently it was the greatest gallantry to kill the general of an army[1], but nothing could make a person more infamous at present than such a practice. When the king of France in person besieged a certain castle, the governor sent to know in what part of the camp the king lodged, that he might not cannonade it[2]. The king of Prussia indeed did not grant the princes of Saxony this request, when they

[1] Grotius, *De iure belli et pacis*, lib. iii. cap. iv. § 18.

[2] 'Le comte de Croui, qui était gouverneur de la ville [Lille] . . . envoya complimenter le Roi, et le supplier de le faire avertir de quel côté il camperait, pour empêcher qu'on ne tirât sur son quartier: Louis XIV le remercia de sa politesse, et lui fit dire que son quartier serait dans tout le camp de son armée.' *Histoire de Henri de la Tour d'Auvergne Vicomte de Turenne*, 1735, tom. i. p. 416.

informed him where the royal tent stood, but this was because he was assured that the chief magazine was there. Now if there be any in a nation who have injured more than others, they are the king and generals. How comes it then that it is not now thought lawful to kill them as well as formerly? The plain reason is that monarchies, whose interest it always is to show respect to those in authority, set the example at present, but republics, whose interest lies in adopting the opposite maxim, formerly led the fashion[1].

The same policy which makes us not so apt to go to war makes us also more favourable than formerly, after an entire conquest. Anciently an enemy forfeited all his possessions, and was disposed of at the pleasure of the conquerors. It was on this account that the Romans had often to people a country anew, and sent out colonies[2]. It is not so now, a conquered country in a manner only changes masters, they may be subjected to new taxes and other regulations, but need no new people. The conqueror generally allows them the possession of their religion and laws, which is a practice much better than the ancient. Modern armies too, are less irritated at one another, because fire arms keep them at a greater distance[3]. When they always fought sword in hand, their rage and fury were raised to the highest pitch, and as they were mixed with one another the slaughter was vastly greater.

[§ 3. *Of the Rights of Neutral Nations.*]

Third, we are next to show what is due to neutral nations from the belligerent powers.

The rule of justice with respect to neutral nations is,

[1] This remark has already occurred above, pp. 55, 56.

[2] *W. of N.* bk. iv. ch. vii. pt. i. vol. ii. pp. 136, 137.

[3] Hume, 'Of the Populousness of Ancient Nations,' *Political Discourses*, 1752. p. 189.

that as they have offended no party, they should suffer no injury. In a war between France and England the Dutch should have the liberty of trading to both countries, as in the time of peace, as they have injured neither party. Unless when they carry contraband goods, or are going to a town that is besieged, they can trade to any part of the country without molestation. A neutral bottom will not, however, protect the goods of the enemy, nor does the hostility of the bottom, so to speak, forfeit the goods of the neutral power. There is some difference between the practice of ancient and modern nations with respect to the *ius postliminii*, or the recovery of what was lost[1]. The maxim in time of war anciently was, we are always in the right, and our enemies always in the wrong; whatever is taken from the enemy is justly taken, whatever is taken from us is unjustly taken. On this account, if a Carthaginian had sold to a Roman a Roman ship taken in war, the former owner, whenever he had an opportunity, took it back, as on the above principle it was unjustly taken from him. Now it is quite otherways; we consider everything done in war as just and equitable, and neither demand, nor would take back any captures made in it. If an English ship be taken by the French and sold to the Dutch, and come to a British harbour, the former owner pretends no claim to her, for he had lost all hopes of it when it had gone into the possession of the enemy.

It is to be observed that there is a very great difference in the conduct of belligerent nations towards one that is neutral, in a land war, from what [it] is in a sea war, which is more the effect of policy than humanity. When an army retreats, and the conqueror pursues into a neutral nation, unless it have power to hold out both, it becomes the seat of war, as is often the case, and little or no satisfaction is given for damages; but in a sea war, a ship taken from the most inconsiderable neutral power is always restored.

[1] Grotius, *De iure belli et pacis*, lib. iii. cap. vi. § 3, cap ix. § 15.

The reason commonly assigned, that it injures their commerce more to take their ships than anything else, is unsatisfactory, for a land war hurts commerce more than it does. The real reason is that a small country has it not in its power to assert its neutrality in a land war, but the smallest is able to do it in a sea war. A small fort can oblige of the greatest nation to respect the neutrality of its harbour.

[§ 4. *Of the Rights of Ambassadors.*]

Four[th], we are in the last place to consider the rights of ambassadors between different nations.

When nations came to have a great deal of business one with another, it was found necessary to send messengers betwixt them, who were the first ambassadors. Anciently, as there was little commerce carried on between different nations, ambassadors were only sent on particular occasions, and were what we now call ambassadors extraordinary, who returned home after their business was transacted. We find nothing like resident ambassadors in Rome or Greece; their whole office was on particular occasions to conclude peace, make alliances, &c. The first time that resident ambassadors were employed, was in the beginning of the seventeenth century, by Ferdinand, King of Spain. Even the word ambassador comes from the Spanish verb, *ambassare*, to send [1]. The Pope, indeed, from the earliest times had residents, or legates, at all the courts of Europe. The very same reason that makes embassies now so frequent, induced the Pope formerly to fall upon this method. He had business in all the countries of Europe, and a great part of his revenue was collected from them, and as they were continually attempt-

[1] 'Le mot d'Ambassadeur, Ambasiadore, ou Embaxador tire son origine de l'espagnol *embiar*, qui signifie envoyer.' Wicquefort, *L'Ambassadeur et ses fonctions*, 1681, p. 4.

ing to infringe the right he claimed, he found it necessary to have a person constantly residing at their courts, to see that his privileges were preserved. The Pope from this custom derived several advantages.

When commerce was introduced into Europe, and the privileges of every country, with the duties payable on goods in another, were settled, the merchants of one country had constant claims on those of another. They themselves were strangers in those countries, and would very readily be injured, and oftener think themselves so. It became necessary, therefore, to have one of their countrymen constantly residing at the courts of different nations to protect the rights of his fellow-subjects. Anciently, as was observed, there was little intercourse with different nations, and therefore no occasion for resident ambassadors, but now, as there is something almost every day to adjust betwixt dealers, it is necessary that there should be some person of weight and authority who has access to the court, to prevent any occasion of quarrel betwixt them. We have already observed that it was Ferdinand of Spain who established this practice. At first it gave great jealousy to the neighbouring nations to keep ambassadors residing at their courts. He, indeed, pretended to have no right to do this, but by sending an ambassador upon a certain occasion, and starting different questions, he found means of keeping him there. This practice was soon imitated, and it immediately became the universal custom of the European princes, and was so far from being taken amiss that it was reckoned a great affront not to send one. Grotius, whose opinions are founded on the practice of ancient nations, declares against resident ambassadors, and calls them resident spies [1], but if he had lived in the present

[1] Grotius, *De iure belli et pacis*, lib. ii. cap. xviii. § 3, says 'optimo iure reiici possunt quae nunc in usu sunt legationes assiduae, quibus quam non sit opus docet mos antiquus cui illae ignoratae,' but does not call permanent ambassadors resident

age, he would have found that extensive commerce renders it impossible to preserve peace a month, unless grievances be redressed by a man of authority, who knows the customs of the country, and is capable of explaining what injuries are really done. The custom of sending ambassadors preserves peace, and by giving intelligence, prevents one country from being invaded by another without timeous notice. When any kind of dispute happens and the ambassador is recalled, you can have intelligence by your communication with other courts, your ambassador there being informed, for ambassadors in general are acquainted with all the business in Europe.

Though one country might attain some kind of pre-eminence by the influence and assiduity of its ambassador, no attention was for a long time given to it, and that balance of power which has of late been so much talked of, was never then heard of. Every sovereign had enough to do within his own dominions, and could bestow little attention on foreign powers. Before the institution of residents they could have little intelligence, but ever since the beginning of the sixteenth century the nations of Europe were divided into two great alliances. On the one hand were England, Holland, Hungary, Muscovy, &c., on the other France, Spain, Prussia, Denmark, Sweden, &c. In this manner a kind of alliance was kept up, sometimes one leaving the one side, and another joining it, as at present Prussia is with England, and Hungary on the other side. A system of this kind was established in Italy about [the] fifteenth century among the great families there. The resident ambassadors of these nations hinder any one country from domineering over another, either by sea or land, and are formed into a kind of council not unlike that

spies. Cocceius' note on the passage, however, quotes Wicquefort, *Memoires touchant les Ambassadeurs*, La Haye, 1677, p. 438, who there mentions acting as a spy as one of the functions of a resident ambassador.

of the Amphictyons in ancient Greece. They have power to advise and consult concerning matters, but not to determine any, and by combining together can threaten any one country pretending to superiority, or making an unreasonable demand. Post offices, too, are of great importance for procuring intelligence, as communication is open through all these countries, both in peace and war, which makes commerce easy, and gives notice of every movement.

An ambassador's person must be sacred, and not subject to any of the courts of justice in the country where he resides. If he contract debts, or do any injury, a complaint must be made to his country. When the Dutch arrested the Russian ambassador in the year 1718, it was complained of as a violation of the laws of nations[1]. The goods which an ambassador buys are not subject to any custom. As a sovereign would be exempted from taxes, so must his ambassador who represents him[2]. When an ambassador makes any attempt to disturb the peace by entering into conspiracies or the like, he may be imprisoned. By way of compliment, and to keep up the dignity of an ambassador, his house is considered as an asylum for offenders. He must be cautious, however, of this privilege, and extend his authority only to the protection of debtors and small delinquents, for the right will be broken through if he harbour those guilty of capital crimes. The servants of ambassadors, too, are entitled to some considerable privileges; if indeed they have contracted debts, they may be arrested, but this is never done voluntarily.

[1] It is probable that two, or possibly three, cases are here confused by the reporter. The Dutch arrested Goertz, the Swedish minister, in 1717; the English arrested the Russian ambassador for debt in 1708; the French arrested the Spanish ambassador in 1718.

[2] Eighteenth century London local rating acts commonly provide that rates on houses let to ambassadors shall be paid by the landlords.

All the words that signify those persons employed by one court at another are derived from the Spanish language. The Spanish court was then the most ceremonious in the world, and Spanish dress was everywhere affected. As ambassadors were obliged to keep up much ceremony, they were hindered in the prosecution of their business. A man that has to negociate matters of the highest importance could not allow so much time to be spent in the endless ceremony of paying and returning visits. Envoys were therefore sent, to whom less ceremony was due, and who could be addressed on any occasion; their dignity, too soon advanced, and incapacitated them to transact business. As they continued for some time, they were called resident ambassadors ordinary, being of an inferior order to the ambassadors extraordinary. Below this rank is the minister, who resides in the country on account of his own business, and has power to transact any little business of the country to which he belongs.

A consul is a particular magistrate who is a judge of all matters relating to the merchants of his own country, and takes care to do them justice in those places where it may not be very accurately administered.

These are the names and offices of the several persons employed in the foreign affairs of the nation, occasioned by the introduction of commerce, and now become absolutely necessary.

Thus we have considered both the laws of nature and the laws of nations.

FINIS

INDEX

F.

G.

H.

I.

S.

T.

U.

V.

W.

EDITOR'S INDEX

THE END

OXFORD: PRINTED AT THE CLARENDON PRESS
BY HORACE HART, PRINTER TO THE UNIVERSITY

Clarendon Press, Oxford.

SELECT LIST OF STANDARD WORKS.

1. DICTIONARIES.

A New English Dictionary on Historical Principles, founded mainly on the materials collected by the Philological Society. Imperial 4to.

Present State of the Work.

				£	s.	d.
Vol. I.	A, B	Edited by Dr. Murray	Half-morocco	2	12	6
Vol. II.	C	Edited by Dr. Murray	Half-morocco	2	12	6
Vol. III.	D	Edited by Dr. Murray	D–Depravation	0	8	6
			Depravative–Distrustful	0	12	6
			Disobst.–Distrustful	0	2	6
		(The remainder of the letter D is far advanced.)				
	E	Edited by Mr. Henry Bradley	E–Every	0	12	6
			Everybody–Ezod	0	5	0
Vol. IV.	F	Edited by Mr. Henry Bradley	F–Field	0	7	6
			Field–Fish	0	2	6
			Fish–Flexuose	0	2	6
		(The remainder of the letter F is far advanced.)				
	G	To be edited by Mr. Henry Bradley. *In Preparation.*				

One Section at least, of sixty-four Pages, is now published Quarterly at Half-a-Crown.

The Dictionary is also, as heretofore, issued in the original Parts, of which the following are already published:—

				£	s.	d.
Series I.	Parts I–VII.	A–Crouching	*each*	0	12	6
,,	Part VIII.	Crouchmas–Depravation		0	12	6
,,	Part IX.	Depravative–Distrustful		0	12	6
Series II.	Part I.	E–Every		0	12	6
,,	Part II.	Everybody–Field		0	12	6

An Etymological Dictionary of the English Language, arranged on an Historical Basis. By W. W. Skeat, Litt.D. *Second Edition.* 4to. 2*l.* 4*s.*

A Middle-English Dictionary. By F. H. Stratmann. A new edition, by H. Bradley, M.A. 4to, half-bound, 1*l.* 11*s.* 6*d.*

An Anglo-Saxon Dictionary, based on the MS. collections of the late Joseph Bosworth, D.D. Edited and enlarged by Prof. T. N. Toller, M.A. Parts I–III. A–SÁR. 4to, stiff covers, 15*s.* each. Part IV, § 1, SÁR–SWÍÐRIAN. Stiff covers, 8*s.* 6*d.*

The Student's Dictionary of Anglo-Saxon. By H. Sweet, M.A., Ph.D., LL.D. Small 4to, 8*s.* 6*d.* *net.* [*Just Published.*]

An Icelandic-English Dictionary, based on the MS. collections of the late Richard Cleasby. Enlarged and completed by G. Vigfússon, M.A. 4to. 3*l.* 7*s.*

A Sanskrit-English Dictionary. Etymologically and Philologically arranged. By Sir M. Monier-Williams, D.C.L. 4to. 4*l.* 14*s.* 6*d.*

A Hebrew and English Lexicon of the Old Testament, with an Appendix containing the Biblical Aramaic, based on the Thesaurus and Lexicon of Gesenius, by Francis Brown, D.D., S. R. Driver, D.D., and C. A. Briggs, D.D. Parts I–V. Small 4to, 2*s.* 6*d.* each.

Thesaurus Syriacus: collegerunt Quatremère, Bernstein, Lorsbach, Arnoldi, Agrell, Field, Roediger: edidit R. Payne Smith, S.T.P. Vol. I, containing Fasc. I–V, sm. fol. 5*l.* 5*s.*

Fasc. VI. 1*l.* 1*s.*; VII. 1*l.* 11*s.* 6*d.*; VIII. 1*l.* 16*s.*; IX. 1*l.* 5*s.*

A Compendious Syriac Dictionary, founded upon the above. Edited by J. Payne Smith (Mrs. Margoliouth). Part I. Small 4to, 8*s.* 6*d.* *net.*

2. LAW.

Anson. *Principles of the English Law of Contract, and of Agency in its Relation to Contract.* By Sir W. R. Anson, D.C.L. *Eighth Edition.* 8vo. 10*s.* 6*d.*

—— *Law and Custom of the Constitution.* 2 vols. 8vo. *Second Edition.*

Part I. Parliament. 12*s.* 6*d.*
Part II. The Crown. 14*s.*

Baden-Powell. *Land-Systems of British India;* being a Manual of the Land-Tenures, and of the Systems of Land-Revenue Administration prevalent in the several Provinces. By B. H. Baden-Powell, C.I.E. 3 vols. 8vo. 3*l.* 3*s.*

Digby. *An Introduction to the History of the Law of Real Property.* By Kenelm E. Digby, M.A. *Fourth Edition.* 8vo. 12*s.* 6*d.*

Grueber. *Lex Aquilia.* The Roman Law of Damage to Property: being a Commentary on the Title of the Digest 'Ad Legem Aquiliam' (ix. 2). By Erwin Grueber, Dr. Jur., M.A. 8vo. 10s. 6d.

Hall. *International Law.* By W. E. Hall, M.A. *Fourth Edition.* 8vo. 22s. 6d.

—— *A Treatise on the Foreign Powers and Jurisdiction of the British Crown.* By W. E. Hall, M.A. 8vo. 10s. 6d.

Holland. *Elements of Jurisprudence.* By T. E. Holland, D.C.L. *Eighth Edition.* 8vo. 10s. 6d.

—— *The European Concert in the Eastern Question;* a Collection of Treaties and other Public Acts. Edited, with Introductions and Notes, by T. E. Holland, D.C.L. 8vo. 12s. 6d.

—— *Gentilis, Alberici, De Iure Belli Libri Tres.* Edidit T. E. Holland, I.C.D. Small 4to, half-morocco, 21s.

—— *The Institutes of Justinian,* edited as a recension of the Institutes of Gaius, by T. E. Holland, D.C.L. *Second Edition.* Extra fcap. 8vo. 5s.

Holland and Shadwell. *Select Titles from the Digest of Justinian.* By T. E. Holland, D.C.L., and C. L. Shadwell, B.C.L. 8vo. 14s.

Also sold in Parts, in paper covers:—
Part I. Introductory Titles. 2s. 6d.
Part II. Family Law. 1s.
Part III. Property Law. 2s. 6d.
Part IV. Law of Obligations (No. 1), 3s. 6d. (No. 2), 4s. 6d.

Markby. *Elements of Law considered with reference to Principles of General Jurisprudence.* By Sir William Markby, D.C.L. *Fifth Edition.* 8vo. 12s. 6d.

Moyle. *Imperatoris Iustiniani Institutionum Libri Quattuor;* with Introductions, Commentary, Excursus and Translation. By J. B. Moyle, D.C.L. *Third Edition.* 2 vols. 8vo. Vol. I. 16s. Vol. II. 6s.

—— *Contract of Sale in the Civil Law.* By J. B. Moyle, D.C.L. 8vo. 10s. 6d.

Pollock and Wright. *An Essay on Possession in the Common Law.* By Sir F. Pollock, Bart., M.A., and Sir R. S. Wright, B.C.L. 8vo. 8s. 6d.

Poste. *Gaii Institutionum Juris Civilis Commentarii Quattuor;* or, Elements of Roman Law by Gaius. With a Translation and Commentary by Edward Poste, M.A. *Third Edition.* 8vo. 18s.

Raleigh. *An Outline of the Law of Property.* By Thos. Raleigh, M.A. 8vo. 7s. 6d.

Sohm. *Institutes of Roman Law.* By Rudolph Sohm, Professor in the University of Leipzig. Translated by J. C. Ledlie, B.C.L. With an Introductory Essay by Erwin Grueber, Dr. Jur., M.A. 8vo. 18s.

Stokes. *The Anglo-Indian Codes.* By Whitley Stokes, LL.D.

Vol. I. Substantive Law. 8vo. 30s.

Vol. II. Adjective Law. 8vo. 35s.

First and Second Supplements to the above, 1887–1891. 8vo. 6s. 6d.

Separately, No. 1, 2s. 6d.; No. 2, 4s. 6d.

3. HISTORY, BIOGRAPHY, ETC.

Adamnani *Vita S. Columbae.* Ed. J. T. Fowler, D.C.L. Crown 8vo, half-bound, 8s. 6d. *net* (with translation, 9s. 6d. *net*).

Baedae *Historia Ecclesiastica,* etc. Edited by C. Plummer, M.A. 2 vols. Crown 8vo, half-bound, 21s. *net.*

Boswell's *Life of Samuel Johnson, LL.D.* Edited by G. Birkbeck Hill, D.C.L. In six volumes, medium 8vo. With Portraits and Facsimiles. Half-bound, 3*l.* 3s.

Casaubon (Isaac). 1559–1614. By Mark Pattison. 8vo. 16s.

Clarendon's *History of the Rebellion and Civil Wars in England.* Re-edited from a fresh collation of the original MS. in the Bodleian Library, with marginal dates and occasional notes, by W. Dunn Macray, M.A., F.S.A. 6 vols. Crown 8vo. 2*l.* 5s.

Crawford. *The Crawford Collection of Early Charters and Documents.* Now in the Bodleian Library. Edited by A. S. Napier and W. H. Stevenson. Small 4to, cloth, 12s.

Earle. *Handbook to the Land-Charters, and other Saxonic Documents.* By John Earle, M.A. Crown 8vo. 16s.

Freeman. *The History of Sicily from the Earliest Times.*

Vols. I. and II. 8vo, cloth, 2*l.* 2s.

Vol. III. The Athenian and Carthaginian Invasions. 24s.

Vol. IV. From the Tyranny of Dionysios to the Death of Agathoklês. Edited by Arthur J. Evans, M.A. 21s.

Freeman. *History of the Norman Conquest of England; its Causes and Results.* By E. A. Freeman, D.C.L. In Six Volumes. 8vo. 5*l.* 9s. 6d.

—— *The Reign of William Rufus and the Accession of Henry the First.* 2 vols. 8vo. 1*l.* 16s.

Gardiner. *The Constitutional Documents of the Puritan Revolution,* 1628–1660. Selected and Edited by Samuel Rawson Gardiner, M.A. Crown 8vo. 9s.

Greswell. *History of the Dominion of Canada.* By W. Parr Greswell, M.A. Crown 8vo. With Eleven Maps. 7s. 6d.

—— *Geography of the Dominion of Canada and Newfoundland.* Crown 8vo. With Ten Maps. 6s.

—— *Geography of Africa South of the Zambesi.* With Maps. Crown 8vo. 7s. 6d.

Gross. *The Gild Merchant;* a Contribution to British Municipal History. By Charles Gross, Ph.D. 2 vols. 8vo. 24s.

Hastings. *Hastings and the Rohilla War.* By Sir John Strachey, G.C.S.I. 8vo, cloth, 10s. 6d.

Hodgkin. *Italy and her Invaders.* With Plates and Maps. By T. Hodgkin, D.C.L.

Vols. I. and II. *Second Edition.* 2*l.* 2s.

Vols. III. and IV. *Second Edition.* 1*l.* 16s.

Vols. V. and VI. 1*l.* 16s.

Hodgkin. *The Dynasty of Theodosius; or, Seventy Years' Struggle with the Barbarians.* By the same Author. Crown 8vo. 6*s.*

Johnson. *Letters of Samuel Johnson, LL.D.* Collected and edited by G. Birkbeck Hill, D.C.L., Editor of Boswell's 'Life of Johnson' (see Boswell). 2 vols. half-roan, 28*s.*

Kitchin. *A History of France.* With Numerous Maps, Plans, and Tables. By G. W. Kitchin, D.D. In three Volumes. *Third Edition.* Crown 8vo, each 10*s.* 6*d.*

Vol. I. to 1453. Vol. II. 1453–1624. Vol. III. 1624–1793.

Ludlow. *The Memoirs of Edmund Ludlow, Lieutenant-General of the Horse in the Army of the Commonwealth of England,* 1625–1672. Edited, with Appendices and Illustrative Documents, by C. H. Firth, M.A. 2 vols. 8vo. 1*l.* 16*s.*

Lucas. *Introduction to a Historical Geography of the British Colonies.* By C. P. Lucas, B.A. With Eight Maps. Crown 8vo. 4*s.* 6*d.*

—— *Historical Geography of the British Colonies:*

Vol. I. The Mediterranean and Eastern Colonies (exclusive of India). With Eleven Maps. Crown 8vo. 5*s.*

Vol. II. The West Indian Colonies. With Twelve Maps. Crown 8vo. 7*s.* 6*d.*

Vol. III. West Africa. With Five Maps. Crown 8vo. 7*s.* 6*d.*

Vol. IV. South and East Africa. Historical and Geographical. [*Immediately.*]

Machiavelli. *Il Principe.* Edited by L. Arthur Burd, M.A. With an Introduction by Lord Acton. 8vo. 14*s.*

Prothero. *Select Statutes and other Constitutional Documents, illustrative of the Reigns of Elizabeth and James I.* Edited by G. W. Prothero, M.A. Crown 8vo. 10*s.* 6*d.*

—— *Select Statutes and other Documents bearing on the Constitutional History of England, from* A.D. 1307 *to* 1558. By the same Editor. [*In Preparation.*]

Ralegh. *Sir Walter Ralegh.* A Biography. By W. Stebbing, M.A. 8vo. 10*s.* 6*d.*

Ramsay (Sir J. H.). *Lancaster and York.* A Century of English History (A.D. 1399–1485). 2 vols. 8vo. With Index, 37*s.* 6*d.*

Ramsay (W. M.). *The Cities and Bishoprics of Phrygia.* By W. M. Ramsay, D.C.L., LL.D. Vol. I. The Lycos Valley and South-Western Phrygia. Royal 8vo. 18*s.* *net.*

Vol. I. Part II. West and West-Central Phrygia. [*Immediately.*]

Ranke. *A History of England, principally in the Seventeenth Century.* By L. von Ranke. Translated under the superintendence of G. W. Kitchin, D.D., and C. W. Boase, M.A. 6 vols. 8vo. 63*s.*

Rashdall. *The Universities of Europe in the Middle Ages.* By Hastings Rashdall, M.A. 2 vols. 8vo. With Maps. 2*l.* 5*s.*, *net.*

Rogers. *History of Agriculture and Prices in England,* A.D. 1259–1702. By James E. Thorold Rogers, M.A. 6 vols. 8vo. 7*l.* 2*s.*

Smith's *Wealth of Nations.* With Notes, by J. E. Thorold Rogers, M.A. 2 vols. 8vo. 21*s.*

—— *Lectures on Justice, Police, Revenue and Arms.* Edited with Introduction and Notes. By Edwin Cannan. 8vo. 10*s.* 6*d.* *net.*

Stephens. *The Principal Speeches of the Statesmen and Orators of the French Revolution*, 1789–1795. With Historical Introductions, Notes, and Index. By H. Morse Stephens. 2 vols. Crown 8vo. 21*s.*

Stubbs. *Select Charters and other Illustrations of English Constitutional History, from the Earliest Times to the Reign of Edward I.* Arranged and edited by W. Stubbs, D.D., Lord Bishop of Oxford. *Eighth Edition.* Crown 8vo. 8*s.* 6*d.*

—— *The Constitutional History of England, in its Origin and Development. Library Edition.* 3 vols. Demy 8vo. 2*l.* 8*s.*

Also in 3 vols. crown 8vo, price 12*s.* each.

Stubbs. *Seventeen Lectures on the Study of Mediaeval and Modern History.* Crown 8vo. 8*s.* 6*d.*

—— *Registrum Sacrum Anglicanum.* An attempt to exhibit the course of Episcopal Succession in England. By W. Stubbs, D.D. Small 4to. 8*s.* 6*d.*

Swift (F. D.). *The Life and Times of James the First of Aragon.* By F. D. Swift, B.A. 8vo. 12*s.* 6*d.*

Vinogradoff. *Villainage in England.* Essays in English Mediaeval History. By Paul Vinogradoff, Professor in the University of Moscow. 8vo, half-bound. 16*s.*

4. PHILOSOPHY, LOGIC, ETC.

Bacon. *The Essays.* With Introduction and Illustrative Notes. By S. H. Reynolds, M.A. 8vo, half-bound. 12*s.* 6*d.*

—— *Novum Organum.* Edited, with Introduction, Notes, &c., by T. Fowler, D.D. *Second Edition.* 8vo. 15*s.*

Berkeley. *The Works of George Berkeley, D.D., formerly Bishop of Cloyne; including many of his writings hitherto unpublished.* With Prefaces, Annotations, and an Account of his Life and Philosophy. By A. Campbell Fraser, Hon. D.C.L., LL.D. 4 vols. 8vo. 2*l.* 18*s.*

The Life, Letters, &c., separately, 16*s.*

Bosanquet. *Logic; or, the Morphology of Knowledge.* By B. Bosanquet, M.A. 8vo. 21*s.*

Butler. *The Works of Joseph Butler, D.C.L.*; sometime Lord Bishop of Durham. Divided into sections, with sectional headings, an index to each volume, and some occasional notes; also prefatory matter. Edited by the Right Hon. W. E. Gladstone. 2 vols. Medium 8vo. 28*s.*

Fowler. *The Elements of Deductive Logic, designed mainly for the use of Junior Students in the Universities.* By T. Fowler, D.D. *Tenth Edition,* with a Collection of Examples. Extra fcap. 8vo. 3*s.* 6*d.*

—— *The Elements of Inductive Logic, designed mainly for the use of Students in the Universities.* By the same Author. *Sixth Edition.* Extra fcap. 8vo. 6*s.*

—— *Logic;* Deductive and Inductive, combined in a single volume. Extra fcap. 8vo. 7*s.* 6*d.*

Fowler and Wilson. *The Principles of Morals.* By T. Fowler, D.D., and J. M. Wilson, B.D. 8vo, cloth, 14*s.*

Green. *Prolegomena to Ethics.* By T. H. Green, M.A. Edited by A. C. Bradley, M.A. 8vo. 12*s.* 6*d.*

Hegel. *The Logic of Hegel.* Translated from the Encyclopaedia of the Philosophical Sciences. With Prolegomena to the Study of Hegel's Logic and Philosophy. By W. Wallace, M.A. *Second Edition, Revised and Augmented.* 2 vols. Crown 8vo. 10s. 6*d.* each.

Hegel's *Philosophy of Mind.* Translated from the Encyclopaedia of the Philosophical Sciences. With Five Introductory Essays. By William Wallace, M.A., LL.D. Crown 8vo. 10s. 6*d.*

Hume's *Treatise of Human Nature.* Edited, with Analytical Index, by L. A. Selby-Bigge, M.A. *Second Edition.* Crown 8vo. 8*s.*

Hume's *Enquiry concerning the Human Understanding, and an Enquiry concerning the Principles of Morals.* Edited by L. A. Selby-Bigge, M.A. Crown 8vo. 7*s.* 6*d.*

Locke. *An Essay Concerning Human Understanding.* By John Locke. Collated and Annotated, with Prolegomena, Biographical, Critical, and Historic, by A. Campbell Fraser, Hon. D.C.L., LL.D. 2 vols. 8vo. 1*l.* 12*s.*

Lotze's *Logic,* in Three Books; of Thought, of Investigation, and of Knowledge. English Translation; Edited by B. Bosanquet, M.A. *Second Edition.* 2 vols. Cr. 8vo. 12*s.*

—— *Metaphysic,* in Three Books; Ontology, Cosmology, and Psychology. English Translation; Edited by B. Bosanquet, M.A. *Second Edition.* 2 vols. Cr. 8vo. 12*s.*

Martineau. *Types of Ethical Theory.* By James Martineau, D.D. *Third Edition.* 2 vols. Cr. 8vo. 15*s.*

—— *A Study of Religion: its Sources and Contents. Second Edition.* 2 vols. Cr. 8vo. 15*s.*

5. PHYSICAL SCIENCE.

Chambers. *A Handbook of Descriptive and Practical Astronomy.* By G. F. Chambers, F.R.A.S. *Fourth Edition,* in 3 vols. Demy 8vo.

Vol. I. The Sun, Planets, and Comets. 21*s.*

Vol. II. Instruments and Practical Astronomy. 21*s.*

Vol. III. The Starry Heavens. 14*s.*

De Bary. *Comparative Anatomy of the Vegetative Organs of the Phanerogams and Ferns.* By Dr. A. de Bary. Translated by F. O. Bower, M.A., and D. H. Scott, M.A. Royal 8vo. 1*l.* 2*s.* 6*d.*

De Bary. *Comparative Morphology and Biology of Fungi, Mycetozoa and Bacteria.* By Dr. A. de Bary. Translated by H. E. F. Garnsey, M.A. Revised by Isaac Bayley Balfour, M.A., M.D., F.R.S. Royal 8vo, half-morocco, 1*l.* 2*s.* 6*d.*

De Bary. *Lectures on Bacteria.* By Dr. A. de Bary. *Second Improved Edition.* Translated by H. E. F. Garnsey, M.A. Revised by Isaac Bayley Balfour, M.A., M.D., F.R.S. Crown 8vo. 6*s.*

Goebel. *Outlines of Classification and Special Morphology of Plants.* By Dr. K. Goebel. Translated by H. E. F. Garnsey, M.A. Revised by Isaac Bayley Balfour, M.A., M.D., F.R.S. Royal 8vo, half-morocco, 1*l.* 1*s.*

Sachs. *A History of Botany.* Translated by H. E. F. Garnsey, M.A. Revised by I. Bayley Balfour, M.A., M.D., F.R.S. Crown 8vo. 10s.

Fossil Botany. *Being an Introduction to Palaeophytology from the Standpoint of the Botanist.* By H. Graf zu Solms-Laubach. Translated by H. E. F. Garnsey, M.A. Revised by I. Bayley Balfour, M.A., M.D., F.R.S. Royal 8vo, half-morocco, 18s.

Annals of Botany. Edited by Isaac Bayley Balfour, M.A., M.D., F.R.S., Sydney H. Vines, D.Sc., F.R.S., D. H. Scott, M.A., Ph.D., F.L.S., and W. G. Farlow, M.D.; assisted by other Botanists. Royal 8vo, half-morocco, gilt top.

Vol. I. Parts I–IV. 1*l.* 16*s.*

Vol. II. Parts V–VIII. 2*l.* 2*s.*

Vol. III. Parts IX–XII. 2*l.* 12*s.* 6*d.*

Vol. IV. Parts XIII–XVI. 2*l.* 5*s.*

Vol. V. Parts XVII–XX. 2*l.* 10*s.*

Vol. VI. Parts XXI–XXIV. 2*l.* 4*s.*

Vol. VII. Parts XXV–XXVIII. 2*l.* 10*s.*

Vol. VIII. Parts XXIX–XXXII. 2*l.* 10*s.*

Vol. IX. Parts XXXIII–XXXVI. 2*l.* 15*s.*

Vol. X. Parts XXXVII–XL. 2*l.* 16*s.*

Biological Series.

I. *The Physiology of Nerve, of Muscle, and of the Electrical Organ.* Edited by J. Burdon Sanderson, M.D., F.R.SS. L.&E. Medium 8vo. 1*l.* 1*s.*

II. *The Anatomy of the Frog.* By Dr. Alexander Ecker, Professor in the University of Freiburg. Translated, with numerous Annotations and Additions, by G. Haslam, M.D. Med. 8vo. 21*s.*

IV. *Essays upon Heredity and Kindred Biological Problems.* By Dr. A. Weismann. Authorized Translation. Crown 8vo.

Vol. I. Edited by E. B. Poulton, S. Schönland, and A. E. Shipley. *Second Edition.* 7*s.* 6*d.*

Vol. II. Edited by E. B. Poulton, and A. E. Shipley. 5*s.*

Elliott. An Introduction to the Algebra of Quantics. By E. B. Elliott, M.A. 8vo. 15*s.*

Prestwich. *Geology, Chemical, Physical, and Stratigraphical.* By Sir Joseph Prestwich, M.A., F.R.S. In two Volumes.

Vol. I. Chemical and Physical. Royal 8vo. 1*l.* 5*s.*

Vol. II. Stratigraphical and Physical. With a new Geological Map of Europe. Royal 8vo. 1*l.* 16*s.*

Price. *A Treatise on the Measurement of Electrical Resistance.* By W. A. Price, M.A., A.M.I.C.E. 8vo. 14*s.*

Smith. *Collected Mathematical Papers of the late Henry J. S. Smith, M.A., F.R.S.* Edited by J. W. L. Glaisher, Sc.D., F.R.S. 2 vols. 4to. 3*l.* 3*s.*

Oxford
AT THE CLARENDON PRESS
LONDON: HENRY FROWDE
OXFORD UNIVERSITY PRESS WAREHOUSE, AMEN CORNER, E.C.

Printed in Dunstable, United Kingdom

85717238R00198